Labor Unions, Partisan Coalitions, and Market Reforms in Latin America

Why do labor unions resist economic restructuring and adjustment policies in some countries and in some economic sectors while they submit in other cases? And why do some labor leaders fashion more creative and effective roles for labor unions? This book addresses these critical questions in an in-depth elegant comparative study of Argentina, Mexico, and Venezuela in the 1990s. In each case, this book studies the role of both national confederations and individual unions in specific economic sectors in each country. It demonstrates the importance of the presence and nature of alliances between political parties and labor unions and the significance of competition between labor unions for the representation of the same set of workers. This work opens new horizons for appreciating the intellectual and practical importance of the variation in the interactions between workers, unions, political parties, and economic policies.

Maria Victoria Murillo is Assistant Professor of Political Science at Yale University. She has published articles on labor politics in both English and Spanish, in journals such as *World Politics*, *Journal of Inter-American Studies and World Affairs*, and *Desarrollo Economico*.

Cambridge Studies in Comparative Politics

General Editors

Peter Lange *Duke University*
Margaret Levi *University of Washington, Seattle*

Associate Editors

Robert H. Bates *Harvard University*
Ellen Comisso *University of California, San Diego*
Peter Hall *Harvard University*
Joel Migdal *University of Washington*
Helen Milner *Columbia University*
Ronald Rogowski *University of California, Los Angeles*
Sidney Tarrow *Cornell University*

Other Books in the Series

List continues on page following index

Labor Unions, Partisan Coalitions, and Market Reforms in Latin America

MARIA VICTORIA MURILLO

Yale University

CAMBRIDGE
UNIVERSITY PRESS

PUBLISHED BY THE PRESS SYNDICATE OF THE UNIVERSITY OF CAMBRIDGE
The Pitt Building, Trumpington Street, Cambridge, United Kingdom

CAMBRIDGE UNIVERSITY PRESS
The Edinburgh Building, Cambridge CB2 2RU, UK
40 West 20th Street, New York, NY 10011-4211, USA
10 Stamford Road, Oakleigh, VIC 3166, Australia
Ruiz de Alarcón 13, 28014 Madrid, Spain
Dock House, The Waterfront, Cape Town 8001, South Africa

http://www.cambridge.org

First published 2001

Printed in the United States of America

Typeface Janson Text Roman 10/13pt.   *System* QuarkXPress [BTS]

A catalog record for this book is available from the British Library.

Library of Congress Cataloging in Publication Data
Murillo, Maria Victoria, 1967–
    Labor unions, partisan coalitions, and market reform in Latin America /
Maria Victoria Murillo.
        p.   cm. – (Cambridge studies in comparative politics)
    Includes bibliographical references and index.
    ISBN 0-521-78072-1 – ISBN 0-521-78555-3 (pb)
    1. Labor unions – Venezuela – Political activity.   2. Labor unions –
Mexico – Political activity.   3. Labor unions – Argentina – Political activity.
I. Title.   II. Series.
    HD6653.5 .M87   2001
    322'.2'098–dc21   00-048631

ISBN   0 521 78072 1   hardback
ISBN   0 521 78555 3   paperback

Contents

Abstract

Presidents leading populist labor-based parties came to power almost simultaneously in Argentina, Mexico, and Venezuela in the late 1980s. Although their respective parties promoted protectionism and state intervention in the postwar period, once in office all three presidents advanced trade liberalization and state retrenchment. The parallel convergence of labor-based parties into neoliberalism challenged the policies on which their long-term alliance with labor unions had been built. Despite the strong partisan loyalties between labor and governing parties in all three countries, labor reactions to this common challenge were diverse and so was the permeability of governments to labor demands. Moreover, the patterns of union-government interactions in Argentina, Mexico, and Venezuela varied not only across the three countries, but also across economic sectors within each country. Some unions endorsed market-oriented reforms whereas others rejected these policies. Sometimes unions were able to exercise policy input and other times the government ignored labor demands.

Political dynamics are crucial to understand the interaction between unions and labor-based governments implementing market reforms. First, in a context of economic uncertainty, partisan loyalties made unions more likely to restrain their militancy when partisan allies were in the government. Secondly, leadership or partisan competition for the control of unions increased the incentives for militancy. Even loyal union leaders who believed that workers' discontent about their collaboration with the government would lead to their own replacement become more militant. Additionally, interunion competition for membership created incentives for labor unions to break their own coordination efforts in their bids for affiliates, thus weakening all of them and reducing government's incentives to yield to labor demands. The combination of these three variables explains four patterns of union-government interaction: effective restraint (cooperation), ineffective restraint (subordination), effective militancy (opposition), and ineffective militancy (resistance). In sum, partisan loyalties, leadership, and interunion competition influenced the shape and pace of market reform implemented by labor-based parties, thus demonstrating how political forces redefined economic interests in the construction of policy coalitions.

Acknowledgments

There are many people and institutions who aided and encouraged me to undertake and carry out this project. Although mentioning them will not pay my debt to them, it gives me a chance to acknowledge it. My interest in politics, labor, and unions emerged in my adolescence during the Argentine transition to democracy. It took a more analytic turn when I began the study of political science at the Universidad de Buenos Aires. At that stage, several Argentine scholars inspired my interest in different ways including Atilio Borón, Claudia Hilb, Guillermo O'Donnell, and Juan Carlos Portantiero. During my years as a graduate student at Harvard University, I benefited from the guidance and support of my advisor, Jorge I. Domínguez. Jorge taught me the many complications of searching for general arguments to understand the complex diversity of political phenomena while keeping my enthusiasm for the study of politics. Alberto Alesina, Robert Bates, Peter Hall, and Deborah Yashar also provided crucial intellectual support during the process of writing my dissertation, and they taught me the value of social scientific research from very different perspectives that have enriched my work and worldview. At Harvard, I also benefited from a larger intellectual community that challenged my ideas and made me enjoy my work. This community expanded as a result of my subsequent affiliations with the Government Department, the Weatherhead Center for International Affairs, the Harvard Academy for International and Area Studies, and the David Rockefeller Center for Latin American Studies. I cannot mention everyone, but I need to thank Imelda Cisneros, John Coathworth, Javier Corrales, Edward Gibson, Jeanne Kinney Giraldo, Miguel Glatzer, Merilee Grindle, Virginie Guiraudon, Frances Hagopian, Peter Lom, Daniel Posner, Karissa Price, and John Womack for being generous with their time and ideas and to the late Julie Goldman for setting an example.

During my fieldwork in Argentina, Mexico, and Venezuela, I benefited from the help and support of many people and the generosity of numerous union leaders, activists, labor lawyers, policy makers, and managers who I interviewed. The Institute Torcuato Di Tella in Argentina, the Institute for Higher Studies in Administration (IESA) in Venezuela, and Latin American School of Social Sciences (FLACSO-Mexico), the Mexican Autonomous Technological Institute (ITAM), El Colegio de México, and Intelmex provided institutional support that made my research possible and pleasant. At the Instituto Di Tella, Juan Carlos Torre was a mentor who helped me understand Latin American politics and gave critical comments on an early version of the manuscript.

A long list of individuals helped to acquire the material presented in this book or shared their ideas with me. Ricardo Kirshbaum granted me access to the archives of *Diario Clarín*, Rosendo Fraga provided me data on union elections, and James McGuire shared his data set on Argentine strikes. *Entorno Laboral*, *Veneconomy*, and *El Nacional* provided access to their archives. Francisco Iturraspe shared his Venezuelan chronology with me. Carlos Acuña, Enrique Deibe, Rodolfo Díaz, Sebastián Echemendi, Rosendo Fraga, Pedro Matheu, Marta Novick, Alvaro Orsatti, Hector Palomino, Noemi Rial, Ricardo Ríos, Enrique Rodriguez, Cecilia Senén González, Santiago Senén González, and Federico Sturzenegger helped me with my research and discussed their ideas about Argentina with me. My family and friends reminded me I was at home. In Mexico, Graciela Bensusán, Ilán Bizberg, Marcelo Cavarozzi, Rafael Fernández de Castro, Enrique De La Garza, José Domínguez, Javier Elguea, Carlos García, Blanca Heredia, James Samstad, Mónica Serrano, Leonardo Valdez, and Francisco Zapata generously facilitated my quest for information and taught me about Mexican politics. Antonieta Mercado provided helpful research assistance and Hilda Rodríguez gave me her friendship and support. Finally, Imelda Cisneros, Rolando Díaz, Steve Ellner, Consuelo Iranzo, Francisco Iturraspe, Hector Lucena, Gustavo Márquez, Juan Carlos Navarro, Francisco Rodríguez, and Emiliana Vegas generously offered their time, contacts, and insights into Venezuelan politics. Robert and Ruth Bottome did that and more; they made me feel at home.

Several institutions granted me financial support for this endeavor: the Mellon Foundation, the Institute for the Study of World Politics, the Ministry of Education in Argentina, the Organization of American States, the

Acknowledgments

Graduate School of Arts and Science, the Center for International Affairs, the Fundación Mexico in Harvard, the David Rockefeller Center for Latin American Studies, and especially, the Harvard Academy for International and Area Studies at Harvard University.

The Department of Political Science at Yale University provided a collegial environment and intellectual stimulus for putting all the pieces together. In particular, my students at the seminar "Labor Politics in a Globalized Era" were a source of inspiration to finish the last stages of this project. The comments and suggestions of Arun Agrawal, David Cameron, Geoffrey Garrett, Ian Shapiro, and James Scott sharpened my ideas and provided new ways of looking at this theme. Pauline Jones-Loung read the whole manuscript, made useful insights and criticisms, and, most importantly, gave me her generous friendship.

I also benefited from a larger intellectual community of people who discussed these ideas at different points in their elaboration. I want to thank Jeremy Adelman, Katrina Burgess, Ernesto Calvo, Ruth Collier, Miriam Golden, Robert Kaufman, Steven Levitsky, Scott Martin, Nicoli Natrass, Phillip Oxhorn, Hector Schamis, Jeremy Sikkins, and Bill Smith. Pablo Boczkowski, Javier Corrales, David Flechner, Edward Gibson, Stephanie Golob, Frances Hagopian, and Mario Pecheny read parts of the manuscript and made useful comments. James McGuire and an anonymous reviewer read the entire manuscript and considerably sharpened my thinking on numerous points for revising it into its final form. I am grateful to Kay Mansfield who helped bring clarity to my prose while making me laugh and to David Flechner who provided invaluable assistance in the final stages of writing the manuscript. *World Politics* published an article that summarized the argument in the book. Finally, I wish to acknowledge the editorial assistance of Alex Holzman and Lewis Bateman at Cambridge University Press.

Most of all, I deeply appreciated constant and unlimited love, support, and encouragement from my parents, Susana Rozenblum and Renato Murillo, through the whole process. My deepest gratitude is reserved for my husband Ernesto Cabrera. We traveled together intellectually and geographically. Without his comments (to several iterations of the manuscript), patience, and encouragement, this project would have never been completed. The thought of dedicating this book to him has finally become a reality.

List of Acronyms

AD: Democratic Action
AMET: Association of Vocational Teachers
ANECP: National Agreement for the Promotion of Quality and
    Productivity
ATE: Association of State Employees
CADAFE: Company for the Administration and Development of Electricity
CADE: Argentine Company of Electricity
CAMMESA: Company for the Administration of the Wholesale
    Electricity Market
CANTV: Venezuelan National Company of Telephones
CFE: Federal Commission of Electricity
CGT: General Confederation of Labor
CIAE: Italian-Argentine Company of Electricity
CLFC: Light and Power Company of Center Mexico
CNTE: Coordinating Committee of Education Workers
CONASUPO: National Company for the Provision of Basic Staples
COPARMEX: Employers Confederation of Mexico
COPEI: Independent Committee for Political Organization
COPRE: Commission for the Reform of the State
COR: Revolutionary Labor Confederation
CROC: Revolutionary Confederation of Workers and Peasants
CROM: Mexican Regional Labor Confederation
CRT: Revolutionary Workers' Confederation
CT: Congress of Labor
CTA: Congress of Argentine Workers
CTERA: Teachers' Confederation of the Argentine Republic
CTM: Mexican Workers' Confederation
CTV: Venezuelan Workers' Confederation

CVF: Venezuelan Corporation of Development
ECLAC: Economic Committee for Latin America and the Caribbean
EMASA: Company of Environmental Issues, Inc.
ENTEL: National Company of Telecommunications
EVARSA: Resource Evaluation, Inc.
FATLyF: Argentine Federation of Light and Power Workers
FEB: Federation of Buenos Aires' Teachers
FEDEPETROL: Federation of Oil Workers
FENATEV: Venezuelan National Federation of Education Workers
FESEBES: Federation of Goods and Services Unions
FETEN: Federation of Workers of the National Education
FETRAELEC: Federation of Electricity Workers
FETRAMETAL: Federation of Metal Workers
FETRATEL: Federation of Telephone Workers
FETRAUTOMOTRIZ: Federation of Automobile Workers
FOETRA: Federation of Telephone Workers and Employees of the Argentine Republic
FONACOT: National Fund for the Development of Workers' Consumption
FREPASO: Front for a Country with Solidarity
FSTSE: Federation of Public Service Workers' Unions
GATT: General Agreement on Trade and Tariffs
GDP: Gross Domestic Product
IADB: Inter-American Development Bank
ILO: International Labor Office
IMF: International Monetary Fund
IMSS: Mexican Institute for Social Security
INFONAVIT: Institute for the Worker Housing National Fund
INP: National Port Institute
IVSS: Venezuelan Institute of Social Security
LFT: Federal Labor Law
MAS: Movement Towards Socialism
MEM: Wholesale Electricity Market
MEP: People's Electoral Movement
MTA: Movement of Argentine Workers
NAFTA: North American Free Trade Agreement
OECD: Organization for Economic Cooperation and Development
OSTEL: Telephone Workers' Welfare Fund
PAN: National Action Party

List of Acronyms

PARM: Authentic Party of the Mexican Revolution
PCV: Communist Party of Venezuela
PDVSA: Venezuelan Oil, Inc.
PEMEX: Mexican Oil
PLM: Labor Party of Mexico
PNR: Revolutionary National Party
PRD: Party of the Democratic Revolution
PRI: Institutional Revolutionary Party
PRM: Mexican Revolutionary Party
PROHINSA: Engineering Projects, Inc.
PRONASOL: National Program of Solidarity
PSE: Pact of Economic Solidarity
PST: Socialist Workers' Party
PURN: Single Party of the National Revolution
SAR: System of Savings for Retirement
SEGBA: Electricity Services of the Great Buenos Aires
SEP: Public Education Secretariat
SITRAFORD: National Union of the Ford Motor Company
SMATA: Related Trades of the Automobile Industry
SME: Mexican Union of Electricity Workers
SNTE: National Union of Education Workers
STPRM: Oil Workers' Union of the Mexican Republic
STRM: Telephone Workers' Union of the Mexican Republic
SUPE: Union of State-Owned Oil Workers
SUTERM: Single Union of Electricity Workers of the Mexican Republic
TELMEX: Mexican Telephones
TRANELSA: Electricity Transmission, Inc.
UCEDE: Union of the Democratic Center
UCR: Radical Civic Union
UDA: Union of Argentine Teachers
UIA: Industrial Union of Argentina
UNT: National Union of Workers
UOM: Union of Metal Workers
URD: Republican Democratic Union
UT: Telephonic Union
VIASA: Venezuelan International Airlines, Inc.
YPF: Fiscal Oil Reserves

1

Unions' Dilemma: How to Survive Neoliberalism

As all the starts shrivel in the single sun,
The words are many, but The Word is one
that becomes uncoded later, with an exchange of capital letters:
The words are many, but the word is One.
Jorge Luis Borges (1932)

In less than seven months, three men named Carlos assumed the presidencies in Mexico, Venezuela, and Argentina and produced the most important policy turnaround of the postwar era in these three countries.[1] In December 1988, Carlos Salinas de Gortari from the Institutional Revolutionary Party (PRI) was inaugurated as president of Mexico. In February 1989, Carlos Andrés Pérez from the Social Democratic Party, Democratic Action (AD), started his term as president of Venezuela. In July 1989, Carlos Menem from the Peronist Party followed suit in Argentina. All three were the candidates of populist labor-based parties, which had supported protectionism and state intervention in the postwar period.[2] Once in office, however, all three presidents actually reduced state

---

[1] These three countries are among the largest and most important in Latin America and the Caribbean. By 1995, they comprised 32% of the total population and 34% of the urban population in the region. They produced 43% of the regional gross domestic product and 48% of regional exports of goods and services, and they were responsible for 43% of total regional consumption according to the Inter-American Development Bank (1996: 357–61).

[2] "Labor-based parties are parties whose core constituency is *organized labor*. Such parties depend to a significant extent on trade union support . . . for their political success, and as a result, trade unions exercise an important degree of influence over the party leadership in terms of strategy, the party program, and candidate selection . . . labor-based parties vary ideologically (from Communism to Social Democracy to various forms of populism). . . ." (Levitsky 1999: 5–6). Populism was a style of campaigning by charismatic politicians who drew masses of new voters into their movements and retained their loyalty even after the leaders died. These charismatic politicians inspired a sense of nationalism and cultural pride

1

intervention and opened their economies, thus moving their labor-based parties away from the policies upon which the historic relationship with their long-term labor allies had been built.

Because these three countries had labor-based parties in power and corporatist labor regulations, the common strain created by their parallel convergence into neoliberalism should have provoked a uniform reaction among labor unions according to the conventional wisdom. However, the patterns of union-government interactions in Argentina, Mexico, and Venezuela varied not only across the three countries, but also within them. Unions' reactions ranged from active resistance to passive quiescence. Some unions endorsed policies that hurt their constituencies and organizations. Others rejected market-oriented reforms despite their alliance with governing parties. In Argentina, Peronist unions had opposed the stabilization and privatization efforts of the previous non-Peronist president to the point of calling thirteen general strikes during his administration in the name of nationalism and social welfare. When President Menem privatized the very same companies nationalized by Perón fifty years before, the Peronist unions not only accepted privatization, but also became private entrepreneurs as owners of public utilities, trains, cargo ships, and pension funds. In Venezuela, union leaders made Pérez win the AD primaries and helped him get elected president. However, after Pérez announced his policy shift, the Venezuelan Workers' Confederation (CTV) put aside a long tradition of labor peace, which had prevented general strikes since the establishment of democracy in 1958, and halted activities in the entire country less than six months into his administration.

Furthermore, labor's ability to obtain concessions from allied governments that implemented market reforms was also varied. Some unions were able to change government policies. Others tried and failed. The Argentine and Mexican teachers' unions were the largest in their respective countries. Both were led by skilled and determined female leaders who had joined efforts in the organization of a Latin American association of teachers' unions. Teachers' unions in both countries were facing government efforts to decentralize the administration of education to the provincial level. The militancy of the Argentine teachers accounted for more than

in their followers while promising to improve their lot. The vast majority of their followers were urban workers and the poor, but middle-class voters and elites also join these cross-class coalitions (Conniff 1999: 4).

one-third of total strikes during the year of this reform. However, the government ignored their demands. In Mexico, teacher opposition to key pieces of the decentralization process not only limited its scope but also served to provide salary and fringe compensations for teachers. This book examines the conditions that explain these variations in union-government interactions and their effect on the transition from close to open economies. Its comparative analysis provides useful implications for understanding similar interactions in other countries where labor-based parties have also shifted away from their traditional policies under the pressure of international shocks.

Labor Politics and Market Transitions

Labor-based parties have a comparative advantage for implementing market-oriented reforms[3] that bring uncertainty to their constituencies because they are more credible when they claim that *need* – provoked by economic distress – rather than *taste* – influenced by their ideology – has induced them to implement these policies (Cukierman and Tommasi 1998). In these three countries, the labor-based incumbents blamed globalization pressures, fiscal deficits, the foreign debt, or macroeconomic imbalances for policies presented as both urgent and indispensable. In the words of President Pérez, in his March 1990 State of the Union address:

We have effectively perceived the unavoidable need to confront our economic reality. Our inefficient, subsidized, and overprotected economy lacked the capacity and the productivity for exporting. Moreover, and more important from my point of view, it lacked the capacity to improve the living standards of the population, which had been continuously declining since the first years of this decade. ... These circumstances did not allow us to keep following the same path and thus we had to propose a deep change. ... It was indispensable to define a new development strategy to rescue the country from stagnation. ...

According to President Salinas (in Cordera and Rocha 1994:15):

The economic reform was done because while the state increased its ownership, the people increased its needs. Therefore, we had to privatize to obtain resources to pay for the debt acquired by the state during all these years.

---

[3] Market-oriented reforms include short-term stabilization measures, fiscal restraint, tax reform, financial liberalization, competitive exchange and interest rates, trade liberalization, privatization, and deregulation of most markets, including the labor market (Williamson 1990).

The sudden conversion of the labor-based parties forced them to deal with business's distrust of their former populist character and attempt to bring capital back into their economies. Hence, their new policies were drastic to show their new commitment to the market. In the words of President Menem (in Baizán 1993:37–38):

The government was becoming weaker and giving in more to lobbies and organized interests . . . everybody was taking advantage of the state to benefit their particular interests. The whole society was financing these subsidies with an uncontrollable inflation. . . . It was clear that we need a shock of hyper credibility to change the economic structure in the most drastic way. To propose a new environment where the private initiative was the engine and the state left the scene. . . .

However, drastic market reforms have costs for labor unions and workers whose influence has developed based on state expansion, protectionism, rigid labor markets, and political clout. Trade liberalization increases differences among workers across and within sectors, making it harder to organize labor unions based on horizontal solidarity. International competition and privatization also provoke labor restructuring and layoffs in sectors that have been among the most highly unionized in the past, thereby reducing the bargaining power of labor unions in these sectors. Higher unemployment hurts union bargaining power and increases job instability for union constituencies.[4] Stabilization policies relying on wage restraint and international competition further reduce unions' wage-bargaining power.[5] The reform of social and labor regulations challenges institutions that have provided unions with legal and political clout (ranging from appointments on social security boards to

---

[4] In Argentina, unemployment increased from 6.5% in 1988 to 18.6% in 1995 (INDEC 1996). In Venezuela, unemployment rose from 6.9% in 1988 to 9.6% in 1989 and 10.4% in 1990 although falling afterward to reach 6.5% in 1993 (Betancourt et al. 1995: 5). In Mexico, unemployment measurements are highly contentious, but open unemployment peaked in 1983 and 1984 (Friedmann, Lustig, and Legovini 1995: 337) and the combined official rate of open unemployment and underemployment grew from 6.8% in 1989 to 8% in 1994 (Salinas 1994).

[5] In Argentina, hyperinflation cut manufacturing real wages by 36.3% between January 1989 and March 1991. Even after the success of stabilization, industrial real wages fell by 12% between April 1991 and June 1995 (Consejo Ténico de Inversiones 1997: 65). In Venezuela, the real industrial wage fell 35% in the 1989–93 period (ILO). In Mexico, real wages in manufacturing had dropped by almost 40% between 1982 and 1988, and despite improving during the Salinas administration, they did not recover to their 1982 level (Pastor and Wise 1997: 432).

monopolies of representation), which they would not be able to achieve based solely on their industrial power. More importantly, market reforms introduce a high degree of uncertainty about the future labor-market positions of union constituencies that often induce workers to distrust these policies despite partisan reassurances. All these effects are more acute in previously subsidized sectors, such as the public and the manufacturing sectors that have enjoyed high levels of protection and constituted the core of populist coalitions pursuing import substitution industrialization.[6]

Students of market-oriented reforms point out that, in developing countries, organized labor has traditionally had its strongholds in the protected sectors of the economy. Because protection from foreign competition and state intervention had benefited labor unions with greater bargaining power, this literature expects their acrimonious rejection of market reforms. Moreover, it is assumed that the costs of reforms are concentrated in protected groups (including labor unions) that are already organized and can mobilize against the reforms. On the contrary, the potential winners of reforms are uncertain about their identity, and the benefits of reforms are diffused among unorganized individuals making it unlikely that they will be able to successfully support these policies (Fernández and Rodrik 1991). Thus, for Nelson (1989), Williamson (1994), and Haggard and Kaufman (1994), it was important to understand which institutions insulate policy makers from labor and societal pressures to enable them to implement market reforms.[7] Geddes (1995: 67), however, dissipates their fears when arguing that "working class opposition to adjustment has resulted in neither systematic defeats for incumbent politicians nor the wholesale abandonment of reform policies." The scheduling of reforms and their partial implementation nonetheless have

---

[6] After the Great Depression, Latin American countries followed a development strategy of state-led import substitution industrialization that promoted domestic manufacturing of previously imported goods. Governments originally raised tariffs to compensate for the shortage of foreign exchange produced by the crisis. They gradually moved their protectionism into subsidized exchange rates for importing inputs, nationalizations, and subsidies for the industry based on the transfer of resources from exporters of primary products. Closed markets, though, created few incentives for developing industries competitive enough to export (Diaz Alejandro 1984, Hirshman 1968). These policies allowed the formation of populist coalitions between urban workers and industrialists producing for the domestic market (Cardoso and Faletto 1969, O'Donnell 1973).

[7] In two studies of market reforms in Latin America, Acuña and Smith (1994) and Conaghan and Malloy (1994) point to the combination of repression, co-optation, and insulation of skillful policy makers for the success in the implementation of these policies.

important distributive consequences.[8] An assessment of concessions and changes in the reform process from the perspective of labor organizations will provide an important piece in the debate about the transition from closed to open economies.

The study of union-government interactions during economic liberalization contributes directly to this debate. By shifting the focus from policy makers to organized labor, I show that unions can organize either support for or opposition to the reforms, thus changing the costs of reforms for policy makers. I also provide empirical evidence to assess the effect of union action on the feasibility, design, and implementation of reforms; that is, the ability of unions to obtain concessions in their bargaining over market reforms.[9] The delays in modifying labor-market regulations in Argentina, Mexico, and Venezuela despite publicly announced intentions by governments to undertake this reform are but one example of labor influence on the pace of policy implementation.

Concessions to unions, however, do not explain the militancy of some unions and the restraint of others. Because strikes are costly for both parties, strong unions should be able to obtain concessions without exercising their muscle if governments have complete information about their strength. Weak unions, instead, have more to lose from militancy than from restraint because the cost of militancy is likely to have no payoff. Kennan (1986) discusses the difficulties in finding rational explanations for strikes when complete information is available. With incomplete information in the bargaining, strikes can serve as tools through which labor obtains information about the state of the firm and its ability to pay for labor demands (Hayes 1984) or a bluffing strategy of weak unions pretending strength (Tsebelis and Lange 1997).[10]

[8] Hellman (1998: 232) shows the distributive consequences of partial reforms in post-communist transitions "where actors who enjoyed extraordinary gains from the distortions of a partially reformed economy have fought to preserve those gains by maintaining the imbalances of partial reform over time." Schamis (1999) shows the distributive consequences of certain reform sequencing that benefited entrenched business sectors in Latin America.

[9] According to Hellman (1998), concessions to losers can have positive externalities, such as checking the power of early winners that may oppose further advances in liberalization and deregulation.

[10] Kennan (1986) presents the Hicks's paradox or the impossibility to explain strikes when complete information is available. Hicks suggested two possible explanations. Either the union is trying to maintain a "reputation for toughness" or there is incomplete information in the bargaining. Following Hayes's (1984) idea of strikes to obtain information,

Partisan links, however, facilitate communication about labor and government's intention. Partisan links can cause labor unions to trust the government and make it unnecessary for labor to probe its willingness to concede. Instead, labor cooperation with partisan allies could be based on its trust about the *need* for policies and the alternative legislative gains and favorable state regulations that compensate for industrial restraint.[11] Garrett (1998) and Iversen and Wren (1998) still find that social democratic administrations use state expenditures to compensate their constituencies in Organization for Economic Cooperation and Development (OECD) countries in the 1990s. Such compensations could explain labor restraint. This interpretation is consistent with the Latin American literature on state corporatism, which argues that the combination of state regulations on industrial relations and political affiliations of labor unions created political patterns of strike activity.[12] This literature predicts restraint when labor-based parties are in control of the state apparatus of incentives and constraints in corporatist countries, such as Argentina, Mexico, and Venezuela (Zapata 1987, 1993).

Furthermore, the appropriate institutional settings can facilitate labor peace by enhancing labor unions' control of the behavior of their members when they trust partisan allies. Referring to market reforms, Przeworski (1991: 181) argues that cooperative unions "constitute encompassing, centralized organizations and must trust in the good faith of government." He is applying to developing countries the findings of Garrett and Lange (1985, 1989) and Alvarez, Garrett, and Lange (1991) for OECD countries. They argue that countries with labor governments and a centralized union movement or countries with right-wing government and

Tsebelis and Lange (1997) suggest that strikes may be a bargaining strategy, like bluffing in poker, to pretend strength in the case of weak unions. In such a case, employers may want to probe the union to assess its strength, even at the cost of industrial conflict, to reduce their offers and maximize their profits.

[11] For the literature on *power resources*, partisan allies provide legislative resources that explain the decline in the use of industrial resources (Korpi 1978, 1985).

[12] Schmitter's (1974) definition of *corporatism* refers to a system of interest representation based in functionally differentiated categories, recognized or licensed by the state and with representational monopoly within their respective categories in exchange for controls in the selection of leaders and articulation of demands. It implies functional representation of labor and business combined with state institutions that subsidize and control functional groups. In *societal corporatism*, organized interests constitute themselves in a more autonomous way before they are recognized by the state. In *state corporatism*, state incentives and constraints played a larger role in the organization of societal interests (Schmitter 1974, Collier 1995).

decentralized wage bargaining have a better macroeconomic performance due to wage restraint.[13] In the Latin American tradition, corporatist regulation and controls over labor mobilization are used to explain labor restraint.[14]

However, all three countries – Argentina, Mexico, and Venezuela – had labor-based administrations and corporatist labor regulations. Wage bargaining was predominantly at the industry level in Argentina and decentralized to the company level in Mexico and Venezuela. These patterns of wage bargaining, along with labor-based administrations, were not supposed to lead to wage restraint and good macroeconomic performance. Furthermore, state retrenchment was an essential part of labor-based parties' policy agendas in Argentina, Mexico, and Venezuela, making any compensation through public expenditures difficult. Within this common institutional and partisan context, *What conditions explain labor loyalty to or betrayal of long-term party allies?* Moreover, *Why did government officials grant concessions in some cases and not in others?*

To answer these questions, this book shifts the focus of analysis to the interactions between labor unions and governments at different levels of organization and in different national and sectoral contexts. This multi-level study allows me to overcome the limitation of theories based on system-level variables, which are inadequate to understand the organizational dynamics of individual unions, and to bridge the gap between macrolevel and microlevel explanations.[15] Macrolevel variables provide the context that affects organizational dynamics and define national trends. However, they are insufficient to explain the internal politics of labor unions and their effect on the interaction with government officials. Instead, I analyze a variety of labor organizations, including national con-

---

[13] Centralized union movements had authority to restrain wage militancy and trusted that social democratic allies would provide expansive fiscal policies and full employment in return. This argument is derived from two sources. First, the political exchange and neo-corporatist literature that associates wage restraint in corporatist social democratic countries with the political compensations received by labor (Korpi and Shalev 1980, Cameron 1984). Second, from Calmfors and Driffill (1988) finding of a hump-shaped curve for wage militancy in OECD countries, where both centralized and decentralized labor movements have lower wage militancy than those with medium levels of centralization.

[14] Country studies of labor regulations and their effect include Ellner (1993) for Venezuela, Middlebrook (1995) for Mexico, and McGuire (1997) for Argentina.

[15] Recent political science studies have moved to the study of the microdynamics within labor unions. Most notably Golden (1997) analyzes the effect of organizational dynamics on union-employer interactions during strikes against job redundancies.

federations and industrial unions in Venezuela, Mexico, and Argentina, in terms of their strategic interaction with labor-based governments implementing market-oriented reforms. Based on these empirical findings, this book argues that the incentives created by partisan loyalties, leadership competition, and union competition explain these interactions. Partisan loyalty derived from a long-term union affiliation with the incumbent party facilitates labor restraint and collaboration. The union trusts the government and does not need to strike to probe its intentions. Yet, leadership competition among union leaders affiliated with different political parties for the control of unions can make the incumbent labor leaders fear displacement and resort to militancy. Although militancy may not augment their bargaining leverage, the fear of replacement increases their incentives for militancy as a way of showing their responsiveness to the rank-and-file hurt by market reforms. Militancy, in this case, is not a bargaining tool but the outcome of the union's own internal dynamics. Union competition among labor organizations for the representation of the same workers makes coordination more difficult, thereby weakening unions. Union competition rather than the degree of militancy thus signals to the government the weakness of the union and, in doing so, affects its capacity to obtain concessions.

This theory has broad comparative implications for understanding union-government relations in other countries as well. In Latin America and other regions of the world, unions and labor-based parties exchanged labor support for the party's commitment to provide unions with access to the state. The debt crisis and the failure of inward-oriented development strategies provoked the policy shift of labor-based parties in Latin America.[16] Trade integration and capital mobility made labor-allied parties shift toward market-oriented reforms in other regions of the world (Rodrik 1997). Hence, by focusing on a small number of variables explaining union dynamics in different contexts, my theory can be applied to union-government interactions in other countries facing similar dilemmas. Changes in the partisan identity of the government and its relationship to organized labor, union competition, and leadership competition should also affect the incentives of union leaders in other national contexts.

---

[16] Import substitution industrialization had led to budget and trade deficits by the 1970s due to its reliance on heavy state expenditures and overvalued exchange rates and the lack of adequate tax bases. However, the inflow of capital (mostly in the form of loans) allowed governments to keep these policies until the debt crisis (Frieden 1991, Geddes 1995).

This study contributes to understanding the impact of market reforms on partisan coalitions and partisan identities. In all three countries, the turn to neoliberalism by governing labor-based parties facilitated the growth of electoral contenders who criticized incumbents for the costs of drastic reforms. These same political parties made inroads into the union movement affecting the levels of partisan competition for the control of unions. Hence, the new electoral dynamics and the agenda of institutional change led incumbent labor-based parties to build broad political coalitions to sustain the process of reform and their political power. Labor unions played a prominent role in the success and demise of these coalitions in the case of these labor-based administrations. Moreover, the emergence of new political identities and partisan ties in the labor arena reverberated in the reshaping of the political party systems in these three countries.[17]

---

[17] Collier and Collier (1991) argue that labor incorporation into these labor-based parties shaped the configuration of the party system in all three countries. Changes in the political economy of Latin America have been associated with a redefinition of partisan coalitions and even party regeneration (Roberts 1995, Gibson 1997, Levitsky 1999).

2

A Theory of Union-Government
Interactions

The despotism of the leaders does not arise solely from a vulgar lust of power or
from uncontrolled egoism, but is often the outcome of a profound and sincere conviction of their own value and of the services which they have rendered to the
common cause. **Robert Michels (1966)**

This chapter presents the theory that explains the interaction between
labor unions and labor-based governments implementing market reforms.
The interaction between unions and governments involves the reaction –
either militancy or restraint – of labor unions to market reforms and
the government's response in the form of concessions. Militancy is the
most common measurement of union behavior and refers to organized
protests disrupting production or governance. Although militancy is
usually measured by counting the number, duration, or scope of strikes,
repertoires of protest vary depending on cultural legacies, institutional
opportunities, and political resources. Alternative repertoires of protests
include, among others, threats to strike, demonstrations, boycotts, sabo-
tage, hunger strikes, and sit-ins. In 1997, Argentine teachers shifted their
strategy of protest from strikes and demonstrations to scheduled hunger
strikes accompanied by scattered solidarity pop concerts facing the
National Congress. In 1992, after the failure of strikes and demonstrations, Ford Motors' workers in Mexico decided to attract public
attention by "streaking" through the offices of the Labor Arbitration
Committee.

The interaction does not end with union militancy or restraint because the government can respond by granting or refusing the concessions demanded by labor. Because militancy is costly for unions, union
leaders prefer to threaten industrial action rather than to actually exercise

11

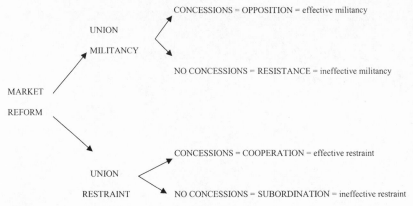

Figure 2.1 Classification of union-government interactions under market reforms.

it.[1] Hence, although strong unions will not need to strike if their strength is recognized, weak unions will not dare to do it if their weakness is known.[2] Therefore, strong unions should be able to obtain concessions even without militancy because conflict also involves costs for the government.[3] Yet, some strong unions indulge in militancy to achieve their demands although the cost seems unnecessary. Indeed, even weak unions sometimes endure "heroic defeats" to borrow Golden's (1997) metaphor. To understand this apparent irrationality in the behavior of militant unions as well the responses of governments, I classify the interactions into four categories that capture labor reactions and their effect in achieving concessions from the government: successful militancy (opposition), unsuccessful militancy (resistance), successful restraint (cooperation), and unsuccessful restraint (subordination) (Figure 2.1).

Unions do not probe allied governments nor do they bluff. Labor unions trust their allies, and union competition or monopoly provides

---

[1] According to Golden (1997: 16), "A strike is costly because workers lose wages and may need or expect strike funds to be paid, or because the union may lose members if scabs enter the enterprise and work in place of striking employees."

[2] They cannot bluff if the government knows about their weakness.

[3] "The organization has become strong enough to derive some power (i.e., control over its environment) from its recognized *potential* of power. In other words, concessions are likely to be made not because members have struck, but in order to avoid a strike" (Offe and Wiesenthal 1985: 216).

signals of their strength and make probing and bluffing unnecessary. Militancy results from the internal dynamics of the union and the leadership's search for political survival, whereas the organizational structure of unions affects their ability to obtain concessions. Partisan loyalty, leadership competition, and union competition, thus, are key factors for understanding union-government interactions.

A Partisan Theory of Union-Government Interaction

This study focuses on the strategic interaction between governments and unions because union leaders rather than workers sit at the bargaining table with government officials and organize strikes. Union leaders make collective action, whether strikes or restraint, possible. They organize workers' behavior and its exchange for concessions.[4] Union members have different preferences regarding wages, work conditions, and job stability derived from their diverse labor-market alternatives. Union leaders, thus, aggregate a particular combination of such preferences into specific union demands. They also articulate and present labor demands to government officials. Hence, union leaders are workers' representatives in any exchange with government officials to discuss labor demands.

However, unions are not perfect agents, and the preferences of union leaders need not be the same as those of workers.[5] Besides those of their constituencies, union leaders also have their own objectives in the exchange.[6] For example, union leaders seek ideological or material rewards while acting as workers' representatives, or they may prefer to maximize the long-term rather than short-term goals of workers. Whatever the objectives of union leaders, their primary constraint is to "remain in power because otherwise they would not be able to pursue their objectives" (Farber 1986: 1080). They want to remain as workers' agents because their

---

[4] Pizzorno (1978: 278) argues that unions organize collective action so as to make possible even intertemporal exchanges of current restraint for future benefits.

[5] The imperfection of the union agency may be a desirable goal for workers who select union leaders not just to carry their demands, but also to articulate them and calculate the benefits of intertemporal exchanges.

[6] Crouch (1982: 161) points out that unions cannot be reduced as agents from their rank and file "because organizations, whether of workers or of anybody else, are not simple embodiments of their members' wishes; they are social institutions in their own right, and develop their own internal patterns of power, goal-seeking and conflict."

13

own payoff derives from the exchange of behavior for demands. Hence, they are constrained by their constituencies' preferences to the extent that they want to avoid replacement by internal or external rivals.[7] That is, they can be replaced by new leaders who propose a different set of union demands (leadership competition) or their members can defect to other unions whose banners have become more attractive for them (union competition).[8]

Union leaders have built long-term alliances with political parties that reduced their replacement fear in the past. Labor leaders entered into the alliances seeking to complement industrial strategies with political influence to provide benefits for their constituencies and themselves, including restrictions to their replacement. Political parties channeled their demands through the state and helped them mobilize support from other sectors, thus facilitating the survival of labor leaders. Politicians, in turn, tried to attract labor allies to gain electoral and policy support for their parties, thus incorporating labor into the political arena. Union leaders provided electoral machines for labor-based parties and social consensus or support in return for political influence (see Chapter 3). The alliance with political parties created partisan bonds that shaped the expectations and behavior of both actors. Thus, the identity of the party in government influences the attitudes of union leaders toward incumbent politicians and their ability to bargain with them. Other things being equal, union leaders are more willing to restrain their militancy when their allied parties are in the government and increase it when their allies are in the opposition.[9] That is, unions may need strikes to probe governments they distrust, but not their allies in power. Strategic politicians, in turn, also expect allied unions to facilitate the implementation of government policies and provide electoral support. Thus, incumbent politicians prefer to reward the loyalty of allied unions rather than to give in to unions who have no attachment

[7] Farber (1986) argues that the democratic constraints on the leadership range from cases where the limits are so loose that the leadership can maximize their objective function without regard to the constraints of the political process (dictatorship) to those where the leadership is severely constrained by the political process and the need to answer the rank and file. Yet, he shows that the possibility of insurgency constrains leaders even in imperfect democracies.

[8] In a Hirshmanian (1968) sense, replacement by alternative leaders can be assimilated to "voice" within the same organization whereas the abandonment of the union by members is similar to his concept of "exit."

[9] Zapata (1987) shows political patterns of strike similar to those argued by the political exchange literature for Latin America.

14

to the governing party and fewer incentives for restraint.[10] It follows that if allied union leaders are replaced by others associated with opposition political parties, the change should also affect the terms of union-government interactions. Hence, the identity of the party in government affects the preferences of union leaders in their interaction with government officials.[11]

Partisan loyalty facilitated the fulfillment of constituencies' demands under the original alliance. However, if market reforms implemented by labor-based parties increase the uncertainty of workers about their future, partisan loyalties can become contradictory to constituencies' demands, thereby affecting leadership survival and the incentives of labor leaders in their interaction with governments. In this context, two conditions influenced the interaction between partisan allies in the government and in the labor unions: leadership competition and union competition.

Leadership Competition

Diversity in labor partisan affiliations implies that various parties appeal to organized labor. Whereas in the European context, these parties tend to be Communist, Socialist, and Christian Democrats, in Latin America strong populist labor parties have historically competed with left parties for union influence. The higher costs of leadership competition in a less democratic context also increase the value of subsidies provided by political parties in Latin America. Leadership competition between rivals associated with different political parties can take place within a single union in the form of partisan competition. It can also appear as a competition for leadership among rivals associated with diverse factions of the same party. When diverse factions of the same party compete for union leadership, allied union leaders still risk being replaced as representatives. For the incumbent labor-based parties, partisan competition implies the threat of allied union leaders being replaced by hostile activists allied with the electoral opposition. Leadership competition among factions will imply

---

[10] The cost of bargaining with nonallied union leaders is higher due to the lack of mutual trust, whereas part of the agency costs may indirectly feed the coffers of opposition parties.

[11] Allied labor unions prefer cooperation to opposition to subordination to resistance because they value both concessions for themselves and collaboration with partisan allies. Nonallied union leaders prefer opposition to cooperation to resistance to subordination because they value both concessions and weakening the incumbent party.

15

such a threat only if the winning faction is likely to defect from the party and join the opposition.

Partisan competition can be combined with union competition for membership when different parties control rival organizations. For example, different partisan loyalties separated the competing federations of Venezuelan teachers making both partisan competition and union competition for members overlap. In contrast, the uncontested leader of the single Mexican telephone union was allied with the PRI, thus providing an example of leadership monopoly. Partisan competition could also be contained within a single organization as in the CTV where activists of diverse parties competed for and share leadership positions through proportional representation.

If allied union leaders perceive that leadership competition grows (e.g., by losing local union elections), they will try to recover the following of their constituencies to avoid replacement. If they believe that rival leaders are taking advantage of their restraint vis-à-vis market reforms, their incentives for militancy will increase to avoid replacement. Calls for militancy are aimed to show their constituencies that they have not sold out. Leadership survival thus increases incentives for militancy not as a bargaining strategy, but due to the internal dynamics of the union. Militancy is not irrational. Nor is it a bargaining strategy to obtain information. It is a leadership tactic for political survival.

Union Competition

Union competition, or organizational fragmentation, refers to the rivalry among unions for the representation of workers in the same sector. In some cases, there is a union monopoly, and a single union represents all the workers in the sector. For example, the Mexican teachers' union was the only one in the education sector, and teachers had no other option but to affiliate with it. In other cases, there is union competition, and several organizations vie for the membership of the same workers. For instance, thirteen federations competed for the representation of Venezuelan teachers in 1991.

Union competition introduces the need to coordinate the actions of different unions so as to organize collective action, whether militancy or restraint. The larger the number of unions competing for the same members, the harder is coordination for collective action (Olson 1971: 48). Union competition makes coordination and its enforcement more difficult by creating incentives to attract members from rival organizations, thereby increasing coordination costs for unions engaging in collective action.[12] Unions trying to attract members from rival organizations are more likely to employ tactics that differentiate them in order to become the most appealing to members. This situation is sharpened if unions have diverse partisan identities that generate not only different attitudes toward the government, but also different bargaining costs among competing unions. In addition to coordination costs, each union is also weaker than a single monopolistic union because their leaders control the militancy or restraint of only a share of the involved workers.[13]

Regardless of partisan affiliation, governments should be less likely to make concessions to competing unions because they are weaker than monopolistic unions. Therefore, government reaction in the interaction is more related to the strength of the union than to labor-militancy. Union competition informs the government about the strength of the union, thereby avoiding the need to explore union bargaining power. Since allied government officials know that the probability of militancy increases as a result of leadership competition, they use union competition as an indicator of whether the union is strong or weak and thus whether they should concede.

Labor-based Parties, Market Reforms, and Union-Government Interactions

The effect of union competition and leadership competition on the interaction between union leaders and government officials varies according to the identity of the party in government. When labor-based parties implement market-oriented reforms, allied union leaders are willing to collaborate – despite the uncertainty and distress of their constituencies – due to their loyalty to long-term allies. In fact, high uncertainty created by the opening of the economy and state retrenchment makes interest less clear. Therefore, partisan loyalties become useful indicators of government

---

[12] Golden (1993: 441) shows that coordination in wage bargaining is most likely when union monopoly is high, because the competition for members "provides a strong incentive for unions to try to maximize their wage gains in order to retain members or to attract them away from competitors."

[13] Government officials put less value on the exchange with each union because they have to enter multiple interactions in their negotiations with the sector, thereby increasing bargaining costs.

intentions and political interests because they are based on past interactions that provided benefits to labor unions and workers.[14] Moreover, partisan links facilitate the communication to labor unions about the commitments and constraints of their partisan allies and the need to implement these policies.

Yet, the policy shift of labor-based parties creates a vacuum for populist opposition to market-oriented policies. Political parties from the left or disgruntled politicians splitting from the governing party (on ideological grounds) can take advantage of the policy shift to fill this void. This movement may facilitate the emergence of militant union activists allied with political parties or partisan factions opposing market-oriented reforms and may enhance leadership and partisan competition. Indeed, in all three countries studied, new political parties fitting this description emerged in the electoral arena.[15] These electoral changes facilitate the transformation of factional competition among union leaders into partisan competition by supplying new partisan allies. Partisan competition, in turn, increases the likelihood of labor militancy. Some workers are more uncertain about the effect of the sudden shift from public to private or from protection to exposure or they are less productive and fear competition. These workers are more likely to follow the new populist union leaders into militant protest against market reforms. If their discontent facilitates the control of unions by militant union leaders protesting market reforms, it increases the replacement threat for incumbent union leaders.

Market-oriented reforms can also sharpen union competition by provoking splits over how to respond or aggravating the conflict among rival unions about the appropriate strategies to capture diminishing resources. In the attempt to attract members from rival organizations to increase their representation in these disputes, unions have more incentives for boycotting coordination efforts as a strategy of differentiation, thereby weakening all the unions within the sector.

[14] Referring to market reforms in developing countries, Bates and Krueger (1993: 456) point out that "under conditions of uncertainty, people's beliefs of where their economic interests lie can be created and organized by political activists; rather than shaping events, notions of self-interest are instead themselves shaped and formed."

[15] The emergence of the Argentine Front for a Country with Solidarity (FREPASO) and the Mexican Party of the Democratic Revolution (PRD) originated in ideological disputes generated by the neoliberal turn of populist parties. In Venezuela, Causa R, a party originally organized by union leaders, grew to become a national political party due to its opposition to Pérez's reforms but they also had union followers.

Table 2.1. *Predicted Background Conditions for Loyal Unions and Labor Governments*

		Partisan Competition for Leadership	
		MONOPOLY (one party)	COMPETITION (many parties)
Union Competition For Members	MONOPOLY (one union)	COOPERATION effective restraint	OPPOSITION effective militancy
	COMPETITION (many unions)	SUBORDINATION ineffective restraint	RESISTANCE ineffective militancy

The explanatory factors are not fixed. The identity of the party in government changes with elections. Union competition and partisan competition within the union movement can also change. Governments, however, cannot usually manipulate these variables in the short term, although their market reforms can influence how these variables change. These policies can improve or damage the electoral opportunities of incumbents, affect the likelihood of challenges to labor leaders, and make it harder for unions to coordinate their strategies. Therefore, the explanatory variables can change during the period studied here. These changes, in turn, should generate shifts on the patterns of union-government interactions making them more fluid, even in the short term. Table 2.1 summarizes the conditions predicted by my theory for the four union-government interactions when a labor-based party implements market-oriented reforms:

- *Cooperation* or *effective restraint* is more likely in the absence of union and partisan competition – when only one union organizes all workers and is affiliated with the governing party. Partisan loyalty reduces the incentives for militancy and facilitates bargaining, whereas union monopoly boosts the bargaining power of the union because government officials want the collaboration of a strong and loyal union.
- *Opposition* or *effective militancy* is more likely in the presence of growing partisan competition and union monopoly – when leaders affiliated with different parties compete for the control of a single union. Growing partisan competition based on protesting the consequences of a policy shift increases the incentives for "irrational" militancy. This is because allied union leaders are afraid of being

19

replaced and the sections controlled by contenders have already turned militant. Because the union is strong, government officials are more likely to grant concessions so that allied union leaders can show a better record than their contenders.

- *Subordination* or *ineffective restraint* is more likely to result from competition among different unions affiliated with the governing party. Whereas partisan loyalty facilitates restraint, union competition weakens all unions despite their loyalty. Government officials may also choose among unions to reward only the most compliant because they do not fear feeding partisan competition that would benefit the electoral opposition. This selection should also prompt rival unions toward compliance to avoid losing resources or members if they become less attractive than other competing unions.

- *Resistance* or *ineffective militancy* is more likely to happen when partisan competition and union competition overlap – when competing unions are affiliated with different parties. Union competition weakens all unions and, with partisan competition, makes coordination more difficult. Unions associated with opposition parties protest to differentiate themselves from cooperative loyal unions. If they succeed in attracting members due to their bellicose stance, loyal unions will turn more militant to avoid losing members although union competition makes them all weak and unlikely to be effective in obtaining concessions from the government.

Research Design: A Multilevel Comparison

To test my theory as well as alternative explanations, I devised a research design that allowed me to apply the classification of union-government interactions to cases in three different countries and five sectors of the economy. I selected eighteen unions in Argentina, Mexico, and Venezuela, including the main national confederations and unions in five economic sectors: automobile, education, electricity, oil, and telecommunications.[16]

[16] In Argentina, the individual unions were the Related Trades of the Automobile Industry (SMATA), the Argentine Federation of Light and Power Workers (FATLyF), the Federation of Telephone Workers and Employees of the Argentine Republic (FOETRA), the Union of State-Owned Oil Workers (SUPE), and the Teachers' Confederation of the Argentine Republic (CTERA) with its rival unions. In Mexico, the individual unions were the Telephone Workers' Union of the Mexican Republic (STRM), the Oil Workers' Union

A Theory of Union-Government Interactions

Individual unions were selected based on their exposure to market-oriented reforms in a similar context of labor-based parties turning from populism into neoliberalism. Whereas the national context enhanced cross-country comparability, the previous protection from competition or state ownership in these sectors made their workers more likely to suffer high uncertainty due to the economic opening and state retrenchment.[17] Electricity, oil, telecommunications, and education were under state management whereas the automobile sector had enjoyed preferential protection in all three countries.[18] Additionally, nationwide unions usually organized workers in these sectors across all three countries, further enhancing the comparability of case studies. Finally, national labor confederations provide a picture of national tendencies because they organize unions in every economic sector. A comparison of these confederations to sector-specific individual unions permits me to assess the effects created by different types of labor organization.[19] The main labor confederations

of the Mexican Republic (STPRM), the Mexican Union of Electricity Workers (SME), the National Union of Education Workers (SNTE), and the local union of Ford Motors' Workers at Cuatitlán. In Venezuela, the individual unions included the Federation of Telephone Workers (FETRATEL), the Federation of Electricity Workers (FETRAELEC), the Federation of Oil Workers (FEDEPETROL), the Ford Motors' Section of the Federation of Automobile Workers (FETRAUTOMOTRIZ), and the multiple unions in the education sector. In all cases, I analyzed the process of industrial restructuring and reform that involved bargaining with the specific union studied.

[17] These sectors were hit hard by reforms allowing me to control for the effect of economic hardship on militancy or workers' reaction and predict a tendency toward militancy that could be used by leaders with private information for their internal competition. Because these workers were privileged under closed economies, they should feel the effect of *relative deprivation* when they lost previously acquired rights as a result of the actions of those who had originally granted them (Gurr 1969). In particular, these were highly unionized sectors that tended to have nationwide unions despite variations in national patterns of collective bargaining due to the effect of state expansion and homogenization. Thus they proved a similar context in terms of organizational resources, which could affect their behavior (Franzosi 1995).

[18] Those in the public sector were under soft budget constraints and often had legal guarantees of job security. These conditions strengthened their bargaining power during the period of protectionism granting unions with management prerogatives that they could use as selective incentives. According to theories based on the economic interest of unions (Frieden 1995), we can infer their policy preferences against economic liberalization and state adjustment that affects their bargaining power, and therefore, the wages and work conditions of their members.

[19] Golden (1997) argues that different levels of organization involve fundamentally diverse dynamics regarding strike decisions.

were the Argentine General Confederation of Labor (CGT), the Mexican Workers' Confederation (CTM), and the CTV.[20]

This multilevel research design that combines comparison across countries and within countries (across different sectors and levels of organization) permits me to control for macrolevel effects while testing my microlevel theory. Hence, the comparison across nations and sectors has the advantage of multiplying the number of cases within the three countries and providing variation in macrolevel variables to test alternative theories.[21] At the same time, the small number of cases made feasible the qualitative study that was necessary to gather data on the internal dynamics of labor organizations – for which there was no previous record – to test my microlevel theory.[22] The theoretical benefit of this research design is that it provides the possibility to test macrolevel and microlevel hypotheses while assessing their interaction within different contexts, thus incorporating the effect of both types of variables into the analysis. Its empirical advantage is that it provides the information necessary to test a hypothesis based on multiple interactions around the organizational dynamics of individual unions.

The evidence used to test alternative hypotheses was behavioral and is presented in Chapters 4 through 6. Militancy was measured using the number of strikes as well as other forms of organized protest in the cases where strike activity was limited by the state.[23] Concessions implied the

---

[20] The CGT was the only state-recognized labor confederation. The CTM claims 85% of unionized workers according to the U.S. Department of Labor (1993) or almost 64% of the union members affiliated with the PRI labor movement according to Zazueta and De La Peña (1981: 810). The CTV affiliated 74% of unions and was the largest of the four Venezuelan confederations. The next larger had only 4% of its membership (U.S. Department of Labor 1992, Ellner 1993, and Betancourt et al. 1995).

[21] King, Keohane, and Verba (1994) suggest using subnational units and time divisions to multiply the number of observable implications within the same country when the theory applies to units of analysis that can be disaggregated to those levels.

[22] The absence of information on individual cases prevented case selection bias but required extensive fieldwork to collect the data.

[23] In Argentina, Mexico, and Venezuela, the "right to strike" does not entitle workers to wage replacement while on strike, but firms cannot hire nonunionized workers (Cox Edwards 1997: 132–4). Striking costs were increased by the need of governmental approval for "legal" strikes in Mexico and Venezuela. In Argentina, McGuire (1997: 299) argues that jurisprudence on the right to wage replacement while on strike was confused, and back pay for days spent on strike was a usual practice through the 1980s. Thus, measures of militancy took into account contextual effects because the probability of going on strike should be higher in Argentina than in Venezuela or Mexico due to the different costs involved for workers.

inclusion of union demands into the planned reforms and were assessed by comparing the original and final design of reforms. Concessions were confirmed with interviews with government and company officials (also taken as an expression of their public position), journalistic accounts, and secondary literature.[24] The instances for measuring union reactions and government concessions included a common set of policies (stabilization, privatization, trade liberalization, social security, labor organization, and labor flexibility) for a national labor confederation. Company or activity-specific reforms triggered by state reform and economic opening were used for individual unions (e.g., privatization, industrial restructuring, and administrative decentralization). Moreover, to assess the effect of changes in the explanatory factors on union-government interactions during the period studied, two observations are reported for each union, thus doubling their number (N = 18 × 2 = 36).[25] Table 2.2 summarizes all observed interactions. Arrows show the passing of time between the first and the second observation.

This table shows that the cases studied provide an array of observations of different union-government interaction with no apparent national or sector-level explanations regarding the dependent variable. The marginal cells at the bottom of the table show that each of the studied countries presented at least three different types of interaction despite common national contexts. National macroeconomic conditions and political institutions are not sufficient to explain subnational variation. Shalev (1992) shows the correlation between national employment levels and labor militancy in the OECD, but, even at the national level, unemployment growth coincides with increasing militancy in Venezuela and restraint in Argentina

---

[24] Union demands regarding each reform were collected from union documents, journalistic accounts, and interviews with union leaders (used as a public expression of the official union position). Concessions were measured based on analyses of the original design of reforms; the public demands of unions with regard to the reforms; the number of such demands that were included in the final design of reforms; and the evaluation of policy makers, company decision makers, and union leaders on the reasons for design modification. Union demands were measured using press chronologies, union documents, and interviews; labor militancy was measured using both official statistics and interviews with government officials and industrial relations managers; and reform designs were analyzed using interviews with policy makers and union leaders as well as official and union documents, press chronologies, and secondary sources.

[25] Changes in the independent variable from one category to another were used as cut-off points when possible. When there were no changes in the independent variable, the cut-off was based on two diverse reform initiatives (e.g., privatization and restructuring) when possible. Otherwise, a single observation was doubled.

Table 2.2. *Observed Union-Government Interactions by Country and Sector*

Sectors	Countries			Sectoral Variation	Total Cases
	Venezuela	Mexico	Argentina		
Oil	C → O	S → S	C → C	C = 3, O = 1, S = 2	6
Automobile	C → C	R → S	O → C	C = 3, O = 1, S = 1, R = 1	6
Telecommunication	C → O	C → C	O → O	C = 3, O = 3	6
Electricity	C → O	C → O	O → C	C = 3, O = 3	6
Education	R → R	O → O	R → R	R = 4, O = 2	6
NAT'L CONF.	O → O	S → S	S → C	C = 1, O = 2, S = 3	6
Nat'l Variation	C = 5, O = 5, R = 2	C = 3, O = 3, S = 5, R = 1	C = 4, O = 4, S = 1, R = 2		
Total Cases	12	12	12		36

Note: C = cooperation = effective restraint; S = subordination = ineffective restraint; O = opposition = effective militancy; R = resistance = ineffective militancy

24

at the national level in contrast to predictions based on business cycle theories.[26] Peter Hall (1986) introduces the idea of national patterns of policy making related to the domestic institutions. Garrett and Lange (1995) make a general argument about the effect of socioeconomic and formal institutions on social actors and government responses to their demands. In the Latin American literature, numerous country studies remark on the effect of labor institutions and political regime in shaping the political opportunities for labor strategies (Ellner 1993, Cook 1995, Middlebrook 1995, McGuire 1997, and Burgess 1998). Although these national-level variables help to understand national-level patterns, they cannot explain subnational variation.

The marginal cells at the right of the table also show diversity in the interactions within each of the analyzed economic sectors. Hence the similarity of economic interests is not sufficient to provide an alternative explanation to national-level variation. Economic pluralism could explain sector-level patterns across nations, based on the common link with international markets of sector-specific assets or factor endowments of different countries (Rogowski 1989, Frieden 1995). In these middle-income developing countries, trade liberalization and deregulation have a stronger effect on the tradable sectors (such as oil and automobile) than in the nontradable public services (such as electricity, telecommunications, and, to a larger extent, education). Shalev (1992) and Garrett and Way (1995) found that, in the OECD countries, unions in the public services were more militant than those in manufacturing. Their findings are consistent with the patterns emerging from this table that show a predominance of militant interactions in electricity, telecommunications, and, in particular, the education sector. However, these theories are insufficient to understand variation within each sector and, in particular, the different ability of unions to obtain concessions. My theory, instead, proposes to recover the political dynamics. It takes into consideration the uncertainty of the transition created by political and economic change by examining three variables that shape the choices of union leaders and government officials: partisan loyalty, leadership competition, and union competition.

Chapter 3 shows the role played by the essential elements of my theory on the original alliance between labor unions and populist labor-based

---

[26] The costs of strikes are also affected by the business cycle. High employment improves the bargaining opportunities of workers, and unemployment increases risks and diminishes their probability of gains (Ashenfelter and Johnson 1969).

parties, whose legacies, in particular partisan loyalty, were key to understanding subsequent interactions. Industrial weakness and union leaders' fear of replacement laid at the origin of partisan loyalties that caused their original alliances with populist labor-based parties and influenced the choice of labor regulations in each country. Whereas the emerging political systems shaped the possibility for leadership competition, labor regulations molded opportunities for both leadership competition and union competition. The political system and the labor regulations resulting in each country, in turn, defined the institutional context for union-government interactions during the conversion of labor-based parties from populism into neoliberalism. Chapters 4 through 6 apply the theory presented here to analyze union-government interaction in the three countries whereas Chapter 7 brings all the pieces in the puzzle together in a cross-sectoral and cross-national comparison of all case studies.

3

The Populist Past and Its Institutional Legacies

We are not united by love, but by dread. **Jorge Luis Borges (1964)**

To you, whose lot it is to sow what others may reap, to labor and obey, and ask no more than the wages of a beast of burden, the food and shelter to keep you alive from day to day. It is to you that I come with my message of salvation, it is to you that I appeal. **Upton Sinclair (1990)**

On October 17, 1945, three hundred thousand workers marched into downtown Buenos Aires to demand the release of imprisoned Colonel Juan Perón. In the elections of February 1946, the union-organized Labor Party led the political coalition that brought Perón to the presidency. Most workers voted for Perón and taught their children to be Peronist, creating one of the strongest partisan loyalties in Latin America. After all, Perón and the Peronist unions had changed their lives by providing better wages and labor benefits, social security, and even paid vacations in union resorts. Because the labor benefits compensated unions for their previous frustration in dealing with indifferent employers and hostile governments, they identified with Peronism and served as Peronist political machines. In addition to turning unions into key players in the political system, Peronism promoted import substitution industrialization and state-led development, which further reinforced unionization and labor bargaining power.

In 1989, a Peronist candidate, Carlos Menem won the presidential election. During his populist electoral campaign, Menem had promised wage hikes and social justice and threatened not to pay the external debt. However, after his inauguration, he delivered austerity followed by trade liberalization, privatization, and adjustment of the public sector. As state intervention had done forty years before, the retreat of the state and

27

market-oriented reforms reshaped state-society relations. The national labor confederation, the Peronist-dominated CGT, although surprised by the policy turnaround, accepted the market-oriented reforms and reduced the number of general strikes from thirteen against the previous administration of the Radical Party (1983–9) to one during the first Menem administration (1989–95). Peronist unions, though, were able to negotiate concessions on the reforms of social security, labor legislation, and privatization.

A similar story took place in Mexico. Mexican unions had entered the political arena during the Mexican Revolution. They first formed six Red Battalions that fought with the army of President Venustiano Carranza in 1915. In 1919, they organized a Labor Party, which supported the elections of Presidents Alvaro Obregón and Plutarco E. Calles. In return, unions obtained political appointments and favorable labor legislation to compensate for their weakness in collective bargaining with private employers. In 1938, President Lázaro Cárdenas founded the Party of the Mexican Revolution (PRM) and integrated labor into its functional structure. Unions became political machines for the PRM, which became the PRI, and were included into the party structure. Workers received social benefits, and union leaders gained political influence they could use in bargaining with employers. Like Peronism, the PRI pursued policies of import substitution industrialization and state-led development.

Half a century later, PRI labor leaders witnessed a PRI president, Carlos Salinas, becoming the champion of economic liberalization, state shrinkage, and market-oriented reforms. The main national confederation, the PRI-dominated CTM, explicitly supported Salinas's stabilization plan and structural reforms in the annual corporatist pacts signed by government and business representatives, and an agreement to increase labor productivity signed in 1992. Moreover, the CTM campaigned for Salinas's proposal to integrate Mexico into the North American Free Trade Agreement (NAFTA). In spite of CTM's acquiescence, the administration ignored most of its demands even while paying lip service to the alliance between the PRI and the labor movement.

The story was repeated in Venezuela, where AD had traditionally been a champion of democracy and nationalism as well as union organization. During its first administration (1946–8), AD promoted union organization, wage hikes, and labor rights. AD union leaders advanced the foundation of the CTV, and the AD labor bureau integrated union leaders into the party structure. Unions provided AD with political machines while channeling workers' loyalty and supporting AD development policies also based on state intervention and import substitution industrialization.

In 1988, AD union leaders endorsed the populist Carlos Andrés Pérez in the primaries of AD and in his campaign for the presidency. Pérez had extended state intervention, established a minimum wage, and made dismissals more difficult during his first administration in the 1970s. However, after his inauguration in February 1989, he surprised foes and followers with his announcement of the "Great Turnaround." The "Great Turnaround" included trade liberalization, macroeconomic adjustment, and structural reforms of the state. Pérez encountered a very different response from his union allies than his Argentinean and Mexican counterparts. The AD-controlled CTV responded to his policy shift by organizing the first economic general strike in Venezuelan history, followed by a series of demonstrations and other strikes that boycotted most of Pérez's reforms in the labor and social sector. CTV opposition resulted in diverse concessions related to labor market and social security reforms until the government reformist intentions receded under the pressure of social protests and two failed military coups.

More than a repeated story, the convergence of these three countries explains the choices of labor leaders for political strategies and their consequences in terms of labor regulations and partisan loyalties. Labor unions chose political strategies to compensate for their industrial weakness and to cope with the replacement threat. Trying to build a political coalition and looking for electoral constituencies, populist leaders provided the opportunity of an alliance for labor leaders. The alliance provided policies that benefited workers, confirming the benefits of political strategies and reinforcing their allegiance to populist labor-based parties. Subsidies to labor organization further showed the value of political strategies to labor leaders who had faced previous repression or ignorance by employers. These benefits justified the partisan loyalties of workers and labor leaders. The labor regulations emerging from the alliance shaped patterns of leadership competition and union competition. Limitations to leadership competition, in particular, reduced the replacement threat for allied labor leaders to keep them in control of unions. That is, the incentives created by the fear of replacement were already working at the time of the original alliance. Furthemore, Collier and Collier (1991) argue that these alliances have shaped party systems in these three countries. Party systems, in turn, shaped the opportunities of labor leaders to seek for new allies if populist politicians failed to perform in subsequent interactions. In a similar way, limits to leadership competition also helped politicians control the growth in influence of nonallied labor leaders.

This interpretation is consistent with Valenzuela's (1992) "freezing" effect due to the consolidation of the party-union link after the expansion and institutionalization of collective bargaining and Collier and Collier's (1991) "critical junctures" of labor incorporation. Whereas Collier and Collier focus on the state's goal of controlling and/or cultivating labor support for new political parties, this chapter centers on the incentives for union leaders to join the alliance. For them, labor incorporation in Latin America involved the legalization and institutionalization of an organized labor movement shaped by political parties and state regulations. The legal incorporation of labor through labor codes involved subsidies related to the strength of organized labor and politicians' need of labor support as well as controls for labor organization (Collier and Collier 1979). This chapter looks at the incentives of labor leaders for joining the alliance, giving up their autonomy, and accepting controls in return for subsidies on labor organization.

The Value of Political Alliances

The Argentinean Peronism, the Mexican PRI, and the Venezuelan AD included labor unions in their party structures while establishing legal institutions that subsidized labor organization and provided benefits for union constituencies. These political parties legitimized labor political participation, provided access to the state for labor leaders, and implemented economic policies that benefited organized labor. Political strategies compensated labor unions for their weakness in the industrial arena of late industrializing countries, starting a process of politicization of labor relations that would remain for the rest of the century. In return, these emerging political parties received a loyal core constituency and political machines for electoral support and policy implementation.

In the three countries, the economic policies promoted by populist parties, such as protectionism and state growth (in particular through nationalizations) indirectly benefited labor. Nationalizations expanded employment in a union-friendly environment, and closed economies strengthened the bargaining power of organized labor because employers could pass higher labor costs to consumers. Additionally, in the three countries, corporatist labor codes resulting from the alliance provided limits to union competition and controls for partisan competition. Subsidies to labor organization included the obligation of employers to accept collective bargaining, strike activity, and labor participation in tripartite bodies. Other subsidies also affected patterns of union competition (e.g., monopolies of representation) and partisan competition in the unions (e.g., state registration). Subsidies, however, were double-edged because they could be either granted or withdrawn, thereby reducing labor autonomy from the state for future interactions (Collier and Collier 1979, Offe and Wiesenthal 1985). Incumbent labor leaders accepted this loss of autonomy because these institutions reduced their fear of being replaced by giving them an advantage over challengers nonallied with the governing party. Legal institutions, thus, reinforced the partisan loyalties forged by the alliance although the terms of the exchange differ across countries.[1] The terms of the alliance varied according to the particular conditions involved during the "engagement" period in each country.

From Seduction to Engagement

The partnership between labor unions and populist labor-based parties in Latin America seems evident ex post, but was not so obvious ex ante. Multiclass populist labor-based parties had a more diffused ideology than their Marxist counterparts seeking a proletariat revolution. The charismatic politicians who organized these populist parties sought to foster national development through industrialization and looked for broad multiclass coalitions (Drake 1991, Conniff 1999). Populist politicians needed political support and labor unions provided an organized constituency and helped to promote industrialization by delivering labor peace. Despite the convenience of this marriage for politicians and labor leaders, the seduction was not always immediate. The matchmaking was certainly accelerated by the need of populist politicians to build a power base and their willingness to give concessions to attract labor partners into their

---

[1] Labor *power resources* (Korpi 1978) or relative leverage with regards to politicians (Collier and Collier 1979) explains variation in institutional benefits across Latin American countries and across regions. Informal institutions, though, are more fluid than formal ones in the long run (Levitsky 1999).

political parties. In Mexico, the violence of the revolution accelerated the process. The Constitutionalist army required the military aid of the Red Battalions (organized by the House of the International Worker) before Alvaro Obregón sought the political support of the Mexican Regional Labor Confederation (CROM) in 1919. In the 1930s, Lázaro Cárdenas also resorted to labor for consolidating his national power by reediting the alliance with the CTM. In Argentina, labor leaders had long refused to make alliances with political parties until Juan Perón came to deliver "facts rather than words" to gain their support in his race for the presidency in the 1940s. In Venezuela, Rómulo Betancourt needed labor support to accelerate democratization in the 1940s and to carry the popular vote and provide labor peace after the 1958 transition to democracy.

This seduction process turned labor unions into core constituencies of Peronism in Argentina, the PRI in Mexico, and AD in Venezuela.[2] Because labor support brought these parties to power and allowed them to deliver their programs, unions gained access to government officials and obtained benefits to deliver to their constituencies. Labor's voice was included (formally or informally) in the party structure, and political influence was institutionalized in labor legislation that shaped industrial relations even when allies were out of power. Indeed, labor codes compensated for the relative weakness of labor unions vis-à-vis employers by using political resources not directly dependent on labor market conditions. Thus, politicians extending the influence of the state over different markets used these corporatist regulations to gain support of labor allies (by reducing their uncertainty about the future of industrial relations) and control social unrest that could distort their industrialization drives. In all three countries, the state exercised a strong influence in the outcome of labor relations because it defined domains for collective bargaining and union organization, rights for automatic check-off systems, permissions for closed-shop arrangements, and prerogatives for the administration of publicly provided selective incentives. These laws not only increased the rigidity of labor markets, but also highlighted the importance of political resources for labor and reinforced union partisan loyalties. Moreover, the use of inducements and constraints that reduced labor autonomy from the state also made leader-

---

[2] Gibson (1996: 10) develops the concept of "core constituencies" as a fact that recognizes an implicit hierarchy among members of a coalition. I use the concept to recognize the symbolic value of organized labor in the multiclass coalitions behind Peronism, PRI, and AD.

ship competition harder for challengers to allied union leaders, thereby reducing their fear of replacement.

Finally, Collier and Collier (1991) argue that the process of labor incorporation that originated in these labor-based parties also shaped the political systems of the three countries. These processes, they claim, explain the legacy of stability in Mexico and Venezuela and instability in Argentina. Their "shaping of the political arena," though, had an additional consequence for labor unions by providing them with different political alternatives to their populist partners. The seventy-year dominance of the Mexican PRI made it harder for labor leaders to risk access to the state by courting other political parties. The Venezuelan multiparty democracy provided diverse alternatives for labor leaders, although AD dominance in the political and union arena enhanced their partisan loyalty. In Argentina, despite the existence of other political parties, the proscription of Peronism enhanced the importance of labor unions as the forebears of the banned party, making their partisan loyalty resilient in sickness and in health.

In sum, the alliance between labor union and populist political parties provided labor unions with political resources that compensated for their industrial weakness, thus creating strong partisan loyalties in the three countries. Simultaneously, the political system influenced the availability of alternative electoral allies. Finally, in all three countries, the alliance resulted in corporatist labor regulations that shaped the possibilities for leadership competition and union competition, thus constraining the replacement threat although at the cost of labor autonomy. The rest of the chapter describes these processes and their legacies.

The Multiparty Democracy and the Venezuelan Union Movement

Venezuela was a latecomer to democracy and industrialization in the region. During the dictatorship of Juan Vicente Gómez (1908–35), when Venezuela became a large oil exporter, repressive labor legislation hindered union organization (Lucena 1982). A process of political liberalization under the moderate military rules of Eleazar López Contreras (1935–41) and Isaías Medina Angarita (1941–5) followed after Gómez's death. Exiles returned, and political activists started organizing political parties and labor unions (in the oil fields and urban centers) in an effort to accelerate the democratic transition by mobilizing civil society (Levine 1973, Lárez 1992, Coppedge 1994).

In September 1941, Rómulo Betancourt, a leader from the student opposition to Gómez's dictatorship founded AD.[3] On October 18, 1945, one day after the official birth date of Peronism in Argentina, AD supported a military uprising by young officers that established a revolutionary junta of seven members headed by Rómulo Betancourt. The junta called for free and universal elections, and after AD obtained landslide victories it passed power to the first elected president, Rómulo Gallegos, in February of 1948 (Ellner 1980: 95).[4] During the period from 1945 to 1948, labeled as the *trienio*, there was an upsurge of civil society organization promoted both by AD and its opponents who were trying to provide alternatives for AD's hegemony (Levine 1973). The opposition to AD organized two main parties: the radical Republican Democratic Union (URD) in 1945 and the Social-Christian Independent Committee for Political Organization (COPEI) in 1946. AD fostered the creation of the CTV and used its state prerogatives to promote union organization.[5] Moreover, AD controlled three-quarters of the unions registered during this period because the administration granted faster registration to AD-led unions thereby reducing the influence of their main contender in the union movement, the Communist Party of Venezuela (PCV) (Ellner 1980: 96, Melcher 1992). This manipulation of labor regulations not only reduced

[3] Student opposition based in the Central University of Caracas led to some uprisings and resulted in an abortive coup in April 1928. The student leaders of the "28 generation" provided founders for all the political groups and parties emerging after Gómez's death including several precursors to AD in the 1930s (Levine 1973: 22–4). AD was formally social-democratic. Its nationalism (and consequent antiimperialism) marked its original differences with the internationalism of the Communists (Ellner 1980: Chapter 2). Ellner (1993: 1) argues that AD "was a typical Latin American populist party in that it defended a radical program of income redistribution, its long-term goals were not clearly defined, and it based its popular appeal to a considerable degree on the charismatic qualities of its *jefe máximo*, Rómulo Betancourt." In 1985, AD's Labor Secretary Manuel Peñalver acknowledged the crossclass coalition behind AD. He said, "Might the workers of Acción Democrática have made a mistake when they joined the Party in that multiclass front? . . . No, here a labor party has never been intended. . . . Rómulo Betancourt analyzed . . . that the economic conditions for a class party did not exist then. . . ." (cited in Coppedge 1994: 32).

[4] In the 1947 presidential elections, Rómulo Gallegos received 74.45% of the votes (Kornblith and Levine 1995: 49).

[5] The annual average of unions registered during the *trienio* was 273 whereas in the previous 7 years it had been 36. During the military period (1948–57), the average dropped to 40 unions per year (calculations based on official figures provided by Central Bank of Venezuela 1993, II: 113).

the threat of replacement for AD union leaders, but also increased their possibilities of rising to leadership in new unions.

The 1947 AD-sponsored constitution guaranteed the right to strike and organize unions whereas a reform of the labor law set mechanisms for the resolution of industrial disputes. Meanwhile the AD government established a Ministry of Labor and pressured employers to enter into collective bargaining with unions. This sharply increased the number of signed collective agreements, which included an impressive expansion of fringe benefits. Subsidies for consumption and rent reductions also benefited workers (Collier and Collier 1991: 265). Additionally, the rise in oil prices and production until 1947 facilitated considerable wage increases under the pressure of the Ministry of Labor. A policy of industrialization directed by the new Venezuelan Corporation of Development (CVF), also increased employment, which further reinforced labor bargaining power. Labor leaders, thus, gained benefits to deliver to their constituencies that enhanced their leadership positions and paid the government by providing social peace (Ellner 1980: 113–15). However, the success of the alliance could not prevent a military coup, which imposed a new dictator, General Marcos Pérez Jiménez, in November of 1948.

A popular uprising forced Pérez Jiménez to flee Venezuela in January of 1958. In October, the leaders of the main political parties, AD's Rómulo Betancourt, COPEI's Rafael Caldera, and URD's Jovito Villalba signed the Pact of Punto Fijo to guarantee the success of the new democratic transition. They pledged respect for the electoral outcome and committed themselves to power-sharing arrangements – regardless of election results – and to a Common Minimum Program. The Common Minimum Program included the eventual nationalization of oil fields (by nonrenewal of concessions); guarantees for business sectors, the church, and the military; and promises to pursue full employment, housing programs for the poor, new labor regulations, and widespread social legislation in health, education, and social security (Karl 1986: 212–14). Although Punto Fijo would exclude the PCV, a committee of Communist, AD, COPEI, URD, and independent union leaders – who had coordinated the opposition to the dictatorship – approved a Worker-Employer Accord six months before the pact. The accord established "harmonious collaboration" through the establishment of commissions with equal labor and employer representation for the resolution of labor disputes; respect for labor organization and collective bargaining; protection of job security; and the exhaustion of conciliatory mechanisms before confrontation (McCoy 1989: 40, Karl 1997: 99).

AD won every presidential election but two and held the largest number of seats in Congress until 1989, although it shared power with other parties and in particular with COPEI (Kornblith and Levine 1995: 45). The Suffrage Law of 1959 established an electoral system of proportional representation that reinforced the consensual and multiparty character of the regime. Oil revenues also enhanced democratic stability through generalized subsidies and fostered a development strategy based on import substitution industrialization promoted by higher tariffs and the expansion of state-owned enterprises (Karl 1986: 210–12, Frieden 1991: 184, and Karl 1997: 95). Thanks to this successful formula, the Venezuelan economy grew steadily until 1978 while its democracy survived the waves of authoritarianism that swept over Latin America in the 1960s and 1970s (Karl 1986: 215, Rodriguez 1991: 241). Union constituencies benefited from social policies while labor organization advanced with the state-driven industrialization. Public companies had higher unionization rates, more centralized collective bargaining, and usually resorted to partisan influence for the resolution of industrial conflict (Iranzo and Penso 1993, Márquez 1994). The state also provided the CTV unions with direct subsidies and participation in tripartite institutions ranging from social security to state-owned company boards, which were distributed according to partisan criteria (McCoy 1989, Betancourt et al. 1995: 84).

The use of partisan criteria and the extension of proportional representation to union elections permitted the coexistence of labor leaders affiliated with different political parties. Its numerical predominance facilitated AD's control of labor militancy and the fulfillment of Punto Fijo goals. AD labor leaders were important allies for the party, and AD politicians became very receptive to their demands.[6] AD's regional labor bureaus usually proposed labor authorities at the state level, and the influence of the AD national labor bureau has been crucial in most AD primaries (Betancourt et al. 1993: 84). It was a decisive factor for the presidential nominations of former Minister of Labor Raúl Leoni against the objec-

---

[6] Referring to the importance of labor for AD, Coppedge (1994: 33) states that "no group is more useful than the labor unions for getting out the vote in general, as well as, internal elections. The human resources of the labor unions and federations of the state are at the disposal of the state labor secretary (frequently because he is a leader of the state labor federation), and this power allows him to act as a power broker in state politics. Labor leaders even become [party] general secretaries at the state level."

tions of President Rómulo Betancourt in 1963, Jaime Lusinchi (in exchange for the appointment of AD's labor secretary as AD secretary general) in 1983, and Carlos Andrés Pérez in 1988 (Ellner 1993). All three candidates became Venezuelan presidents.

Labor influence in AD and its policies thus reinforced the partisan loyalty of union leaders to the party whereas the success of political strategies increased the politicization of labor relations. AD's predominance explains a political pattern of strike activity in which labor militancy picked up during COPEI administrations and receded under AD's governments (Coppedge 1994: 34). Additionally, the CTV had a centralized authority because it had considerable leverage over industrial conflict by its affiliates and avoided challenges from strong members by giving a vote to each member in confederate elections. Despite this centralized authority and AD predominance, partisan competition in the union movement was more salient in Venezuela than in Mexico or Argentina. Proportional representation allowed for the coexistence of diverse parties, and AD lost control of the CTV in 1968 when a group of disgruntled union leaders left the party and founded the People's Electoral Movement (MEP). AD recovered control of the CTV in 1970, and the MEP remained a minor party after many of the dissidents returned to AD (Ellner 1993: 41, Coppedge 1994: 55).

Summing up, multiparty democracy, proportional representation, and partisan criteria in the distribution of state subsidies reinforced partisan loyalties for labor leaders. In addition to AD, COPEI, URD, MEP, and the PCV, other parties with labor influence included the Movement Towards Socialism (MAS) and the "new unionism" of Causa R, which challenged the traditional political parties.[7] Hence, whereas in Argentina and Mexico a single party has traditionally commanded the partisan loyalties of labor leaders, in Venezuela, labor leaders owed loyalties to a variety of parties despite the predominance of AD. Hence, leadership competition in the unions generally adopted the form of partisan competition linking labor leaders' partisan identities with those of political allies in the electoral arena. Proportional representation also mitigated union competition

---

[7] The *new unionism* emerged during the 1970s in a state-owned steel factory in the region of Guyana. Although the new unionism won the union election in 1979, two years later the national and state federations seized control of the union taking advantage of a contract dispute. The federations imposed a provisional commission until the CTV pressed for open elections in the union, which were won again by the new unionism in 1987 (López Maya 1997).

by facilitating the inclusion of various political parties within the same union, thereby reducing the incentives for the creation of parallel unions competing for the same constituencies.

Venezuelan Labor Regulations. The Venezuelan labor code was passed in 1936 after the death of Gómez. It predated the organization of most labor unions that emerged from the unionization drive of the 1940s and was maintained with reforms until 1990. The labor code included social security, profit sharing, and severance payments that benefited union constituencies. Yet, it also established union registration and labor ministry prerogatives for the resolution of collective conflicts about the legality of strikes after the submission of a "petition to strike" and the exhaustion of conciliatory mechanisms. The partisan use of state intervention favored AD union leaders by reducing their replacement threat at the cost of relinquishing autonomy from the state and the party.[8] Additionally, the labor code excluded the public sector and limited the scope of unions to the state level, thus requiring unions to form federations for achieving a national scope and increasing union fragmentation.

Job stability guarantees for the leaders of registered unions, and, until 1973, the right to belong to more than one union facilitated union competition (Lucena 1982, Melcher 1992).[9] Union competition, though, was not rampant because employers were obligated to bargain only with the union that represented the majority of workers. The contract was then applied to all workers in the bargaining unit (regardless of whether they were members of the union). Hence, there could be various unions but a single negotiating agent (International Labor Office [ILO] 1996: 61). Moreover, the 1961 constitution allowed collective contracts to include "union clauses" that provided unions with input into the selection of personnel (ILO 1991: 85), which made membership in the bargaining union more attractive. Additionally, the labor code limited union scope to the state level, thus making aggregation into federations the only option for nationwide or industrywide organizing. Federations, in turn, provided

---

[8] The AD leadership controlled access to closed lists and used this access to enforce party discipline, although the importance of the labor bloc in the presidential nomination increased the internal leverage of labor unions (Crisp 1998, Burgess 1998a: 60–1).

[9] For instance, guarantees of job stability for the seven members of the local executive committees of each union and the practice of paying each union participating in collective bargaining a monetary reward (*costa contractual*) for its representation increased the incentives of union leaders to maintain the existing labor organizations.

multiple instances for leadership competition at the local level by multiplying the number of union elections. However, indirect elections at the federal and confederate level facilitated the elaboration of unified slates.[10]

In short, the alliance with AD provided union leaders with benefits they could deliver to their constituencies and access to a highly interventionist state, which they could use to improve their leadership position and avoid replacement by challengers (mainly Communists in the 1940s). In turn, the success of the political strategies explains the enduring politicization of labor relations. Additionally, proportional representation and federative structures facilitated partisan competition in the union movement and, along with collective bargaining regulations, mitigated union competition.

The Institutionalized Revolution and the PRI Monopoly of Mexican Labor Unions

The legacy of the violent Mexican Revolution (1910–17) and its nonreelection banner permeated the one-party dominant system that emerged in the 1930s (Molinar 1991). This inclusive authoritarianism combined strong presidential powers, mass mobilization, and electoral manipulation.[11] PRI-related organizations canalized the mobilization of workers and other social sectors; executive discretion overrode legal boundaries to sustain political stability; and a history of fraudulent electoral practices limited party pluralism.[12] Electoral fraud permitted the PRI to achieve unified government (control of the presidency and Congress). Additionally, discipline within the ruling party (related to the nonreelection of legislators who depended on the president for their future careers) and the

---

[10] The informal practice of agreeing on unified slates for union elections among many competing parties followed the logic of power-sharing emerging from Punto Fijo, but often reduced leadership competition in union elections by providing workers with a single choice (Arismendi and Iturraspe 1990). Yet, it did not formally restrict the possibility of competition if rival leaders did not reach an agreement.

[11] There is a very large amount of literature on the Mexican Revolution and the development of Mexican political system. Among other works, see Carr (1976), Pellicer and Reyna (1978), Garrido (1982), Knight (1986), Hart (1987), and Collier (1992).

[12] Molinar (1991: 37) shows how, after 1946, electoral registration was used to limit electoral competition. Craig and Cornelious (1995: 255) describe PRI strategies for committing electoral fraud, which include "stuffing ballot boxes, intimidating potential opposition supporters, disqualifying opposition party poll-watchers, relocating polling places at the last minute, and issuing multiple vote credentials for PRI supporters."

presidential leadership of the ruling party further reinforced the powers of the executive beyond the formalism of the constitution (Weldon 1997: 227). These informal institutions made the presidency stronger than in the other two countries. The violence of the revolution also fostered an alliance between the revolutionary elites and labor leaders in the House of the World Worker. They organized six Red Battalions to fight with the Constitutionalist army of Generals Venustiano Carranza and Alvaro Obregón in return for labor rights established in the Constitution of 1917. A second alliance followed in 1919 between the CROM and President Alvaro Obregón. CROM leader Luis Morones organized the Labor Party of Mexico (PLM), which served as a political machine first for Obregón and then President Plutarco Elías Calles. Additionally, the CROM controlled labor unrest during these administrations (Middlebrook 1995: 78–9). In return, President Calles appointed Morones as minister of industry, commerce, and labor. Morones used political resources to compensate for the numerical and organizational weakness of labor unions and advanced the organization of CROM unions at the expense of other groups.[13]

This was not a happy marriage though. In 1929, Calles decided to organize the Revolutionary National Party (PNR) to maintain his hold on state power despite the nonreelection clause, but Morones remained in his Labor Party and was later forced to resign under suspicion for the assassination of Obregón (Alvarado 1990).[14] President Lázaro Cárdenas (1934–40) refused to accept Calles's maneuvering behind the scenes. He sought political allies to build an alternative power base to the regional caciques that supported Calles. Seeking labor support, Cárdenas established a populist coalition that included labor unions (Cornelius 1973: 440–3, León and Marbrán 1985). His labor policies included a call for a single organization of industrial workers that resulted in the most impor-

---

[13] Bensusán (1992) and Clark (1934) analyze Morones's political strategy to compensate for industrial weakness. Middlebrook (1995: 90) describes the expansion of the CROM during Morones's tenure as minister: "In 1926, CROM members held 11 of 58 positions in the federal Senate and 40 of 272 seats in the federal Chamber of Deputies. The confederation used its government positions to enforce dues deductions from public employees' salaries . . . [and] . . . CROM's control over many labor conciliation and arbitration boards were also the base from which it compelled employers to recognize its union affiliates and undermined its labor rivals."

[14] Calles's successors worked systematically to undermine the CROM by favoring other unions and replacing pro-CROM personnel in the Federal Labor Office (Roxborough 1984: 16, Aziz Nassif 1989: 60–61, and Middlebrook 1995: 81).

tant unions organizing the CTM in 1936.[15] The affinity between Cárdenas and labor unions turned the latter into important instruments for policy implementation.[16] Cárdenas also incorporated labor unions into the PRM, which preceded the PRI.[17] The CTM joined the new party as an organization, thus establishing a formal alliance.[18] Cárdenas used the functional structure of the party to limit the influence of regional caciques (León and Marbrán 1985). Labor leaders gained seats in both houses of Congress, governorships, and political appointments at all levels while playing an important role in the nomination and election of officials (Collier and Collier 1991: 240). Additionally, Cárdenas promoted state expansion by nationalizing oil and railroads, as well as import substitution industrialization. He also implemented an extensive land reform and extended workers' rights (Aziz Nassif 1989: 63). He established mandatory payment of wages for the seventh day of the week thus raising salaries by 17%, and set up commissions to establish the ability of companies to pay wage hikes threatening noncompliance with expropriation and worker management (Collier and Collier 1991: 241). As a result, real salaries grew 43% between 1934 and 1940 (Lara Rangel 1990: 87). The alliance provided labor unions with access to the state and benefits for their constituencies, showing the value of political strategies, creating a strong partisan loyalty to the PRI, and contributing to the politicization of labor relations in Mexico.

[15] The unions in the CTM included both local unions and regional federations and national industrial unions, such as those in railroads, mining, metalworking, electricity, telecommunications, and oil. The CTM also included Communist and independent unionist (Acedo Angulo 1990, Middlebrook 1995: 203).

[16] For instance, unions provided Cárdenas with an excuse for oil nationalization. When the new union of oil workers entered a labor conflict with the foreign-owned companies and the companies did not accept the Supreme Court ruling in favor of workers, Cárdenas nationalized them (Aziz Nassif 1989: 76–7).

[17] In his defense for the incorporation of the CTM into the new party, CTM-secretary general, Vicente Lombardo Toledano argued that the new party could not be restricted to the labor class and should include other sectors of the Mexican people (cited in Acedo Angulo 1990: 116).

[18] The PRM was a multiclass coalition with a functional structure including organized labor, peasants, bureaucratic, and military sectors. The party identified itself with the Mexican Revolution, drawing in symbols of social justice and economic nationalism despite its catch-all nature. It included mass organizations and territorially based clientelistic bosses. Cárdenas radicalized its appeal by courting labor and peasant support while he exercised a charismatic leadership characteristic of Latin American populism. President Miguel Alemán abolished the military sector in 1940 (León and Marbán 1985, Craig and Cornelious 1995: 253–4, Basurto 1999).

Cárdenas's successors drifted away from his radical populism, although they continued with policies of state-led industrialization and sustained the alliance with organized labor. They retained the functional representation in the party and continued distributing elective and appointed positions to labor leaders. They also expanded the number of state institutions with labor participation by creating the Mexican Institute for Social Security (IMSS) and the Institute for the Worker Housing National Fund (INFONAVIT) among others. They reinforced PRI loyalty by helping allied union leaders displace their Communist competitors from the union movement, thus further reducing partisan competition in the unions.[19] Allied labor leaders reduced the replacement risk as the expense of losing autonomy from the state. The most dramatic example of the drop in the replacement risk was the fifty-year tenure of CTM leader, Fidel Velázquez, who died as such in 1997. Political stability and labor peace permitted high rates of growth although at the cost of considerable restrictions to political pluralism.

The prevalence of the one-party regime curtailed the labor unions' options to look for alternative partners and further reinforced their partisan loyalty to the PRI. The limited partisan competition provided the PRI with a near monopoly over the affiliation of union leaders. The exception was a small movement of unions nonaffiliated with the PRI, which called themselves independent. However, a crisis provoked by the violent repression of a massive student demonstration seeking democratization in 1968 resulted in a process of political liberalization during the 1970s. The 1977 electoral reform attempted to bolster the legitimacy of the regime and the mobilization capacity of the PRI. The CTM, though, was suspicious of its effects on partisan competition in the unions and its share of elective position (Middlebrook 1986: 132). The CTM was allied with the PRI and thus wanted the party in power to provide access to the state.

---

[19] For the sake of labor unity, the Communist union leaders who followed a popular front strategy and other left-wing groups had accepted the predominance of the governing party in the CTM. In 1936, the Communist leaders relinquished the bid for the secretary of organization, supported by national industrial unions. In the late 1940s, though, PRI union leaders replaced the electoral procedures of the CTM that linked votes to membership size with a process that gave one vote to every union, regardless of membership. This reform was targeted at the large national industrial unions in which the Communists and other left-wing groups had more influence and was followed by the expulsion of these groups. Subsequent rebellions of national industrial unions led by left-wing or independent leadership was repressed by the state until the unions were controlled by PRI-affiliated leaders (Medina 1979: 130–43, Basurto 1984: 124–32, Assiz Nassif 1989: 98–104).

Political liberalization, instead, fostered the electoral growth of the National Action Party (PAN) linked to business sectors of northern Mexico and the Catholic Church, and minor left-wing parties previously allied to the PRI also benefited (Middlebrook 1986: 123–31, Craig and Cornelious 1995: 269–79).

Despite monopolistic control by the PRI over most unions, seven national confederations embodied the alliance with the PRI. Besides the CTM and the CROM, these confederations included the Revolutionary Confederation of Workers and Peasants (CROC), the Revolutionary Workers' Confederation (CRT), the Revolutionary Labor Confederation (COR), CGT, and the Federation of Public Service Workers' Unions (FSTSE). With the exception of the FSTSE, the other national labor confederations registered affiliates in a broad range of economic activities, and the largest confederations – CTM, CROC, and CROM – maintained a national presence with important numbers of affiliates registered in every major region (Middlebrook 1995: 178–9). The emergence of this array of national confederations competing for institutional space within the party structure was related to the internal power struggles that characterized the PRI. The competition among these PRI-related national confederations for the affiliation of local unions and federations did not create risks for PRI politicians because their partisan loyalties were restricted within the boundaries of the party. In fact, PRI politicians could take advantage of this competition to reinforce partisan loyalty by threatening to decrease the share of candidacies or appointments of less loyal confederations. PRI-related national labor confederations made some unification attempts including the establishment of the Congress of Labor (CT) as an umbrella organization in 1966. Yet, the CT's consensual mechanisms for decision making failed to centralize the Mexican confederations and avoided the hegemony of its largest member, the CTM.[20] In the end, it could only coordinate their participation in the corporatist institutions of the state, thus providing a new arena for union competition within the boundaries of the party.

Within confederations, however, discipline was usually tight. The CTM, in particular, imposed a centralized authority over affiliated unions. This authority derived from sanction power included in its constitution and its influence in the institutions regulating industrial relations,

---

[20] In 1979, the CTM affiliated 63.9% of the Congress of Labor union members (Zazueta and De La Peña 1981: 810).

approving collective contracts, and distributing social security. Furthermore, the CTM avoided challenges to centralized leadership by weakening its strongest members. Like the CTV, it counted all unions equal, thus imposing the predominance of small unions over nationwide industrial organizations (Camacho 1980: 112, Aguilar García 1986: 134). This centralized authority further reinforced the limits on partisan competition within the confederation.

Mexican Labor Regulations. The 1917 Constitution guaranteed the right to strike and organize unions. However, before the enactment of the Federal Labor Law (LFT) in 1931, union organization was fragmented, and decentralized collective bargaining was regulated at the local level (Bensusán 1992, Middlebrook 1995: 76). The law remains in place although it has been amended. It introduced obligatory collective bargaining and labor representation on Conciliation and Arbitration Boards, which regulated collective bargaining and established union registration and monopolies of representation within the bargaining unit (LFT, art. 386, 387, and 388). Cárdenas allowed the introduction of closed-shop arrangements through exclusion clauses in collective contracts and established monopolies of representation and a single confederation for the public administration (Mexican Constitution, art. 123, clause B).[21] Outside the public administration, however, diverse national confederations competed for the organization of multiple local unions even if exclusion clauses restricted the leadership competition within individual unions. Moreover, the law retained the decentralization of collective bargaining and regulated strike activity. Legal strikes needed state approval, and requirements included support from a majority of workers, a formal petition, and the exhaustion of state-led conciliation efforts.[22]

In sum, the combination of a one-party system, executive discretion, and state intervention in industrial relations reduced the replacement threat for allied union leaders at the expense of their autonomy from the

---

[21] Closed-shop clauses forced workers to become union members and employers to fire workers who had been dismissed from the union. They allowed the development of patronage networks that could also be used to curtail leadership competition within the union (Coppedge 1993: 255) or the sale of *protection contracts* to employers who sought to avoid more militant unions (La Botz 1992: 55).

[22] Employers could also appeal a strike by demanding that it be declared "nonexistent" within seventy-two hours of its start, thus forcing workers back to work (Middlebrook 1995:69).

state. The discretion of the Mexican executive to implement labor regulations facilitated its use of legal inducements and constraints to foster the fear of replacement among disgruntled allied labor leaders. Union registration, in particular, could be used to change the conditions for union competition among national confederations.[23] The creation of tripartite state institutions sharpened the stakes of union competition among PRI-affiliated national confederations. Meanwhile, closed shops (through exclusion clauses in collective contracts) allowed union leaders to restrict leadership competition since internal opposition could be punished with job loss thereby reinforcing the limitations to partisan competition created by the one-party regime.

The Legacy of Perón and the Argentine Unions

Argentina has one of the oldest democracies in Latin America. The 1912 electoral law guaranteed the secrecy of universal suffrage to all adult males, amidst a propitious economic environment derived from its export boom. A predominantly middle-class party, the Radical Civic Union (UCR) won the 1916 presidential election and governed the country until 1930 when President Hipólito Yrigoyen was overthrown by the military. In spite of early industrialization and labor organization in Argentina, the Radicals failed to win the support of organized labor. The influence of Socialist and Syndicalist ideas among union leaders and the foreign citizenship of numerous workers have been associated with this failure (Rock 1977).

After 1930, conservative politicians returned to power and excluded the Radicals by committing electoral fraud. Another military coup ended this restrictive democracy in 1943 and paved the way for Perón's entrance onto the political scene. During the 1930s, the influence of the Syndicalist ideology declined while Socialist and Communist union leaders tried to organize industrial unions, centralize collective bargaining to the industrial level, and develop union-run systems for the provision of social and health services. However, the labor movement was very fragmented and weak vis-à-vis employers despite the rapid industrialization. As a result, the incipient labor legislation was not enforced and workers continued to suffer

---

[23] Middlebrook (1995: 172–3) notes that union registration is a highly political issue because affiliates of different confederations compete in the same geographical area, and the registry officials can support one of these confederations at the expenses of the others.

social and political exclusion (Horowitz 1990).[24] The 1943 coup, however, made Colonel Juan Perón the new secretary of labor and social security. During his tenure as secretary of labor, Perón gave legal and technical assistance to unions, consulted union leaders on social and labor legislation, enforced existing labor laws in the whole country, and generalized paid holidays and vacations to the entire labor force. He also created labor courts to handle worker grievances, restricted firing, and improved working conditions and severance payment. Additionally, he enforced collective bargaining with government-recognized unions and intervened often on workers' behalves when negotiations broke down (Little 1988, McGuire 1997: 52–3).

Most analyses of the origin of Peronism argue that the social and political exclusion suffered during the 1930s explains why labor leaders allied with Perón after he implemented prolabor policies as the secretary of labor from 1943 to 1945.[25] On October 17, 1945, which has traditionally been considered the official birth date of Peronism, union leaders organized a general strike and a massive rally to obtain the freedom of Perón who had been put into prison by his colleagues a few days before (Torre 1988). They also founded a Labor Party. In an alliance with splinter groups from the UCR, some independent groups, and conservative provincial leaders, this party won the presidential elections of 1946 with Perón as its candidate. After his inauguration, Perón dissolved the Labor Party and unified all the parties in the alliance into the Single Party of the National Revolution (PURN). In January 1947, the PURN was renamed as the Peronist Party (Torre 1990: 194–202). The Peronist Party finished with the autonomous project of a class party embodied in the Labor Party and imposed a multiclass coalition, such as those behind the PRI and AD although with

[24] Gaudio and Pilone (1988a) show that although employment grew by 40% from 1929 to 1942, real salaries only grew by 6% (p. 44). They also analyzed the strike data for 1935 and point that workers won only 17% of all strikes (p. 31).

[25] There is a large literature on workers' political and social exclusion during the 1930s and its effect on the subsequent alliance with Perón. This corpus begins with Germani's (1966, 1973) seminal view of the effect of industrialization on migrant workers as a mass available for the appeal of Peronism. Di Tella (1981) considers Peronism a mobilization of workers from above. Murmis and Portantiero (1971) argue that unions exchanged political support for regulations that favored working conditions. Matsushita (1983) and Tamarin (1985) study the ideology and attitudes of union leaders to explain their alliance with Perón. Torre (1989, 1990) argues that, although unions led the political exchange, they were bypassed by Perón after he was elected president because he also offered political and cultural inclusion for workers.

a lower degree of formal institutionalization.[26] Indeed, after women were granted the vote in 1949, Perón organized his party as a movement and promised shares of one-third of the elective positions to the labor, political, and female branches.[27]

During Perón's tenure as president (1946–55), unionization grew dramatically and real wages increased.[28] Perón not only increased state intervention in the regulation of labor relations, but also increased protectionism and state expansion. He controlled foreign trade and transferred hard currency from agricultural exports into industrial promotion. He nationalized railroads, ports, and telecommunications. These policies increased employment and unionization, especially after Perón made it compulsory for the public sector in 1950 (McGuire 1997: 58). Labor leaders also saw their salaries grow and gained elective and appointed positions, including membership in the cabinet showing the value of political strategies (Collier and Collier 1991: 341). In addition, Perón institutionalized union privileges into laws and then used these regulations – such as monopolies of representation over collective bargaining and union dues through employer withholding – to increase the Peronist control over unions. Hence, left-wing or dissident labor leaders lost state subsidies or were replaced by government or CGT trustees and deprived of the right to exercise monopolies of representation (Zorrilla 1983: 36–9, Doyon 1988, McGuire 1997: 59). Due to the combination of subsidies and constraints, the Peronist loyalty expanded enormously whereas partisan competition dropped dramatically thus reducing the replacement threat for allied union leaders at the expense of labor autonomy from the state.

---

[26] Mackinnon (1998) describes the internal conflicts led by labor leaders who wanted to hang on to their class autonomy in the internal elections of the Peronist Party in 1947 and the first midterm elections of 1948. This process reinforced the multiclass nature of the populist coalition behind the charismatic and nationalistic leadership of Perón as expressed in the literature cited in the previous footnote and studies of the Peronist vote (Mora y Araujo and Llorente 1980).

[27] The 1948 party charter established territorial and union branches. The 1951 structure as a *movement* rather than a party granted one-third of candidacies and leaders to labor but was not formalized into a party charter nor rigorously practiced before Perón's overthrow in 1955 (Levitsky 1999: 48–9).

[28] According to Doyon (1988: 178), union members grew from 877,333 in 1945 to 2,256,580 in 1954. The Ministry of Labor registers 45% of Argentine unions as organized between 1943 and 1956 (Lamadrid, n.d.: 75). According to James (1988: 11), the labor share of national income grew from 40% to 49% between 1946 and 1949.

In 1955, a military coup ousted Perón and banished the Peronist Party, starting a period of political and economic instability. Neither civilian nor military presidents lasted more than a few years, and military coups became the usual mechanism of presidential succession. When it became obvious that Peronism still was the first plurality, democratic transitions failed. Moreover, the political conflicts among industrial groups and agricultural exporters resulted in multiple devaluations and mounting inflation.[29] Perón's successors failed to erase his mark among workers, and labor leaders retained their partisan loyalty to Peronism despite harsh repression and increasing incentives for partisan competition by the government.[30] Instead, Peronist unions learned how to create industrial distress with political objectives and adapt to different political environments to a much greater degree than labor leaders in Mexico and even Venezuela. Additionally, the banning of the party turned the unions into the only legal forum for political activities for Peronists, thereby reinforcing the partisan links between the unions and Peronism and increasing the factional competition within the movement (James 1988: 74–6, McGuire 1997: 98–9).[31]

In 1983, Argentina reestablished democracy with the Radicals and the Peronists alternating power in a competitive two-party system. Electoral rivalry resulted in thirteen general strikes of the Peronist CGT against the economic policies of the Radical president, Raúl Alfonsín, until he was replaced by the Peronist Carlos Menem in 1989. In spite of the pluralism of the Argentine party system, union leaders retained their partisan loyalty to Peronism to the point that leadership competition usually remained within partisan boundaries, adopting a form of factional competition, even when occasional defections from the party turned it into partisan compe-

[29] O'Donnell (1977 and 1982), Waissman (1982), Rouquie (1982 and 1975), Sábato and Schwartzer (1985), Cavarozzi (1987), Smith (1989), Collier and Collier (1991), and McGuire (1997) analyze this period of Argentine history as well as the causes of political and economic instability.

[30] By 1956 the military government had come to accept the impossibility of erasing Peronism from the unions by legal decree or simple repression. It was also convinced of the lack of viability of alternative candidates (mainly Socialist and Communist) for working-class leadership. The government then tried to weaken the union movement, provide for minority representation, permit more than one union to represent workers in a single industry, allow for multiple confederations, and help anti-Peronists in union elections. However, this policy was also unsuccessful in eroding the partisan loyalty to Peronism (Cavarozzi 1984: 63–86, James 1988: 66–8).

[31] In spite of the strong partisan loyalty of labor unions, the independent political projects of union leaders who wanted to occupy the space left by the exile of Perón met with his resistance to lose control of "his" movement (McGuire 1997: chapters 4 and 5).

tition. Factional competition in the CGT was more usual, though, because it was a very decentralized confederation. The largest ten unions organized 52% of unionized workers. The CGT electoral system weighted membership for union vote giving the ten largest unions control of 47% of the delegates to CGT conventions (Thompsom 1993: 130). They also sustained the CGT financially making it difficult for the CGT leadership that had very limited sanction power to discipline them (CGT 1994c). This decentralized authority and factional competition contributed to the many institutional ruptures and divisions that plagued the CGT except for the period from 1945 to 1955.

Argentine Labor Regulations. Perón's labor laws were often amended and even suspended during military rule, but they were reenacted after the return of democracy.[32] The law on labor organizations established union monopolies of representation per activity or industry. Unions controlled their own elections, and there was no provision for minority representation. The law on collective bargaining established compulsory collective bargaining at the industrial level and the right of unions to retain as an extraordinary quota a percentage of every wage increase after the signing of a new contract, which applied to members and nonmembers alike. Moreover, collective contracts had no term limit until a new deal was reached covering unions from negotiations during recessions or politically inhospitable conditions. Finally, the social security law extended the monopolies of representation to a compulsory health insurance system run by union-administered health or welfare funds.[33] They provided unions with funds charged as administrative fees. Their services also became selective incentives for members, who received a larger range of services despite the obligation of welfare funds to cover all workers regardless of union membership.[34]

---

[32] Perón's decrees as secretary of labor became laws during his presidency and continue to regulate Argentine labor relations and union organization as law 14,250 of collective bargaining; law 14,555 and later law 23,551 on union organization; and law 18,610 and later law 23,660 on welfare funds (Gaudio and Pilone 1988b: 87, James 1988: 10).

[33] Welfare funds also expanded to other activities, such as social tourism, recreation, complementary pensions, and educational and training services. The fact that law 14,250 also excluded unions from paying taxes when pursuing activities that benefited their members further enhanced the development of welfare funds.

[34] The provision of nonhealth services and even more extensive health services to union members than to nonmembers was used as a selective incentive (union leader O. Raitano, personal interview, 1995).

These regulations shaped the patterns of union competition and leadership competition. Monopolies of representation for collective bargaining and social security administration curtailed union competition. The lack of minority representation and the industrial centralization of monopolistic resources occasionally induced union leaders to agree on single slates for union elections, thereby restricting leadership competition within the unions. However, there was internal competition within unions, in particular under non-Peronist administrations.[35]

In short, the alliance with Peronism and the importance of unions during Peronist proscription sustained Peronist partisan loyalty in the labor movement and reduced the incentives for partisan competition. Meanwhile, monopolies of representation curtailed union competition, and the absence of minority representation made leadership competition more difficult although possible and often adopted the form of factional competition.

The Legacies of the Alliance

In all three countries, the alliance between unions and labor-based parties provided inducements for labor organizing that reduced the replacement threat for allied union leaders, although at the expense of their autonomy from the state or the party. The institutions that emerged from the alliance created corporatist systems of state-labor relations. The state had the power to shape the relationship between management and unions, thus making it more attractive for both groups to channel their demands through the state to obtain a better outcome. Labor regulations and partisan structures sustained this alliance between unions and labor-based parties while shaping the opportunities for union competition and leadership competition, thus curtailing the replacement threat for allied union leaders. Moreover, protectionism and state intervention facilitated unionization and labor bargaining with employers who could pass higher labor costs onto consumers. Thus, political strategies proved valuable for labor, explaining the subsequent politicization of labor relations that would

---

[35] In the period between 1965 and 1968, when Radical president Arturo Illia was in power and the Peronist party was banned, 55.9% of union elections had a single slate. During the 1973–6 Peronist administration, the number of uncontested union elections grew to 67.4%. After democratization, leadership competition increased, and only 21.6% of union elections were uncontested in 1984 and 1985 after Peronism was defeated for the first time in fair elections (Gaudio and Thompsom 1990: 79).

provide a common context for the policy shift of populist labor-based parties.

In spite of the comparability across countries, different trends in leadership competition and union competition emerged from the diverse history of the alliance in each country. Union competition was more prevalent in Mexico at the national level than in Argentina and Venezuela, although factional struggles within Peronism have resulted in divisions within the CGT. Leadership competition was easier in Venezuela, in the form of partisan competition, than in Argentina and was most restrictive in Mexico.

In these three countries, however, the alliance generated partisan bonds that tied labor unions and populist political parties. Union leaders exchanged their autonomy for institutional arrangements that reduced the replacement threat by providing policies that benefited their constituencies and limited leadership competition and union competition. As described in the following three chapters, the legacies of the alliance, in terms of partisan loyalty, union competition, and leadership competition, shaped the interactions between labor unions and populist partisan allies implementing market reforms. Labor-based parties in government took advantage of the institutional legacies of the original exchange to implement market-oriented reforms because partisan loyalties and state regulations of industrial relations facilitated the transition toward more open economies. Hence, none of these governments enacted reforms of labor organization, which could have radically transformed the opportunities for union competition and leadership competition. Governing labor-based parties were afraid of undercutting their own comparative advantage in their interaction with labor unions. Therefore, union competition was more resilient than leadership competition during the reform process because it was more regulated by labor legislation that has remained largely unchanged since the original "marriage" between labor unions and their allied parties. Finally, although the legacies of labor institutions and party systems influenced all unions within each country, different patterns of union-government interactions emerged within Venezuela, Mexico, and Argentina during the implementation of market reforms. These variations are more related to political dynamics that not only explain the different interactions observed in each country, but also provide a richer picture of the transition in each of them.

4

A Tug of War: Labor Unions and Market Reforms in Venezuela

Pérez's conversion from populism to neoliberalism set the stage for a dramatic change in the Venezuelan political system established by the Pact of Punto Fijo in 1958. Democratic stability had traditionally set Venezuela apart from the less democratic Mexico and highly unstable Argentina. The other particular trait of Venezuela has been its strong dependence on oil production for most of the twentieth century. Since World War II, oil exports have accounted for more than 90% of the foreign exchange earnings, two-thirds of government revenue, and one-fifth of gross domestic product (GDP). High taxes and royalties on oil profits and production have been the largest sources for government revenue for generalized subsidies after democracy was reinstalled in 1958 (Karl 1986: 215, Rodríguez 1991: 241, Frieden 1991: 186). Oil revenues were used to foster a development strategy based on import substitution industrialization and state intervention, which succeeded in promoting growth with low inflation. Between 1954 and 1978, the average annual real growth in nonoil gross domestic product was 7.4%, and the annual inflation rate was only 3% (Rodríguez 1991: 238). Oil revenues, thus, fostered both economic development and a stable bipartisan democracy. Since 1958, two political parties, AD and COPEI, have won all presidential elections that produced three partisan turnovers. These two parties received approximately 60% of presidential votes until 1973 and more than 85% from 1973 to 1988 (Kornblith and Levine 1995: 49).

Carlos Andrés Pérez had already been president of Venezuela between 1974 and 1979. In this period, Venezuela benefited from the oil boom, which not only generated revenues but also increased its credit worthiness and provided foreign loans. Pérez nationalized oil and iron ore with full compensation, subsidized the import substitution industries, and expanded

52

social programs. He invested oil revenues and borrowed funds in infrastructure, intermediate inputs, and petroleum-related industries. He instituted a massive program to open the Amazon frontier and expand the output of mineral raw materials and hydroelectric power (Frieden 1991: 199, Rodríguez 1991: 254–7, McCoy and Smith 1995: 123–5).[1] However, the large capital inflow – and the Venezuelan commitment to a fixed exchange rate – provoked an overvaluation of the currency. In addition, free convertibility and capital movements permitted an exit toward foreign-denominated assets and provoked a large capital flight subsidized by government indebtedness. When international interest rates grew, and especially after Mexico pulled the trigger of the debt crisis by declaring a unilateral moratorium, Venezuela could not sustain the exchange rate parity. In February 1983, COPEI president Luis Herrera Campins devalued the currency. In December of that year, COPEI lost the election to AD's Jaime Lusinchi.

Like Alfonsín in Argentina and De La Madrid in Mexico, Lusinchi inherited an economy in shambles. In 1983, the external debt reached almost $40 billion (U.S. billion), the GDP dropped 5.3%, and unemployment hit 10.2% (ECLAC 1993: 432, Betancourt et al. 1995: 3). However, in contrast to the election of De La Madrid in Mexico, the inauguration of Lusinchi represented a partisan turnover. Additionally, unlike Alfonsín in Argentina, Lusinchi belonged to a labor-based party. President Jaime Lusinchi obtained the AD's nomination because of the support of AD labor leaders. In exchange, they obtained the nomination of one of them, Manuel Peñalver, as secretary-general of the party in 1981. Lusinchi even proclaimed in 1983 that he had been elected president "on the shoulders of the workers" (Ellner 1993: 71).

AD partisan loyalty made the CTV serve as a transmission belt for the AD labor bureau and increase militancy against COPEI administrations (Coppedge 1994: 88). As a result, from 1960 to 1985, an annual average of 1.8 million worker-hours was lost to strikes during COPEI administrations whereas the same annual average dropped to 400,000 worker-hours during AD governments (McCoy 1989: 48–9, Coppedge

---

[1] During the oil boom (1974–81) public spending expanded from 20.1% to 29.1% of GDP and peaked in 1982 when it reached 37% of GDP (McCoy and Smith 1995: 127). Most of this expansion was financed with foreign credits. The state owed or guaranteed over 80% of the external debt, which grew from $2 billion in 1972 to more than $33 billion (U.S. billion) in 1982 (Frieden 1991: 78, McCoy and Smith 1995: 127).

1994: 34).[2] Indeed, during the previous COPEI administration of Luis Herrera, the CTV had organized numerous mobilizations in different states and sectors, public-sector strikes against layoffs – alleging discrimination to AD activists – and even threatened a general strike. In addition, the CTV had drafted a bill to raise salaries, taking advantage of the fact that COPEI did not control the congress and could not avoid its enactment (Ellner 1993: 67, Naim 1993). COPEI union leaders "criticized some of the CTV-sponsored mobilizations for being politically motivated" (Ellner 1993: 68).

President Lusinchi devalued the currency and implemented a stabilization program based on fiscal austerity and exchange and price controls. To foster social support for his stabilization plan, Lusinchi attempted to implement a short-lived social pact with the CTV and business associations. However, the fiscal deficit kept growing and hindered the state's ability to deliver basic services and pay for growing subsidies. Price and interest failed to control inflation and created scarcity (Naim 1993, Navarro 1994, McCoy and Smith 1995: 123).[3] In this context, AD's control of the CTV paid for Lusinchi. Although CTV president Juan José Delpino demanded wage hikes, union leaders affiliated with COPEI and other parties maintained that the militant rhetoric of the AD-led CTV was insincere because it did not organize the type of protest that had been promoted during the Herrera administration (Ellner 1993: 71–81).[4] Lusinchi rewarded labor restraint with compensatory bonuses, salary hikes in the public sector, and a law to improve work conditions.[5] Additionally, a reduc-

---

[2] Referring to Venezuela, Crisp (1997: 168) argues that because of the influence of party identity on interest groups, "when AD controls both the government and the CTV, laborers may be less capable of pressing for their demands because union leaders are responsive to the party. On the other hand, if the president is from COPEI, labor unrest and conflict with the government may be exacerbated because the union is ruled by AD."

[3] The fiscal surplus of 1984 became a fiscal deficit of 9.4% of GDP by 1988 (Table 4.1). A system of multiple exchange rates served to foster capital flight, which was estimated as between $30 to $80 billion (U.S. billion) (McCoy and Smith 1995: 125).

[4] When asked about the measures that would be used to achieve a 34% wage hike in 1985, Delpino answered, "First we will discuss things with the government and with Fedecámaras in the Tripartite Commission without resorting to coercive measures like strikes and public demonstrations, because the situation of the country requires equilibrium among its principal forces, and the CTV wants to become an example of equilibrium" (El Nacional, October 16, 1985, cited by Coppedge 1994: 89).

[5] At the onset of his administration, Lusinchi had also issued a decree mandating employers to increase their workforce by 10%. He had also established transport subsidies for workers,

Table 4.1. *Selected Macroeconomic Indicators for Venezuela*

Year	Real GDP Growth	Unemployment (2nd semester)	Minimum Real Salary[a]	Inflation (%)	Fiscal Balance (% of GDP)	Current Account Balance[b]
1984	−1.4	13.4	18,852.3	11.6	2.2	4.7
1985	1.4	12.1	28,248.2	11.4	0	3.3
1986	6.3	9.3	33,936.8	11.5	−7.4	−2.2
1987	4.5	8.5	26,420.6	28.1	−6	−1.4
1988	6.2	6.9	26,554.8	29.5	−9.4	−5.8
1989	−7.8	9.6	22,068.1	84.4	−1.1	2.5
1990	6.5	10.4	15,668.1	40.7	0.1	8.3
1991	9.7	8.7	17,513.1	34.2	−2.2	1.7
1992	6.8	7.1	19,985.1	31.4	−5.9	−3.4
1993	−0.4	6.5	14,472.0	38.1	−1.3	−2.2
1994	−3.3	8.7	15,000.0	60.8	−13.3	4.1

[a] At 1994 prices, deflated by the consumer price index.
[b] Billions of U.S. dollars.

Sources: International Financial Statistics (IMF 1996), Economic and Social Report (IADB 1992, 1996), and Betancourt et al. (1995: 3).

tion in unemployment accompanied his shift toward expansionary policies in 1986 (Table 4.1). Moreover, COPEI union leaders did poorly in the CTV elections thereby proving they were unable to foster a credible threat to replace AD union leaders. Hence, the CTV did not organize or threaten with any general strike against Lusinchi despite mounting inflation, the failure of the Social Pact, and conflicts over the CTV-run Workers' Bank (Coppedge 1994: 87).[6] Instead, AD union leaders decided to use political rather than industrial resources to express their discontent and endorsed Carlos Andrés Pérez against Lusinchi's candidate, Octavio Lepage, in the AD primaries. According to Ellner (1993: 79), "the presence of as many as 12,700 trade unionists in AD's 52,000-member electoral college facilitated Pérez's easy triumph over Lepage." After his nomination, Pérez ran

a program of workers' cafeterias, a new employment program of public works, social programs for the poor, increases in the minimum wage, and appointed CTV advisor, Raul Matos Azócar, as minister of development (Burgess 1998b: 16–17).

[6] In 1966, the CTV established the Workers' Bank, which received numerous state subsidies. After the debt crisis hit it hard, Lusinchi bailed it out but also put it in receivership, provoking a conflict with the CTV over the control of the bank (López Maya 1989).

a "populist" campaign and won the 1988 elections by a landslide (Little and Herrera 1995).[7]

Pérez's Administration (1989–93): The "Great Turnaround"[8]

President Pérez was inaugurated on February 2, 1989 and resigned in May 1993 – after two unsuccessful coup attempts – under corruption charges. A provisional president finished his term until January of the following year. In spite of his populist campaign, even before his inauguration, President Pérez surprised AD union leaders with his cabinet appointments, which included many non-AD technocrats and entrepreneurs. He also signed a "letter of intent" with the International Monetary Fund (IMF) although he had previously characterized this institution as "assassins to the service of economic totalitarism" (Kornblith 1998: 15). Moreover, his planning minister, Miguel Rodríguez, unveiled an economic package called "The Great Turnaround," which proposed a drastic change in the inward-oriented and state-based development strategy of postwar Venezuela. However, this conversion from populism to neoliberalism was more pragmatic than ideological. In a private meeting with AD politicians in 1989, Pérez portrayed the market reforms as necessary evils claiming that he was not neoliberal but a true social democrat with no alternative (Corrales 1996: 201). Even as late as March 1993, Naím (1993: 46) cites Pérez as saying, "I am a man with only one ambition – history. I want to go down in history as a man who was capable of overcoming the worst crisis in Venezuela's contemporary history."

The new policies included a liberation of exchange rates, interest rates, prices (on all but eighteen basic food items), and trade (reducing tariffs and eliminating nontariff barriers), and the implementation of a restrictive monetary policy, a tax reform, and a program of privatization. To

[7] President Pérez was elected with 52.9% of the votes, but his party obtained only 43.3% of the votes at the legislative level. Lusinchi had obtained 58.4% of the votes and AD candidates obtained almost 50% in the legislative elections (Korblith and Levine 1995: 49–51).

[8] The analysis of the reforms of the Pérez administration and the union responses to these reforms is based on field research done in Venezuela in 1994 and 1996. Sources include union, government and company documents, collective-bargaining contracts, a press chronology based on the archives of *El Nacional* and *Veneconomy* and the database of Professor Francisco Iturraspe, and interviews. The interviewees (twenty in 1994 and forty-eight in 1996) included policy makers, managers, and union leaders affiliated with various parties.

reduce the fiscal deficit, the government cut expenditures, froze public employment, and curtailed subsidies for public services. These policies provoked increases of 50% in utility prices, 30% in transport fares, and 100% in the domestic price of oil (Naím 1993, Navarro 1994, Karl 1997: 180).

On February 27, 1989, barely eleven days after Pérez had announced his program to the country and on the day when the new gas prices went into effect, violent urban riots shocked Caracas and other Venezuelan cities. The riots were directed against the buses that had increased their fares more than the established 30% and small shops that had hoarded subsidized foodstuff to sell at marked-up prices after the price liberalization had gone into effect. The 1989 riots, which were violently repressed, demonstrated the popular discontent with the immediate consequences of the "shock" therapy applied by President Pérez. They also shattered the faith of Venezuelans in their long-democratic traditions and reliance on an oil-producing state (Tarre Briceño 1994, Kornblith 1998).

Despite the riots, Venezuelan macroeconomic indicators improved rapidly. The large fiscal deficit of 1988 turned into a moderate fiscal surplus by 1990. The 1988 current account deficit became a surplus by 1989, and reserve accumulation reached $12.5 billion (U.S. billion) in 1990 (Navarro 1994: 12). Despite the 1989 recession and hike in unemployment, growth had resumed and the unemployment rate has started to decline by 1990 (Table 4.1). Moreover, the government had benefited from the increasing price of oil in 1989 and 1990 (Torres 1993: 224).

However, in 1992, Pérez suffered two coup attempts that protested his economic policies. The following year, he left office amid corruption allegations and the stalling of his promarket policies. Romero (1997) blames the "rentier" mentality of the Venezuelans who expected a restoration of the oil bonanza to be distributed by the state and could not accept a reduction of rents. Naim (1994) and Navarro (1993) explain that popular discontent with market reforms arose because of the government's inability to communicate its goals to the population and a lack of collaboration by the media. Corrales (1996) argues, instead, that AD's distrust of a program that attacked traditional sources of partisan patronage and excluded the party from policy making undermined Pérez's reform efforts by reducing their credibility. Kornblith (1998) points out that the simultaneous implementation of market reforms and a political reform (designed by a special commission for the reform of the state under Lusinchi) that established direct elections for governors and majors created a threat for AD. In the

1989 elections, AD won 11 of the 20 governorships and 151 of the 260 majors. Despite AD's good performance, the electoral competition that replaced presidential appointments to lower levels caused the party to lose political offices. Political reforms and economic reforms should have strained the relationship between the party and the president. However, Rodriguez Caballero (1996: 1) argues that "Acción Democrática did not once vote against the Pérez administration in Congress, [and] went to great lengths to block no-confidence votes against its ministers." Moreover, a few days after the riots, the AD National Political Committee and regional secretaries-general reaffirmed their support for Pérez's economic policies.

This analysis of the union-government interactions during the Pérez administration contribute to the previous debate by adding a piece to the puzzle concerning the failure of market reforms in Venezuela and the political earthquake that followed them. In this context, it is remarkable that the AD-led CTV broke its long tradition of restraint under AD administrations. Indeed, CTV militancy peaked compared with its behavior during previous non-AD administrations. On May 18, 1989, the CTV organized the first general strike in Venezuelan history that was not called to defend democracy. Further CTV protests undermined the administration's ability to govern and boycotted most labor and social reforms attempted by Pérez. Union leaders affiliated with other parties also rejected market-oriented reforms, especially those associated with the Causa R, who expanded their labor influence during this period by protesting against these policies. Thus, in contrast to Salinas and Menem, Pérez had to confront labor opposition to his conversion from populism to neoliberalism. The following section analyzes the stimulus created by market reforms and the consequences of labor reactions to these policies. It focuses on the government side of the interaction before shifting the lens to the internal dynamics of unions.

The Policy Stimulus: Market Reforms

This chapter and the following two chapters each begin by focusing at the national level and then on the subnational variation across different sectors of the economy regarding the union-government interactions. In the three chapters, most of the comparisons are restricted to case studies within each country, whereas Chapter 7 focuses on cross-national comparisons. The national-level section analyzes the policy stimulus created by market reforms and the impact of that stimulus on labor and the concessions granted or denied by the government to unions to implement these policies. In the first part of the section, the government takes the initiative by choosing the set of policies that change the status quo for labor and has the opportunity to buy off labor support if necessary. The second part of the section explains labor's reaction and capacity to obtain these concessions.

Pérez inherited an enormous fiscal deficit and a system of price controls that barely controlled inflation and created scarcity. Therefore, he liberalized prices while opening the economy to put pressure on the price of tradable goods. To balance the budget, he privatized state-owned enterprises and cut expenditures instead of resorting to printing money. Trade liberalization and public sector reform provoked layoffs and changes in work conditions to increase competitivity. Thus, workers in previously privileged sectors such as the protected sectors and the public sector were the most threatened by market reforms. Moreover, labor and social reforms included in Pérez's program affected workers' social benefits and unions as organizations. Pensions, severance payments, and work conditions had an effect on workers' expectations. Labor unions also cared for regulations on labor organizing and representation in tripartite state bodies.

Stabilization. Pérez lifted price controls used by Lusinchi to control inflation and instead tackled the fiscal deficit. He increased public-sector prices (including oil), halted public investment, and replaced indirect subsidies with direct ones. He abandoned the multiple exchange-rate system in favor of a unified exchange rate that was left free to float and liberalized interest rates.[9] The immediate effect was a sharp recession accompanied by mounting inflation and unemployment, but inflation went down, and economic growth resumed at a high rate in 1990 whereas unemployment has fallen since 1991 (Table 4.1).

Although the economic indicators in terms of inflation, growth, and unemployment improved, Pérez could not gain the support of the CTV for its stabilization program (Betancourt et al. 1995, Díaz n.d.). In part, the relatively high levels of inflation obscured the early achievements of

---

[9] The liberation of exchange rate controls provoked a devaluation of 170%, and interest rates jumped from 13% to 35%. Government investment fell from 3.2% of GDP in 1988 to 0.1% of GDP in 1989 (Crisp 1998: 22).

the adjustment program (Table 4.1).[10] Additionally, the stabilization did not avoid a deterioration of real wages. Real wages in manufacturing dropped 60% between 1988 and 1994 (UNIDO 1998). Real minimum salaries fell 40% in the same period (Table 3.1). The CTV, thus, rejected price liberalization and demanded compensations. The government granted workers an emergency wage hike and a six-month suspension of layoffs while establishing subsidies for the poor and unemployment insurance. Additionally, it consulted with CTV about the pace of price liberation for basic staples.[11]

Trade Liberalization. Before 1989, Venezuela was a closed country. There were forty-one tariff rates and 57% of the domestic production enjoyed some form of nontariff protection. This made the economy internationally uncompetitive except for the oil sector. Pérez launched a far-reaching trade-liberalization program in April 1989 (decree 238). All quantitative and discretionary restrictions were replaced by a new tariff system based on the degree of product processing. The maximum tariffs dropped from 135% to 20% by 1992 whereas average tariffs dropped from 37% to 10% by 1993. Import licenses that affected almost 48% of manufacturing production in 1989 covered less than 2% of it by 1991 (Corrales and Cisneros 1999: 2102–3). Moreover, Venezuela joined the General Agreement on Trade and Tariffs (GATT) in July 1990. As for the effect of these policies in the short run, the trade deficit of 1988 became a surplus for the period between 1989 and 1994. However, although the value of nonoil exports increased substantially in 1989 after the devaluation, it remained stable or even declined during the rest of the period, and oil continued to have the lion's share of exports (IMF 1996 and 1998).

Trade liberalization was especially costly for the tradable sectors that had previously enjoyed import protection. It affected both producers and workers in these sectors, although the continuous depreciation of the

---

[10] The inflationary outcome could have created the perception that Pérez's policies had created the crisis. Weyland (1996a) points out that President Pérez perceived the imminent crisis due to the huge fiscal deficit. However, the population in general did not perceive the crisis because inflation was contained at almost 30%, and they had not suffered hyperinflation like the populations of Argentina, Peru, or Bolivia who could perceive the high costs of avoiding adjustment.

[11] This account is derived from Naím (1993) and Navarro (1994) and personal interviews with CTV leaders, Rafael Castañeda (1994) and Juan José Delpino (1996), and former Development Minister Imelda Cisneros (1997).

exchange rate provided some compensation for them. Between 1988 and 1994, the number of industrial firms dropped from 11,043 to 8,891, and employment fell from 509,908 to 441,016, although the impact differed across industries (Corrales and Cisneros 1999: 2106). It is remarkable that despite the strong effects of trade liberalization, neither the industrial business sector (Corrales and Cisneros 1999) nor the CTV opposed this reform.[12] Indeed, ignoring the effect of trade liberalization on employment and industrial restructuring, former CTV leader Juan José Delpino said, "We did not oppose the liberalization of import tariffs because they did not have an impact on workers" (personal interview, 1996).

Privatization. Pérez had nationalized the iron-ore and oil industries during his first administration culminating in a sustained process of state expansion, which resulted in state-owned enterprises accounting for 29.4% of GDP by 1982. The importance of the public sector was such that the government employed 22.5% of the workforce by 1984 (Crisp 1998: 9). In spite of his statist past, Pérez's government program called for a reduction in the size of the state in nonstrategic sectors by "transferring to the private sector the propriety or management of public enterprises in diverse areas of the economy" (Cordiplan 1990: 31). The privatization program started in 1989 with the offer of some hotels to a consortium formed by the CTV and a private group. However, the extreme generosity of the offer outraged public opinion. The privatization was halted, and a system of public offers and cash payments was established for the following bids (personal interview with former Venezuelan Investment Fund's president Gerver Torres, 1996). Of the almost thirty firms privatized, the most important were the Venezuelan National Company of Telephones (CANTV), Venezuelan International Airlines, Inc. (VIASA), and the National Port Institute (INP). Privatization proceeds reached $2,471 million (U.S. million) in the period between from 1990 to 1994 (Inter-American Development Bank [IADB] 1996: 171). In March 1992, the Congress approved a privatization law that designated the Venezuelan Investment Fund to define tender terms and assigned proceeds to social investment and debt amortization (Torres 1993: 235).

Privatization affected only workers in the enterprises involved and threatened job stability and work conditions. Yet, these sectors were the

---

[12] Personal interviews with former Development Minister Imelda Cisneros and President Pérez (1996) confirmed this account.

most unionized of the economy (Gamboa 1993: 127, Iranzo 1994: 2). Additionally, privatization challenged the right of the CTV to appoint labor directors in public enterprises. However, in its Tenth Congress of 1990 the CTV accepted the privatization of nonstrategic sectors and proposed worker ownership through *cogestion*.[13] The CTV also demanded labor representation in privatized companies, job stability, and respect for previous work conditions (Iranzo 1994: 9). Accordingly, the 1992 law included a provision for employee-owned stock programs on 10% to 20% of capital under special financing and the stability of collective bargaining conditions after privatization. Both concessions followed the scheme employed in the privatization of CANTV, although President Pérez favored allowing the sale to workers outside the privatized company as well (Ellner 1999). Thus, although the privatization program affected workers in state-owned enterprises, the CTV obtained targeted compensations for those workers. Moreover, the law provided for directors to represent worker shareholders who would replace the CTV-appointed labor directors. Indeed, the union was allowed to present a slate for the election of such directors.

Severance Payment's Reform. The severance payment system worked as compensation for layoff and a complementary lump sum upon retirement. Since 1974, severance benefits had been paid independently of the cause of job termination and doubled for unjustified layoff (Betancourt et al. 1995). Employers protested that because severance payments had been calculated based on final month's salary, this retroactive calculation in an inflationary context made these payments too expensive. Their high cost – employers added – promoted the growth of the informal sector and high turnover rates in an attempt to reduce the accumulation of severance benefits. In 1990, a presidential commission elaborated a proposal to reform the system. This proposal was very similar to a previous project drafted by the Caracas Chamber of Commerce for liquidating severance payments of current employees.

---

[13] The CTV had already pointed out the limited possibilities of state intervention to advance workers interest in its Porlamar Manifesto of 1980. The manifesto points to *cogestion* as an alternative way to advance the interest of workers and increase social equality (CTV 1987: 103–54). Therefore, during the Tenth Congress of 1990, the CTV approved a document called *Privatization* that accepted privatizations provided that they did not involve "strategic" sectors and included workers' and union participation (CTV 1990a).

Because the CTV had rejected the chamber of commerce's proposal, the government blueprint included CTV demands, such as the extension of the original one-year liquidation plan to four years and the establishment of trust funds for half of the involved amount to reduce cash payments to workers. In addition, companies would pay a seniority premium of one day for each year of service, and trust funds would pay the principal and interests to workers upon termination of employment. The commission also agreed to the creation of pension funds with a 25% premium calculated based on the workers' accumulated benefits. Employers were to contribute an additional 10% of workers' salary to this fund. The benefits would be collectable when the worker withdrew from the labor force (Funaro 1990, Congreso de la República de Venezuela 1990).[14] In addition to those concessions to the CTV, President Pérez also offered a 20% across-the-board wage hike that would not be included in the liquidation of severance benefits (González Silva 1990). In spite of these concessions, the CTV continued to reject the reform.[15]

Social Security Reform. The Venezuelan Institute of Social Security (IVSS) was established in 1944. It had limited coverage that was extended during the fifties both geographically and regarding benefits by the introduction of a pension fund and the expansion of the number of medical units and hospitals. However, by 1988 it covered only 35% of the economically active population or 55% of wage earners (IVSS 1993). The IVSS board of directors included CTV representatives providing for union

---

[14] Because this reform mainly involved payroll taxes and the creation of individual savings accounts, it could be assimilated into the pension reforms that took place in Argentina and Mexico. In fact, it was a common practice for employers to use the funds in the severance payment accounts as a source of credit. Hence the reform would create a more legitimate source of savings in the perception of the business sector. The CTV also perceived the savings as a form of pension due to the low coverage of the pension system and thus demanded the creation of the fund to avoid its payment as a lump sum (Iranzo 1994: 7).

[15] Confirmed in personal interviews with President Pérez and CTV union leader José Beltrán Vallejo (1996). Former CTV President Juan José Delpino claimed that although he thought it was necessary to modify the system of severance payments, the rest of the CTV did not agree with him and preferred to keep the existing system (personal interview, 1996). Iranzo (1994: 8) explains the CTV's defense of the system of severance payment because it discouraged layoffs in the medium and small companies as well as among the most senior workers (who were more likely to be unionized). In 1997, President Caldera obtained the support of both business and labor associations for a reform of the system that was later canceled by President Chávez.

participation in its administration, like in the Mexican social security institute or in the Argentine welfare funds. However, the IVSS was very inefficient and nearly bankrupted when Pérez assumed as president. Its problems derived from rampant clientelism, which resulted in overstaffing, and tax evasion, which eroded its finances. Moreover, although the IVSS was based on payroll taxes, the deterioration of the public hospitals induced noncovered patients to overload its medical units. IVSS President Jorge Kamkoff tried to use a never implemented law to reform the institution by turning it into an insurance agency instead of a provider. He also proposed to replace the pension fund administered by the IVSS with a capitalization system in which each worker would fund her/his own retirement plan.

The IVSS reform had costs for both the federation of health workers (Fetrasalud) and the CTV. Over the years, Fetrasalud had secured a generous collective contract while its labor leadership had used access to employment as a source of patronage because IVSS employees had job stability. Additionally, the CTV had the power to appoint IVSS directors. This right not only implied access to patronage but also input into the policy making of the state tripartite institution. The reform would have brought layoffs and changes in work organization resented by Fetrasalud. The change to a private management of pensions would also have affected the CTV management influence on the IVSS. The CTV was not enthusiastic about the reform. Nor did it use its centralized authority to control the active boycotts of Fetrasalud to the reform of the system.[16] Labor delayed the reform until after the 1992 coup attempt when political instability made its legal enactment unfeasible.

Labor Flexibility and Labor Organization Regulations. As in Mexico, the labor code regulated both work conditions and labor organization. Hence, legal reforms could affect labor flexibility and conditions for labor organization. Complaints by business about the rigidity of Venezuelan labor markets and the politicization of labor relations were echoed by the administration. Yet, although the government structural reforms called for increasing the flexibility of regulations on work conditions and hiring and

---

[16] See Commission for the Restructuring of the IVSS (1989, 1992), CTV (n.d.), Bottome (1992), confirmed by personal interviews with Kamkoff, Fetrasalud union leader Edilberto La Riva, CTV union leader José Beltrán Vallejo, and a member of the commission who asked for confidentiality (1996).

firing, the legal reform approved during this period moved in the opposite direction. A new labor code approved in 1990 increased workers' benefits (e.g., expanding pregnancy and motherhood benefits, and raising payment for overtime work and work during holidays from 25% to 50% and for night shifts from 20% to 30%). It imposed new regulations that raised the rigidity of hiring (e.g., 75% of the payroll had to be "head of a family" and the percentage of Venezuelans in the payroll increased from 75% to 90%). It made changes in the organization of work more difficult (e.g., functional mobility became conditional upon notification of the labor inspector and the union of worker consent with double severance payment owed to workers who refused to perform the new task) (*Veneconomy*, June 1989: 1–3). The new labor law explicitly forbade the reduction of benefits through collective bargaining (art. 510). Moreover, it also reinforced subsidies for labor organization. It increased the number of labor directors in the public-sector companies (with one of them appointed by the CTV), introduced incentives for private firms to have worker ownership, and raised the number of union committee members with guaranteed job stability (art. 610, 611, 623, and 451).

President Pérez called for a delay in the passage of the law and labeled it as "populist" because it increased labor-market rigidity and hindered the changes necessary to make the Venezuelan economy more competitive (personal interview, 1996). Employers adamantly rejected this law before its enactment by arguing that it increased labor costs and reduced their incentives for hiring and thus hurt unemployed workers. However, the CTV had rejected the flexibility of regulations on work conditions in the structural reform plan of the government and any change that would undermine the incentives for labor organizing already built into the legislation. As a result, when Senator Rafael Caldera prepared a bill for a new labor code that guaranteed the previously acquired rights, the CTV participated actively in its drafting and rallied support for it in Congress. In spite of the efforts of employers and the government efforts to boycott Caldera's bill, the CTV pressed AD legislators to assign the bill constitutional urgency to boycott the efforts of the executive branch to delay its approval. In 1990, after the CTV organized a public demonstration to demand the sanction of the labor bill, the Congress passed it, and President Pérez sanctioned it to avoid having his veto overridden by Congress.[17]

---

[17] See Corrales (1996: 238). Personal interviews with CTV leaders AD's Beltrán Vallejo and Angel Zerpa Mirabal, COPEI's Carlos Navarro, and MAS's Rodrigo Penso (1994)

Summary

The CTV did not support Pérez's policy shift. Although Pérez granted labor unions an emergency wage hike, a suspension of layoffs, and unemployment insurance, they did not back his stabilization policies. The government was also unable to gain the CTV support for the reform of the severance payment system despite its concessions and changes in the proposal. The government also failed to win the CTV support for the reform of the IVSS. The government not only failed to deregulate the labor market, but was unable to deter a reform that increased the rigidity of labor relations and the incentives for labor organizing. However, the CTV, similar to business organizations, accepted trade liberalization and had already accepted privatization, even at the cost of compensations for the involved workers and subsidies for worker ownership. The next section explains the CTV rejection of Pérez's reforms despite partisan loyalty and CTV's ability to obtain government concessions.

Leadership Competition and CTV Opposition

The interaction between the CTV and Pérez provides an interesting case study for the theory presented in Chapter 2. That is, that partisan loyalty promotes labor collaboration with an allied administration, but leadership competition increases the incentives of allied union leaders for militancy because they fear the replacement threat. The effect of labor militancy or restraint to obtain governmental concessions, however, is related to whether the union is competing with others for the representation of workers. Union competition makes coordination for collective action more difficult and weakens every union, which can control only a share of the involved workers. In Venezuela, the CTV reacted militantly to Pérez's policy shift and was effective in hindering some reforms and obtaining

informed this account. In a personal interview, President Pérez (1996) claimed that the sanctioning of the code "was a very uncomfortable situation for me because it became a sort of national goal. The day I sanctioned it, I said that I was in disagreement with many aspects of that law, although it was useless to reject a law that had been unanimously passed by the Congress. All the attempts to avoid it failed. I wanted the people to be convinced of the need of a modern and less rigid law." The unanimity of the vote prevented his veto because in Venezuela, the presidents' veto power can be overridden by a two-thirds majority or a bare majority if the president sends it a second time to Congress for consideration (Crisp 1997: 179).

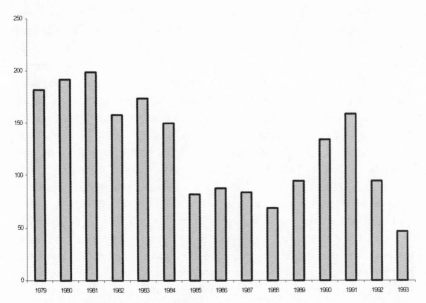

Figure 4.1 Strike petitions, 1979–93.
Sources: Central Bank of Venezuela (1993: 137) and Memories of the Ministry of Labor.

compensation for others (opposition). According to the theory, this reaction should be explained by increasing leadership competition that forces loyal union leaders to become more militant to avoid replacement by rivals, whereas union monopoly should make this militancy effective in retrieving concessions for labor.

In Venezuela, AD union leaders controlled the CTV. Partisan loyalty increased the militancy of the CTV under the COPEI administration of Luis Herrera (1979–83) and induced its restraint during the AD administration of Jaime Lusinchi (1984–8) as shown in Figure 4.1 by the number of strike petitions.[18] However, the use of proportional representation and organization of unions in federation facilitated partisan pluralism, thereby making partisan competition the usual form of leadership competition in the union movement.[19]

---

[18] As in Mexico, strike petitions must be presented to the labor inspectors for the strike to receive legal approval. For that reason, petitions are better measurements of militancy than strikes that must pass the filter of state control to take place.

[19] AD had always had more than 50% of delegates to CTV congresses, except for the congress in 1970 when it had a 34.5% plurality (Ellner 1993: 53). Consequently, AD always

Despite its partisan loyalty, the CTV did not maintain restraint during the AD administration of Carlos A. Pérez (1989–93). The CTV called two general strikes (in May 1989 and November 1991), which were the first since the successful transition of 1958. CTV-affiliated unions increased strike petitions until the 1992 coup (Figure 4.1). The increase in militancy during the Pérez administration coincided with economic growth as predicted by industrial relations theories. However, militancy grew in 1989 despite an almost 8% drop of GDP and mounting unemployment (Table 4.1). Additionally, high growth also coincided with the decline in militancy between 1986 and 1988 (Figure 4.1). Therefore, macroeconomic conditions are not sufficient to explain labor behavior, and political variables must be added to the picture.

The reaction of the CTV began when its president, AD's Juan José Delpino, criticized Pérez's policies and cabinet appointments.[20] AD labor leaders were also displeased that Pérez broke the traditional practice of deferring to the labor bureau for the selection of the labor minister and IVSS director. However, the AD labor bureau and the CTV supported his program in early February despite the criticism of non-AD factions within the CTV and non-CTV unions (Burgess 1998b: 19). In contrast, union leaders affiliated with other political parties demanded a more militant response to the economic program of Pérez, thus targeting the "populist" space left void by AD in a way that could challenge AD's influence on the union movement. This replacement threat became more real for AD union leaders during the urban riots of February 27 and 28, 1989. They perceived the riots as a signal of popular discontent with Pérez's policies that also expressed the views of their constituencies. The replacement threat increased the incentives of AD union leaders for militancy, even against an AD president, as a way to show their constituencies that they were still responsive.

On March 28, the AD labor bureau voted to organize a special CTV congress to discuss labor strategies against market reforms. In the CTV special congress, partisan loyalties were a fundamental factor in influenc-

held the presidency of the confederation except for the period between 1968 and 1970 that followed the split of AD into the MEP (Chapter 2).

[20] Delpino had strongly supported Pérez in the AD primaries and argued that "when Pérez reached his second term he implemented the *paquete* [economic program] to avoid the crisis he thought was going to explode. . . . Therefore, the *paquete* was necessary but it was also necessary to establish policies to prevent its harsh effects for the poor people" (personal interview, 1996).

ing the position of union leaders regarding the strategies to take against market reforms. Delpino said, "there were diverse opinions regarding the general strike among *adecos* [AD activists]. Union leaders from other parties were happy to go into strike because they were in the [electoral] opposition and thus, they wanted to go into strike more than AD union leaders who believed the strike might weaken their own party" (personal interview, 1996). Because AD union leaders could not easily rely on partisan cues, they were divided over the issue of calling a general strike. AD union leaders were torn between supporting an allied administration and showing their union constituencies that they had not sold out. That is, they had to make a decision between risking the governability of their partisan allies or the control of their followers who could be attracted by partisan rivals within the union movement. CTV President Delpino, who was more exposed to partisan competition within the confederation, criticized the stabilization program and pushed for a general strike. AD union leaders based on the labor bureau, such as Federico Ramírez León, Carlos Castañeda, and Angel Zerpa Mirabal, were more exposed to party pressures and wanted to blame "speculators" for price hikes. However, the dramatic effect of the February riots, the approaching renewal of CTV authorities the following year, and the pressure of union leaders affiliated to other parties caused the fear of replacement to prevail. On May 18, Delpino led the CTV into a national general strike against Pérez's economic policies, even though the president of AD had warned that taking such action "would signify pulling the rug out from under the government" (Burgess 1998b: 21). The 1989 general strike reached a pinnacle of militancy not only because it was the first since 1958, but because Venezuelan union leaders have traditionally preferred to avoid industrial conflict.[21]

Delpino resigned from the CTV presidency in January 1990 and was replaced by AD's Antonio Ríos as provisional president.[22] Because the left-wing opposition parties won many elections for governor in December

---

[21] The reports of Gil Yepes (1989a) and Ellner (1989) on the effect of the riots and the discussion of the general strikes were confirmed in personal interviews by union leaders, such as MEP's Olarte, AD's Delpino in 1996, and MAS's Penso and AD's Castañeda and Zerpa Mirabal in 1994. In an attitudinal study of the 1960s, only 2.2% of surveyed union leaders justified a general strike to satisfy economic demands, thus highlighting the drama of the general strike (Ellner 1993: 101).

[22] Delpino resigned over disagreements with other AD union leaders regarding corruption issues (personal interview 1996).

69

1989, CTV leaders became more aware of partisan competition with the union followers of these political parties. Because of this replacement threat, CTV militancy remained high. The CTV organized a national protest against the reform of the severance benefits system and the stabilization program in February. In the May 1 parade, the CTV demanded the quick approval of the new labor code. However, the replacement threat receded in May when AD obtained 61% of the delegates to the CTV Congress, whereas COPEI got only 20%, the MEP received 8%, and other groups had the remaining 3% (Grupo Santa Lucía 1990: 26). The predominance of AD facilitated the confirmation of Ríos as CTV president and reduced the incentives for militancy by AD union leaders. In June, the CTV put down its protests and agreed to analyze the government proposal for a new severance payments system and participate with the business association, Fedecámaras, in a forum to discuss economic reforms. It also participated in setting up a program of day care centers.[23]

This restraint was short-lived, however, because partisan competition reinforced the replacement threat in 1991 when AD union leaders suffered many electoral defeats in local union elections. In most cases, AD lost union elections to Causa R, a new political group that was growing in the unions and in the electoral arena.[24] Causa R and other left-wing parties, such as MAS and MEP, were expanding their influence in the large companies of the public sector, which had been affected by state reforms, perhaps in response to CTV acceptance of privatization and the antiprivatization calls of these groups (Ambrus 1992). The influence of these parties was also growing in CTV regional federations, where they called assemblies to induce the CTV to organize a plan of scheduled strikes.[25] Union elections also attracted the attention of AD union leaders. Afraid of replacement, they reacted by organizing protests to demand wage hikes,

---

[23] See Sweeney (1990a), Sweeney and Funaro (1990), and *Veneconomy* (September 1990: 2).

[24] Although it had originated in the union movement, Causa R had moved into the electoral arena and won the governorship of Bolivar state in 1990 and the mayorship of Caracas in 1992.

[25] *Veneconomy* (June 1992: 16) reported "in the last eighteen months, one hundred and thirty union elections have been held, of which a hundred were AD controlled unions. Today only twenty-five of those unions are under AD control." In personal interviews, union leaders Penso (1994), Olarte, and Beltrán Vallejo (1996) described the regional pressures.

wage indexation, job stability in the public sector, and the resignation of Labor Minister Germán Lairet while denouncing the reform of the severance benefits' system.[26] The CTV also rejected Pérez's decree on wage hikes for the private sector and introduced a bill to legislate a 45% wage increase, repeating an act from the COPEI administration of Luis Herrera.[27] Other CTV actions included a national program of mobilization, a public demonstration in front of the Congress in June (with the three smaller confederations), and a general strike in November (Sweeney 1991).[28]

President Pérez had to choose between giving in to CTV militancy or facing the growing influence of more hostile left-wing union leaders who actively boycotted his reforms and had no partisan loyalty. He gave in to the CTV and replaced his labor minister with CTV candidate, Rubén Rodriguez; raised the transportation bonus; and halted the severance payments' reform. He also promised to avoid massive layoffs and include CTV policy input (Sweeney 1991). Despite his concessions to labor, by the end of 1991, Pérez had lost control of AD, which was won over by the anti-Pérez faction with the support of AD labor leaders (Steve Ellner, personal communication). Moreover, in February 1992, Colonel Hugo Chávez led an unsuccessful military coup against Pérez, which was qualified as "understandable" by former president Rafael Caldera in the Senate. A second military coup failed in November.

After the coup attempt of February 1992, when the challenges to market reforms became a threat for the democratic regime, the partisan loyalty of AD labor leaders proved valuable to Pérez. Despite mounting social unrest, the CTV did not organize more general strikes or demonstrations to avoid endangering the stability of the government. The CTV also did not support protests called by opposition parties (e.g., the civic strike of May 1992 called by left-wing parties). Moreover, AD labor legislators

---

[26] The reports of *Veneconomy* (April–July 1991) were confirmed in personal interviews by Beltrán Vallejo and former Labor Minister Rubén Rodríguez (1996).

[27] However, in this occasion, AD sided with the president and did not support the CTV bill in Congress (Burgess 1998a: 293).

[28] Causa R union leaders boycotted the general strike to differentiate from AD leadership of the CTV. This reaction strengthens the argument on the importance of partisan loyalty for union actions. Burgess (1998b: 25) argues that AD labor leaders extended their influence into the party because their votes were crucial in internal elections. Hence, although the party had supported the reform of severance payments in May, AD legislators postponed the congressional debate in July.

following party discipline did not support a motion for censure against Pérez's cabinet in March 1992.[29]

Thus, the conversion of Pérez from populism to neoliberalism emptied a space that could be taken over by populist rival groups in the union movement and the electoral arena. The urban riots of February 1989 signaled to AD union leaders that the threat of leadership competition was real, thereby increasing their incentives for militancy to appear more responsive to their constituencies. The AD-controlled CTV held a near monopoly of representation and had a strong bargaining power to obtain concessions from an allied government that was afraid of more hostile union leaders, such as those of Causa R, replacing their labor allies. This situation explains both the unusual CTV militancy and its capacity to obtain concessions, although the usual measures of bargaining power such as union density or concentration were lower in Venezuela than in the other two countries. Hence, increasing partisan competition provided incentives for militancy even for loyal AD union leaders, whereas the lack of competition with other national confederations reinforced the capacity of the CTV to obtain concessions thus making opposition (effective militancy) the union-government interaction.

Sector-level Analysis: Introducing Variation within the Same Country

Comparisons both across and within countries are a relatively new endeavor in the comparative study of developing areas. Although used in the study of OECD countries, there are fewer studies of this sort in the developing countries where the lack of reliable statistical information and the higher salience of informal institutions make such studies more urgent. In particular, this format is very useful to test theories based on similar economic interests across different countries. In the case of union-government interactions, political economists explain variation in union behavior based on economic interests around sector-specific assets in open economies (Frieden 1995). That is, preferences for trade liberalization should be different for unions in the tradable and nontradable sectors and

---

[29] Although Pérez had lost control of AD in October 1991, the lack of CTV-organized industrial actions or demonstrations after the coup attempt of February 1992 shows the concern of AD labor leaders with democratic stability in spite of the rupture between the party and the president. Despite the contrast, this attitude is comparable to the Mexican CTM rejection of political liberalization because of fear of a more competitive regime than the one in which labor unions and their partisan allies had defined the terms of their alliance.

views of privatization should be diverse for public-sector and private-sector unions within the same country.

To control for the effect introduced by these sector-level variables, this section provides five case studies in different sectors of the economy that are repeated in the following two chapters for Mexico and Argentina. The sectors studied included the oil and automobile industries, which were tradable goods, and telecommunications, electricity, and public education, which were services under state control. Unions in these sectors presented different interactions with the government during the period studied. They provide case studies to understand the effect of partisan loyalties, leadership competition, and union competition in different economic contexts while holding national conditions constant. Additionally, a comparison of these sector-level case studies with those in the following two chapters provides information for a comparison in Chapter 7 of the explanatory power of the theory across nations.

Oil. Oil was the principal export of Venezuela, and oil-related activities accounted for 23.9% of Venezuelan GDP by 1991 (ECLAC 1993: 440). During his first administration, Pérez nationalized the oil industry creating a state monopoly over oil production, which was run by PDVSA (Venezuela Oil, Inc.) PDVSA was a holding company for three state-owned oil enterprises: Lagoven, Maraven, and Corpoven. The president appointed the head of PDVSA who traditionally managed it similar to a private corporation, although its weight in the Venezuelan economy made this a politically sensitive industry (personal interviews with PDVSA chief economist, Ramón Espinasa 1996, Karl 1997). Because this industry was the main source of foreign exchange for Venezuela, Pérez proposed to open oil exploration and production to international capital in "marginal oil fields" through "strategic associations" between foreign and domestic capital and PDVSA in 1989 (*Veneconomy*, July 1989: 19). However, Congress did not pass his proposal. Nonetheless, the management of PDVSA instituted changes in work organization with the aim of increasing the productivity of the company in preparation for a future opening. In 1991, the management proposed the introduction of a system of merit incentives to partially replace unrestricted wage hikes to stimulate improvements in productivity.[30] Management wanted merit incentives to respond

---

[30] The following account is derived from Maraven (1989, 1991), Corpoven (1991, 1993), Lagoven (1991, 1993), Garip-Bertuol (1993), Iranzo and Penso (1996), and personal

to wage demands with rewards for performance, thus increasing productivity and dealing with labor costs. Additionally, PDVSA executives tried to restrict the hiring and firing prerogatives of the labor union because the hiring of 80% of workers from union lists restricted external flexibility.

Workers were afraid of management discretion over wages hikes through merit incentives, whereas the union would be affected by changes in hiring prerogatives, which were also used by AD labor leaders to reinforce their control of the union. Labor did not react militantly, however. FEDEPETROL was the main union for organizing oil workers and a monopolistic union serving as the representative of labor for collective bargaining.[31] AD controlled FEDEPETROL and did not face partisan competition because left-wing activists, mainly from MEP and MAS, were a small minority although critical of AD leadership and its use of hiring prerogatives to curtail partisan competition (Ellner 1993: 141). In the absence of a serious replacement threat, AD-led FEDEPETROL restrained and accepted merit incentives in return for the maintenance of hiring prerogatives. PDVSA executives wanted to reward AD union leaders to keep labor peace in a sensitive sector of the Venezuelan economy. Hence, partisan loyalty combined with the absence of partisan competition or union competition resulted in cooperation (effective restraint) as the union-management interaction. However, the setting changed during the following round of collective bargaining in 1993.

When the 1991 collective contracts expired two years later, PDVSA's management continued to target the hiring prerogatives of the union and also tried to eliminate the commissary. The commissary was a general store that had originated in the times when oil fields were isolated and provided cheap supplies to oil workers. It constituted a huge subsidy for their salaries because prices changed every two years through collective bargaining at a much slower pace than inflation, creating a financial burden for the corporation. PDVSA wanted to eliminate many items from the commissaries in an attempt to cut the institution altogether and replace it with a bonus, because high inflation made it very expensive for the company to subsidize the prices of commissary merchandise.

---

interviews with PDVSA human resources manager, Alberto Rivas, legal advisor, Juan Vera, and union leaders Rodrigo Penso (1994) and Carlos Ortega (1996).

[31] Fetrahidrocarburos was born from a split of FEDEPETROL in 1961 when URD voluntarily withdrew and Communists were ousted from the federation (following their CTV expulsion) (Ellner 1993: 132–3). PDVSA bargained with FEDEPETROL and Fetrahidrocarburos rubberstamped collective contracts (Vera, personal interview, 1996).

By 1993, partisan competition from left-wing activists had expanded with Causa R joining MEP and MAS and growing at the expenses of AD. These left-wing activists had long criticized AD leaders for their corrupt and politically discriminatory practices regarding the use of hiring prerogatives to limit leadership competition. Indeed, the activists claimed that the defense of such prerogatives at the expense of merit incentives, which they had confronted, was a sellout. Additionally, increasing partisan competition also coincided with the national growth of Causa R at the expense of an AD national crisis in the electoral arena. AD union leaders feared replacement and became more militant by increasing strikes petitions and even threatening a national strike against the changes in the commissaries. They accepted a modification of hiring prerogatives to improve their image among members.[32] The boycott against the changes in commissary items worked, whereas hiring prerogatives were reduced to 60%. Moreover, PDVSA granted the union increased training opportunities for their constituencies. Hence, the absence of union competition and partisan competition led to cooperation between the union and the company regarding merit incentives. However, in 1993, the increase in partisan competition made AD union leaders more militant, but the company still granted concessions to the union to avoid the replacement of loyal union leaders by left-wing partisan groups in a monopolistic union. Thus, the union-management interaction shifted from cooperation to opposition.

Automobiles. The Venezuelan automobile sector has been protected since 1962 when imports of cars were forbidden in an attempt to foster import substitution industrialization. In 1989, Pérez reduced tariffs and scheduled further reductions for the following years. He also abolished most nontariff protection in the automobile sector, including price controls; restrictions on the entrance of assemblers and the introduction of new models; and levels of domestic contents. In 1990, he abolished import licenses and allowed the import of the same vehicles produced domestically. Additionally, he established a minimum percentage of foreign currency contribution scheduled to increase until 1994 to foster exports. In 1991, he approved the importation of used vehicles for transportation of passengers (Sweeney 1990, Iranzo et al. 1996: 196–200, Lucena 1998: 42–3). The combination of the drastic opening of the sector, the

---

[32] The CTV leadership pressed FEDEPETROL leaders to accept the change to improve their image and avoid a general setback of AD in the union (Iranzo and Penso 1996).

effects of the recession, and the impact of the devaluation on the dollar-denominated debts of automakers sent the industry into a dive. Production plunged from the 1978 peak of 182,678 vehicles to 27,637 units in 1989 (Lucena 1996: 32).

The hardest hit of the largest companies was Ford Motors of Venezuela, which had the second highest level of automobile production until 1989. Between 1988 and 1989, Ford sales dropped by 80%, and its share of the market fell from 24.6% to 14.9% (Iranzo et al. 1996: 213, Table A). Thus, Ford was a key case to study the subsequent reaction of the union and its interaction with management. Because collective bargaining was at the company level, the appropriate unit of analysis is the Ford section of Sutra-Automotriz Carabobo. As most state level unions, Sutra-Automotriz Carabobo was affiliated with FetraCarabobo (the state-level federation corresponding to the state where the plant was located) and with the Federation of Metal Workers (FETRAMETAL), the federation of miners, metal, automobile, and similar workers (Chapter 2).[33] Ford's response to the crisis was to lay off half of its workforce and change work conditions within the plant. It reduced work categories from thirty-three in 1989 to six in 1993 and introduced internal flexibility of tasks and a system of paid incentives for training (*pay for knowledge*).

Such dramatic reduction in employment and changes in work conditions did not result in the same militant reaction as that of their counterparts in Mexico and Argentina where workers defended their previous work conditions. When Ford introduced changes in work organization as a response to the 1989 downturn, the local section of the union collaborated with management. Labor leaders not only restrained and accepted the changes, but also persuaded workers of the need to introduce them. In return, management gave the union oversight prerogatives in training, layoffs, and the reincorporation of laid-off workers that followed Ford Motors' recovery after 1990.

Cooperation (effective restraint) followed the expectation of the theory. AD controlled the Ford section, the union, and both federations. In addi-

---

[33] Ford and General Motors were the largest sections of Sutra-Automotriz with one thousand members each. Collective bargaining took place between the Sutra-Automotriz of Carabobo, represented by its section, and the company, although the president of FETRAMETAL also signed contracts. Moreover, the president of the Ford section was also the secretary-general of the union. The contract established the automatic check-off of union dues of which 70% accrued to the union, 20% to FETRAMETAL, and 10% to FetraCarabobo (Ford 1989).

tion to partisan loyalty, AD union leaders who have traditionally attempted to reduce conflicts in the automobile sector faced no leadership competition and held a monopoly of representation over Ford Motors' workers. Indeed, the practice of hiring from union lists reinforced the union monopoly of representation. In the absence of leadership competition or union competition, the union kept labor peace and helped the recovery of the company in return for institutional concessions. Thus, cooperation was the interaction between union and management.[34] This commonality of objectives was expressed by Ford's industrial relations manager, Eduardo Mendoza (personal interview, 1994) who claimed that it was the policy of Ford to have the union as a coparticipant in the action plans related to worker participation. The president of the Ford section of Sutra-Automotriz, Francisco D'Amelio (personal interview, 1994) also identified the union with the modernization of the company and supported the training with pay incentives and changes that would accelerate job recovery. He also argued that the fact that AD controlled the union facilitated collaboration because management and labor wanted to avoid the militant stances of left-wing unions.

Telecommunications. CANTV was originally a private company established in 1930. The state had begun to provide telecommunications services in 1946 and nationalized CANTV seven years later, creating a state-owned monopoly in this industry. The politicization of its industrial relations, corruption, and the lack of investment eroded the efficiency of the company and provoked financial losses in 1989 and 1990 (Francés et al. 1993: 4–5, Iranzo and Richter 1998: 256). Because this industry was fundamental for a competitive open economy, Pérez decreed the creation of the Telecommunications Restructuring Group in the Ministry of Communications and appointed Fernando Martínez Mottola as president of CANTV to prepare it for its privatization in 1990. Five candidates bought the tender terms, but only two consortia led by Bell Atlantic-Bell Canada and GTE-ATT presented bids. In November 1991, the latter won the bid and paid $1,885 million (U.S. million) for 40% of CANTV shares with management rights and an exclusive license for the sector until October 2000.

---

[34] The analysis of Ford is derived from Ford (1989), personal interviews with Mendoza (1994) and D'Amelio (1994), Iranzo et al. (1996), and two Ford Motors' documents: "Impact of pay for knowledge systems" and "Programs for the improvement of quality and productivity in the sector" (n.d.).

Privatization threatened job stability and the generous work conditions of the collective contract, which included scholarships, supplementary pensions, and a variety of welfare benefits, as well as union hiring prerogatives and the right to name labor directors of public companies. The reaction of FETRATEL coincided with the predictions of the theory. Because collective bargaining was centralized in this nationwide state-owned company, FETRATEL organized twenty-nine local unions and held a monopoly of representation for CANTV workers, whereas the national leadership had the authority to approve strikes (FETRATEL 1981). Unionization was almost total among CANTV workers under collective bargaining, in part because the union had control over hiring (Francés et al. 1993). Before privatization, AD controlled the national leadership of the federations, and independent groups headed the unions in Caracas, Cabimas, and Maracaibo. However, there was no partisan competition within the federation.[35]

With no union competition and little leadership competition, FETRATEL accepted the privatization of CANTV after the CTV expressed its support and demanded better conditions for the purchase of workers' stocks in April 1991.[36] The CTV played a key role in an arduous negotiation process permeated by minor unrest.[37] In return for restraining all AD-controlled local unions in 1991 (Table 4.2), the government granted CANTV workers job stability, the improvement of collective-bargaining conditions, and an employee-owned stock program. The program included stocks for 11% of CANTV capital to be paid in nine years with no down payment or interest. The two labor directors who would represent worker shareholders could be elected on the union slate.

Privatization set the stage for the following act. The concessions granted to obtain labor support for the privatization of CANTV prevented

---

[35] Causa R's Alfredo Ramos accused the independent leaders of Caracas of being backed by AD in an attempt to preempt their growth (personal interview, 1996).

[36] The following accounts derive from the press chronology – especially *Ultimas Noticias* (April 25, 1991), *El Universal* (June 30, 1991) – CANTV (1991, 1993), Francés et al. (1993), FETRATEL (1993), Iranzo and Ritcher (1998). They were confirmed in personal interviews with independent union leader, Edmundo Flores (1994); CTV's Olarte; FETRATEL president, AD's Cruz Hernández; Causa R's president of the Caracas union, Alfredo Ramos; CANTV's manager, Ramiro Ruiz; vice president of human resources, Marina Ramiroff; and president, Gustavo Roosen; former CANTV president, Fernando Martínez Mottola; and communications minister, Roberto Smith (1996).

[37] Martínez Mottola and Smith described the process in personal interviews (1996) and acknowledged the support of COPEI and AD as well as the hostility of the Causa R.

Table 4.2. *Conflictive Claims of FETRATEL against CANTV after Privatization (1991–5)*

Local Union	1989	1990	1991	1992	1993	1994	1995
Apure							X
Aragua					X		X
Barinas	X						X
Bolivar							X
Cabimas	X		X	X	X	X	X
Camatagua				X			X
Caracas	X	X	X	X	X	X	X
Carúpano						X	X
Cojedes				X			X
Coro		X		X			X
Cumaná		X				X	X
Guárico							X
El Tigre	X			X			X
La Guaira					X		X
Lara						X	X
Maracaibo		X		X	X	X	X
Mérida				X	X		X
Miranda		X[a]			X		X
Monagas	X						X
N. Esparta							X
Portuguesa					X		X
P. Ayacucho				X	X		X
P. Cabello							X
P. La Cruz							X
Punto Fijo		X					X
Táchira							X
Trujillo							X
Valencia					X		X
Yaracuy					X	X	X
TOTAL	5	6	3	9	11	7	29

[a] Two petitions.

Source: Annual reports of the ministry of labor of 1989 and 1990 and CANTV (1996a).

a restructuring of work conditions before privatization with the exception of a limited program for early retirement. After privatization, management attempted to implement labor restructuring to increase the productivity of the company. Privatization also had an effect on partisan competition. Causa R activists had organized protests in Caracas (demonstrations and takeovers) and initiated legislative and judicial acts to halt privatization to the point that the government excluded them from the bargaining process. However, this intransigent position made Causa R win the elections of the Caracas union – which was the largest in the federation – in 1992. Additionally, it extended its influence in other regions where independent groups controlled the unions, such as Maracaibo and Cabimas. Simultaneously, Causa R also won the first direct election for labor directors representing worker shareholders.

The growing influence of Causa R in the federation signaled an increase in partisan competition for the AD national leadership. Additionally, when the AD president took an offer of early retirement from the company, the perception that he was selling out increased dramatically. As a result, a new and younger AD leadership took over and became more bellicose to avoid the replacement threat. The new leadership brought the union into militancy against restructuring beyond Caracas, Cabimas, and Maracaibo, into the regions controlled by AD. This was revealed by the increase in strike petitions since 1992, which was sustained during the collective-bargaining rounds of 1993 and 1995 (Table 4.2).

The new private management was very hostile to labor. It obtained a judicial injunction to dismiss the president of the Caracas union and Causa R's labor director, Alfredo Ramos, accusing him of selling industrial secrets. Indeed, management did not want to grant concessions to labor, informally targeted union shop prerogatives, and preferred to classify workers as "managerial" to deprive them of collective-bargaining rights. However, the bargaining power of a monopolistic union constrained managerial discretion. Management had to resort to voluntary retirements to avoid breaking the privatization agreement and improved workers' salaries relative to other sectors of the economy between 1991 and 1993 (CANTV 1996b). In short, partisan loyalty, union monopoly, and no partisan competition brought about cooperation regarding privatization. However, the emergence of partisan competition and the subsequent replacement threat for AD union leaders increased the militancy of the union and shifted the interaction to opposition regarding labor restructuring.

Electricity. The Company for the Administration and Development of Electricity (CADAFE) was established in 1958 to unify a variety of nationalized and public companies concerned with generation, transmission, and distribution of electricity around the country. The excessive centralization of operative decisions in Caracas, corruption, and lack of internal flexibility were blamed for the inefficiency of the company. In 1990, in an attempt to revamp infrastructure and cut the fiscal deficit, Pérez appointed Julián Villalba as president of CADAFE to decentralize the company and prepare it for privatization three years later (Torres 1993: 234). Villalba decentralized CADAFE into a holding composed of four regional units plus a coordinating unit in Caracas (personal interview, 1996). Decentralization implied the relocation of numerous workers from the capital city of Caracas to less desirable locations in the interior of the country. Hence, the impact of this reform was different for workers employed in Caracas and those already assigned to interior locations. Workers in Caracas tended to be better paid and trained and preferred their city location to a new one in the interior. Workers in the rest of the country were afraid that the transfer of workers from Caracas would toughen competition in the workplace. The reaction of the union reflected a combination of these conditions and its internal political dynamics.

FETRAELEC organized twenty-six local unions. As in the CANTV, collective bargaining was centralized in a single contract for the whole country signed between CADAFE and FETRAELEC, thus granting the latter a monopoly of representation over CADAFE's workers. The federation was controlled by AD, but Causa R had followers in the Caracas union and had won a seat to the executive committee of that union in 1985. However, AD union leaders in the national federation did not consider that this minority created a replacement threat in the large federation. Because they did not perceive partisan competition, loyalty to AD prevailed. In fact, Villalba argued that although AD union leaders had initially been unhappy with the reform, they supported decentralization to the point that the FETRAELEC president who was an AD representative in Congress voted for it. Labor restraint was effective (cooperation) because workers in the whole country received salary increases to match the wages in Caracas. Additionally, the government guaranteed job stability and kept the generous work conditions of the collective contract and union prerogatives. That is, it did not implement labor restructuring or change work conditions. Finally, the transfer was implemented through a voluntary system that included handsome monetary incentives.[38]

The process of decentralization was to be followed by a restructuring of working conditions through collective bargaining to make workers

---

[38] Causa R union leader, Joaquín Malavé, J. Villalba, and CADAFE's director of personnel, Mirna Bucarito, confirmed this account in personal interviews (1996).

more productive and the company more efficient for privatization. This second reform challenged both work conditions and union prerogatives by granting more power to the management to make the company more efficient and attractive for privatization. As in the previous case, the success of decentralization sowed the seeds for increasing partisan competition. The concessions obtained by FETRAELEC benefited workers in the interior and those transferred from Caracas, but increased discontent among those who remained in Caracas because their relative wages deteriorated compared with those in the interior. The fact that the local unions in the interior were the strongholds of the AD explains this trade-off. Workers in the interior who were represented by AD union leaders who controlled the federation had an advantage. Because Causa R union leaders had rejected decentralization and did not participate in the negotiations over the process, the votes of workers discontent with decentralization helped Causa R win the Caracas union – still the largest in the federation – in 1992.

The victory of Causa R in the Caracas election signaled the increase in partisan competition to AD union leaders in the national federation; in particular, because Causa R was also extending its influence in other public sector unions. Following their victory, Causa R union leaders in Caracas organized a strike against restructuring and privatization, which was not approved by the national federation. Although the strike was declared illegal and repressed, the fear of replacement made AD union leaders more militant. Four AD-led unions in the interior followed their strike petitions into strikes in 1992. In 1992 and 1993, labor unrest was so high that management decided to suspend bargaining for labor restructuring and abandoned any privatization idea (Ministry of Labor 1992, Bucarito, personal interview, 1996). In sum, little partisan competition and no union competition brought about cooperation (effective restraint) as the union-government interaction regarding decentralization. Yet, the hike in partisan competition provoked by the victory of Causa R in Caracas has increased the militancy of AD union leaders since 1992 and has shifted the interaction to opposition (effective militancy) because union monopoly has still allowed FETRATEL to obstruct labor restructuring and privatization.

Education. The Venezuelan public education system grew in a very centralized fashion as a result of the efforts of the national government to expand literacy, which had been very limited until the 1958 democratic transition. In 1936, only 27.8% of the population between seven and four-teen attended school, and by 1981 this percentage had grown to 86.9% (BCV 1990: 173–4). However, by the 1980s the quality of Venezuelan education was coming under attack, and centralization was blamed for its shortcomings. In 1989, the national government concentrated 72.57% of public expenditure on education, compared to the 21.29% spent by state governments and 6.14% by city governments (Navarro 1993). Following the suggestions of the Commission for the Reform of the State (COPRE), Pérez passed a law of decentralization that covered a broad array of activities including education. Pérez also appointed Gustavo Roosen, a private sector manager, as minister of education to improve the quality of education.

Roosen's plans to improve the quality of education included a large administrative reform of the ministry and the fostering of competition between private and public schools. Nonetheless, he became disenchanted with decentralization during his tenure because he distrusted the efficiency of state and city administrations to manage education (Sweeney 1989b, Roosen, personal interview, 1996). Moreover, because decentralization required unwilling governors and majors to demand the transfer of edu-cational responsibilities, decentralization advanced very slowly. The share of national schools in the public system dropped only from 67% to 64% during the Pérez administration (Ministry of Education 1994: 305). Instead, Roosen concentrated on administrative reform, which included a redistribution of expenditures, the extension of the school year and school day, the end of automatic check-off dues for unions, and the creation of a professional teachers' career path by establishing a teachers' statute. He also unified and increased state subsidies to private education because he believed that competition between public and private schools would improve performance.[39]

When Roosen proposed his reforms, he encountered hostile and mili-tant unions that resisted his initiatives. He argued that it was very difficult to deal with so many unions that, in many cases, did not respond to partisan discipline (personal interview, 1996). Teachers' unions rejected decentralization because they were afraid that it would reduce the wages

---

[39] He signed an agreement with the Venezuelan Association of Catholic Educators to provide the Free Catholic Education system, numbering 287,000 students, with a free-standing budget (Soules 1991). Between 1989 and 1993, the share of students in the private sector grew from 14% to 17% (Ministry of Education 1994).

of teachers working for both jurisdictions. They protested the expansion of the private sector (which was not unionized) on the grounds that it invaded the constitutional responsibilities of the state for education and rejected the administrative reform that would change work conditions without compensation and deprive them of dues (Ramírez, personal interview, 1996). They responded with increased militancy, which paralyzed negotiations with the administration.

Teachers' militancy resulted from the fragmentation of the sector in which eleven federations with different partisan affiliations competed for the membership of teachers. That is, each competing federation had a different partisan loyalty and was also trying to expand its membership at the expense of its rivals.[40] The combination of partisan competition and union competition had two effects. Firstly, partisan competition increased militancy because those unions associated with opposition political parties had political incentives to protest. Unions affiliated with the governing party wanted to avoid being perceived as having sold out and losing members to the more militant unions. In fact, the union that grew faster during this period – Venezuelan National Federation of Education Workers (FENATEV) – was the most militant, giving credence to the argument that teachers consider it a more representative union (Iturraspe, personal interview, 1996). Hence, AD teacher unions had to show their militancy as well. Secondly, union competition made coordination of collective action more difficult for all competing unions because a different behavior could serve to attract members from rival unions. Strikes and failed negotiations followed one another due to coordination problems. For example, in 1991, FENATEV and AD-led Fetra-Enseñanza broke negotiations and went to strike. On that occasion, the vice minister of education, Francisco Castillo, complained, "I think that there is a competition among unions, where the one that strikes the most is the one that

---

[40] The fragmentation of the education sector was provoked by the lack of collective-bargaining rights in this sector until 1970. As a result, teachers were organized in professional associations that negotiated agreements outside the jurisdiction of the labor code. After a conflictive strike in 1969, however, they gained the right to organize unions and bargain collectively and were granted job stability through the Civil Service Law (Ellner 1993: 43). The legacy of the pre-1970 period was the division of the sector along professional and degree lines as well as partisan affiliations. There have been efforts to reduce this fragmentation by mergers among unions. However, the process was delayed by the costs involved in terms of loss of union permits, monetary rewards for collective bargaining (*costas contractuales*), and challenges to union leadership (personal interviews with F. Iturraspe, and Fetra-Magisterio union leader, J. Ramírez, 1996).

is the most supported by the rank-and-file."[41] The result has been continuous teacher militancy since the first large strike involving 200,000 teachers in November 1989. None of these federations could command the collective action of all teachers. This made agreements with each of them less valuable than with one monopolistic union and each of them weaker vis-à-vis the government. Therefore, teachers' demands were ignored because none of their unions were strong enough to represent the whole sector.

In sum, the combination of union competition and partisan competition increased the incentives for militancy for union leaders in the opposition. When they broke coordination, they pulled even allied union leaders toward militancy because the latter did not want to lose members to their rivals. As a result, union competition weakened union bargaining power because bargaining arrangements were unstable and each federation represented only a share of the involved teachers. The resulting union-government interaction was resistance (inefficient militancy). Hence, whereas militancy in other public sector unions such as FEDEPETROL, FETRATEL, and FETRAELEC was effective in obtaining concessions, union competition made the militancy of teachers' unions less effective (resistance).

Summary

The three public sector companies, PDVSA, CANTV, and CADAFE, presented a similar picture. Centralized collective bargaining in these state-owned enterprises reinforced the monopolistic power of the AD-controlled unions. In the absence of union competition and with little or no partisan competition, the AD union leadership restrained its militancy and received concessions from the government (cooperation). However, the success of cooperation as the union-government interaction created the conditions that increased partisan competition in all three cases. Left-wing and Causa R rivals increased their appeal among workers by accusing AD union leaders of selling out. The replacement threat made the latter more prone to militancy and shifted the interaction from cooperation to opposition in the following round of collective bargaining thereby making the processes of labor restructuring more difficult in all three cases. It is remarkable that these political dynamics of public or privatized

[41] *El Nacional* (January 9, 1991).

companies held for a tradable good such as oil and for monopolistic telecommunication and electricity services.

To the contrary, both the autoworkers of Ford Motors and teachers presented a different picture. In Ford Motors, the lack of union competition or partisan competition brought about cooperation between management and the union. In the education sector, partisan competition made unions more militant. However, union competition made teachers' militancy ineffective because it weakened every union and made coordination more difficult for the unions. In spite of the different interactions in each of these two cases, both in terms of militancy and union capacity to obtain concessions, there were no changes in the independent variables in these instances, nor any variation in the union-government interaction during the period studied. This last pattern shows the effect that changes in the independent variables provoked on the union-government interaction, thus reinforcing the explanatory power of the theory.

Conclusion and Epilogue

The partisan pluralism of Venezuelan labor unions reflected the multiparty nature of the democratic system established by the Pact of Punto Fijo in 1958. The alliance between labor and AD helped to sustain the electoral predominance of this party and facilitated the implementation of policies that contributed to economic growth and democratic stability until the debt crisis. Labor loyalty to AD and the democratic system proved valuable to Pérez in the critical circumstances created by the 1992 military coups. However, partisan competition within the AD-controlled CTV and the fear of replacement prompted AD union leaders to organize two general strikes and multiple protests against market reforms. The unusual militancy of the CTV against an AD president was even more remarkable, for these general strikes were a unique instance in Venezuelan democratic history. The resulting CTV-government interaction was opposition, where labor militancy was effective in hindering labor and social reforms and obtaining compensation for privatization and stabilization.

Individual unions did not necessarily follow the same path as the CTV. In fact, the three unions of public or privatized companies, FEDEPETROL, FETRATEL, and FETRAELEC, restrained at the beginning of the Pérez administration and only increased their militancy when partisan competition emerged as a result of their initial cooperation with the government. The unions lacked the early signaling provided by urban riots to CTV leaders and did not react until Causa R started winning followers among the local affiliates of these national federations. In the absence of union competition, they retained their capacity to obtain concessions. Sooner in the case of the CTV and later in the case of these three public sector unions, AD union leaders had to increase their militancy to avoid being perceived as sold out to an allied government that was implementing unpopular reforms. Hence, after partisan competition increased, these unions increased their militancy. The lack of union competition in all three cases made this militancy effective for achieving concessions. The interaction thus shifted from cooperation to opposition. In contrast, the local section of Ford Motors had a monopoly of representation over Ford workers, and its AD leader confronted no leadership or partisan competition. In this case, partisan loyalty prevailed because the allied leaders faced no leadership competition and they chose restraint. The lack of union competition made their restraint effective in obtaining concessions thus making cooperation the union-management interaction. Finally, in the education sector, partisan competition made teachers' unions more militant to avoid losing members to more bellicose unions. Yet, union competition weakened them all and made it difficult for them to coordinate either militancy or restraint. As a result, their militancy was ineffective (resistance) in achieving concessions (Table 4.3).

The cases studied in this chapter show the usefulness of focusing on union competition and partisan competition to understand union-government interactions in the context of partisan loyalty that emerges from a long-term alliance between labor-based parties and partisan unions. In Venezuela, leadership competition adopted the form of partisan competition. The pressure created by partisan competition on the replacement threat among AD union leaders was especially obvious in the CTV debate over the 1989 general strike. AD union leaders were torn between their partisan loyalty and their fear of replacement. They had to choose between confronting an administration they helped to gain power and their fear of replacement by discontented constituencies who could desert to rival union leaders associated with opposition political parties. The growth of Causa R in the electoral and union arenas confirmed their fears and justified their protests against market reforms. By leaving the populist space void with his policy shift, Pérez provided a fertile terrain for the growth of partisan competitors. Indeed, his political reform facilitated this competition in the unions by providing viable allies in the electoral arena with access to local administrations.

Table 4.3. *Summary of Union-Government Interactions in Venezuela*[a]

Union	Union Competition	Partisan Competition	Interaction
CTV t-1	no	yes	Opposition
CTV t-2	no	yes	Opposition
FEDEPETROL t-1	no	no	Cooperation
FEDEPETROL t-2	no	yes	Opposition
Ford-section t-1	no	no	Cooperation
Ford-section t-2	no	no	Cooperation
FETRATEL t-1	no	no	Cooperation
FETRATEL t-2	no	yes	Opposition
FETRAELEC t-1	no	no	Cooperation
FETRAELEC t-2	no	yes	Opposition
Teachers t-1	yes	yes	Resistance
Teachers t-2	yes	yes	Resistance

[a] Two observations are reported for each case study to account for the changes in the union-government interaction during the period studied. Changes in the independent variables usually between different rounds of collective bargaining were used as cut-off points between "t-1" (the first observation) and "t-2" (the second observation).

The Pandora's box opened by the combination of market reforms and political reforms affected patterns of partisan competition in the union movement. It had an even more dramatic effect in the electoral arena, especially after the 1992 coup attempts and the resignation of Pérez in 1993. The partisan ties created after Punto Fijo started to unravel, although the protests of the CTV contributed to retention of the partisan attachment among union leaders to a greater extent than among the general population. As a result, Venezuelans were evenly divided in their evaluation of the 1992 coups and their electoral loyalties to the old parties or new antiestablishment candidates in 1993.[42] The outcome of the 1993 presidential election is telling. The votes were divided evenly among four candidates and two political camps. AD's Claudio Fermín and COPEI's Eduardo González ran on political platforms that called for the continuation of market reforms. They obtained 23% and 20% of the votes respectively. On the other hand, Causa R's Andrés Velazquez and the winner, Rafael Caldera, backed by Convergencia and MAS ran populist

[42] In a 1993 national survey of 1,338 subjects, almost 48% supported the February coup whereas 42% rejected it, and the rest remained indifferent or had no opinion (Villaroel 1996).

campaigns that rejected economic liberalization. Velázquez obtained almost 21% of the votes and Caldera received 24% (Molina and Pérez 1996: 222). The Caldera administration hesitated between populism and neoliberalism. It reversed some policies and continued others, mainly by establishing an implicit alliance with AD. Caldera's administration, thus, did not reverse the crisis of Venezuelan political parties.[43]

The call for a break with the past grew louder at the 1999 presidential election. AD and COPEI obtained 32% of the seats in Congress and two-thirds of governorships, but the three presidential candidates had no partisan past (Corrales forthcoming). Irene Saez, a former beauty-pageant winner and major of a rich neighborhood; Henrique Salas-Romer, a businessmen and former state governor; and Hugo Chávez, the colonel who led the military coup of February 1992 ran for president of Venezuela. Electoral absenteeism reached 36% of the electorate. Chávez won with 56% of votes. His election put an end to the democracy established by the Punto Fijo Pact. He called a constitutional assembly and unraveled a process for institutional change with unclear consequences, although it is already obvious that the new constitution has undermined the civilian control of the military and centralized power in the president. Despite AD's collapse, the CTV remained controlled by AD union leaders due in part to their opposition to market reforms. However, President Chávez created a new group of union followers who, with Causa R and MAS union leaders, want to displace AD from its predominant position in the union movement. In February 2000, they reached an agreement with the CTV to call direct confederate elections in which union membership would not be a requisite for participation among workers and with the supervision of the newly created National Electoral Commission. This election will not only increase leadership competition but could also be a critical juncture in defining the future loyalties of Venezuelan workers.

The first stage in this dramatic process of political change was set during the Pérez administration. A unique change in Venezuelan economic policies was followed by a unique popular reaction in the form of urban riots. The CTV continued by calling the first general strike in the democratic history of Venezuela. CTV militancy was effective in obtaining concessions and hindering changes and even driving the party against market reforms. Yet, the CTV was trapped by its own success because its unions

---

[43] A public opinion survey in June 1995 reports that 50% of Venezuelans had no confidence in the political parties and another 32% had only little confidence (Romero 1997: 17).

did not adapt to a new market environment similar to some of its Mexican and Argentine counterparts analyzed in the following chapters. In part, they did not adapt because they did not let the environment change as much as it did in Argentina and Mexico. Venezuelan unions resorted to political resources by playing in the partisan primaries and supporting their embattled government after the 1992 coup, but none of the AD unions studied jumped into a new terrain of organizational or industrial resources. AD union leaders survived the erosion of their political party and still confronted Chávez with an oil strike against his changes in PDVSA in early 2000. The irony is that political resources became more rapidly obsolete in Venezuela than in Mexico and Argentina due to the erosion of the traditional political parties.

In sum, my theory explains the historically unusual behavior of CTV union leaders and the various choices of individual unions studied in Venezuela. The effect of partisan loyalties stressed by Coppedge (1994) and sustained by the use of proportional representation after the Pact of Punto Fijo played an important role in explaining the dynamics of partisan competition in the Venezuelan unions. However, it was not fixed, and partisan competition changed the calculus of union leaders when they feared replacement. The "rentier" mentality (Romero 1997), the dependency on a "rentier" state (Karl 1997), or the initial hike in inflation (Weyland 1996) could explain the shorter patience of Venezuelans that would not allow union leaders to discount the future. The ability of labor unions to ally with antireform sectors in AD – unhappy with electoral losses – reinforced labor's ability to boycott market reforms (Corrales 1996).[44] As a result, partisan competition explains the unusual militancy of the CTV against an AD administration despite the partisan loyalty of the AD union leaders who controlled the confederation. At the same time, the CTV's near monopoly over Venezuelan workers increased its bargaining power thus making its militancy effective in halting some promarket policies and obtaining compensation for others. In contrast, union competition had weakened competing national confederations associated with the PRI in Mexico and the factions in which the Argentine CGT divided before 1992. Although unions showed restraint in both countries, because

---

[44] CTV militancy started before the break between President Pérez and AD, and cannot be attributed only to AD union leaders following a party line. Instead, AD labor leaders with their early opposition contributed to the party estrangement from the Pérez administration.

of partisan loyalty they were not effective in obtaining concessions in return (subordination). In fact, once the factions in the Argentine CGT reunited into a single confederation, the lack of union competition made the restraint of this loyal confederation effective in influencing market reforms under Menem (cooperation).

Partisan loyalties, leadership or partisan competition, and union competition are useful to explain the interactions between the CTV and Pérez compared with their counterparts in Mexico and Argentina. They also account for the variation across the cases studied within Venezuela that cannot be explained by national-level variables. Economic interest falls short of explaining all aspects of this variation. The divide between tradable and nontradable sectors based on their different exposure to the international economy accounts for the militancy of Venezuelan teachers in contrast to the restraint of Ford automobile workers. It is less clear, though, that this divide would serve to explain the increase in militancy of oil workers or the initial restraint of telephone and electricity workers. Economic interests cannot explain the changes in union-government interactions in these three cases during the period studied. In fact, the increase in public-sector militancy is hard to separate from the partisan competition created by the growth of Causa R in public enterprises. Therefore, economic interests are insufficient to explain the puzzle if political dynamics are not also considered. In short, without denying the importance of economic interests, macroeconomic conditions, and political legacies on labor behavior, this chapter shows that partisan loyalty and leadership or partisan competition account for labor reaction in terms of militancy or restraint. Simultaneously, union competition explains the strength of the union and its capacity to turn this reaction into an effective strategy to obtain concessions. Furthermore, these variables apply to the CTV considering an array of market reforms and explain differences across individual Venezuelan unions in different economic sectors better than alternative theories.

5

Divided We Rule: Labor Unions and
Market Reforms in Mexico

The conversion of the PRI from populism to neoliberalism was less dramatic than in Venezuela but it opened a new chapter in Mexico's political and economic history. The Mexican Revolution consolidated in a single-party system beginning in the 1930s. The governing party employed state expansion as a tool for economic development and political stability based on the distribution of subsidies and repression. Although its monetary and fiscal policies varied, the PRI continuously expanded the size of the state and promoted import substitution industrialization. From 1940 to 1956, import substitution industrialization and massive public investment were paid for with inflationary financing leading to frequent devaluations of the currency. After 1956, Mexico followed a strategy of "stabilizing development," which was based on state intervention, high public investment, import substitution industrialization, and conservative fiscal and monetary policies, including a fixed exchange rate. As a result, between 1956 and 1972, the Mexican GDP grew 6.7% annually, but the annual inflation rate was only 3.1% (Lustig 1992: 220, Aspe 1993). Mexico was the first developing country to borrow regularly from international financial markets in the 1960s. This debt further promoted state expansion. About three-quarters of Mexico's foreign borrowing was undertaken by a growing public sector, with most loans going to state-owned enterprises (Frieden 1991: 190). Although the Mexican government was forced to devalue the peso in 1976, the discovery of new oil reserves led to a natural resource–based export boom that further expanded foreign borrowing during a period characterized by high growth and high inflation (Lustig 1992: 226–31).

In the 1980s, Mexico triggered the debt crisis that spread throughout Latin America, creating the conditions that provoked the political conversion of populism into neoliberalism. In 1981, the joint shock of increased international interest rates and a deterioration of the terms of trade in Mexican products put Mexico under significant economic pressure. Mounting government spending and fiscal deficits became unsustainable. The combination of a fixed exchange rate and high inflation contributed to an appreciation of the currency and fostered devaluation expectations. Capital flight was estimated at $9.7 billion in 1981 and $8.2 billion (U.S. billion) in 1982 (Frieden 1991: 198, Hierro and Sanginés 1991: 161–4). With Mexico's foreign debt standing at more than half its 1982 GDP, President José López Portillo declared a suspension of foreign debt payments on its principal in August of that year (Lustig 1992: 25). This moratorium led to an interruption of the flow of commercial lending to Latin America and triggered the region's debt crisis. López Portillo also imposed a freeze on dollar-denominated deposits, devalued the currency, adopted full exchange controls on capital flows, and nationalized the Mexican banking system – alienating the business sector only three months before the inauguration of president Miguel De La Madrid (Maxfield 1990, Lustig 1992: 25–32).

When De La Madrid assumed the presidency in December 1982, he inherited an economy in shambles, similar to Lusinchi in Venezuela and Alfonsín in Argentina. In 1983, the Mexican external debt reached 93.8 billion (U.S. billion), the GDP dropped 4.2%, open unemployment rose to 5.3%, and the annual inflation rate surpassed 100% (Lustig 1992: 32, 40). Moreover, the fiscal deficit reached 12% of GDP (IMF 1997). Until 1985, De La Madrid tried to recover business confidence and to control the macroeconomic variables with an adjustment program based on fiscal and monetary retrenchment and wage restraint. In 1985, he started trade liberalization, and Mexico joined GATT the following year (Heredia 1994). He also sold state-owned enterprises of minor importance and promoted in-bond production (*maquila* sector) (Vega López 1995, Rogozinski 1997).[1] In 1987, the stock market fell, triggering a new round of capital flight and high inflation. In December, De La Madrid devalued the peso and with business, labor, and peasant leaders signed the Pact of Economic Solidarity (PSE). This pact – designed by the Budget and Planning Secretariat – established an adjustment plan through income policies, price agreements, and a fixed exchange rate along with restrictive

---

[1] De La Madrid's privatizations represented less than 0.20% of the annual GDP and less than 1% of the annual public-sector income (Aspe 1993: 185, Edwards 1995: 191).

monetary and fiscal policies. Trade liberalization and privatization were also expected to control the price of tradable goods and curtail the fiscal deficit (Aspe 1993, Lustig 1995). In late 1987, secretary of budget and planning Carlos Salinas was selected among other "pre-candidates" to run on the PRI ticket in the upcoming presidential elections.

De La Madrid's policies hurt labor and created strains within the PRI. Between 1982 and 1988, the real value of minimum wages fell 48.3%, and contractual real wages dropped 47.6% (Aspe 1993: 26).[2] Although open unemployment did not grow, the absence of unemployment insurance and the depth of the recession provoked the growth of the informal sector.[3] Meanwhile, labor unrest increased in January 1983 after the administration lifted price controls and broke a settlement reached with unions in December 1982. In 1983, the CTM demanded an increase in the minimum wage with a threat of a general strike and accepted for the first time that non-PRI independent unions join the May Day parade of the official labor movement in 1983.[4] De La Madrid did not target CTM institutional and legislative positions.[5] He also granted union-distributed compensatory subsidies for workers including food, transportation, and housing.[6] However, the government also repressed the most important strikes by non-PRI–affiliated unions, thus curtailing partisan competition in the unions, whereas the secretary of labor rewarded the support of compliant PRI confederations (Zamora 1990: 114, Campuzano Montoya 1990: 185, Middlebrook 1995: 260). These actions brought

[2] According to Middlebrook (1995), the hike in the minimum salary ceased to be a reference point for collective-bargaining wages and instead became a ceiling. In addition, the labor share of the GDP dropped from 35.2% in 1982 to 26.8% in 1988 (Zepeda 1990).

[3] The low open unemployment was related to wage flexibility and to measurement problems. Specifically, the official urban unemployment statistics are calculated as the difference between the economically active population and those who were employed for at least one hour during the week of reference, even if they received no remuneration or merely provided family help (Friedmann, Lustig, and Legovini 1995: 341).

[4] Cf. Zamora (1990: 135), Campuzano Montoya (1990: 185), Xelhuantzi López (1992: 253), and Middlebrook (1995: 260-1).

[5] According to Reyes del Campillo (1990: 145), the CTM share of PRI candidacies in the labor sector grew from 64% in 1979 to 67% in 1982, 71% in 1985, and 68% in 1988.

[6] The government subsidized the union-run Workers' Bank and union-run stores of production and distribution of basic goods, expanding the union-run sector of the economy. It also increased funding to union-run programs for housing and food (Aguilar Garcia and Arrieta 1990: 698-9, Campuzano Montoya 1990: 188). The PRI introduced a constitutional reform for social housing and price controls for rents, transportation, and basic staples. It also increased profit sharing for workers from 8% to 10% (Aziz Nassiff 1989: 279-81, Zamora 1990: 128).

the CTM to support the PSE although it disagreed with the economic direction.

However, De La Madrid's political problems extended to the PRI. In 1986, PRI politicians who rejected market reforms organized the Democratic Current, in pursuit of a return to the populist roots of the PRI. These politicians included former labor secretary Porifirio Muñoz Ledo and former governor Cuahtémoc Cárdenas, the son of populist President Lázaro Cárdenas. Cuahtémoc Cárdenas was expelled from the PRI after he announced his presidential candidacy for the Authentic Party of the Mexican Revolution (PARM) in October 1987. The following year he ran as the candidate of the National Democratic Front against Carlos Salinas, viewed as the architect of Mexico's new neoliberal policies while De La Madrid's secretary of budget and planning. Cárdenas's platform called for a return to nationalism and state intervention, a suspension of debt-service payments, and a commitment to a mixed economy (Teichman 1995: 173). Some PRI-affiliated union leaders chose to support Cárdenas – most notably oil workers' union leader Joaquín Hernández Galicia – to show their disagreement with the new direction of economic policies.

The Salinas Administration (1988–94): The Neoliberal Revolution[7]

Upon entering office, Carlos Salinas de Gortari faced a crisis of political legitimacy along with difficult economic circumstances. On the political front, the 1988 presidential election was very contested. Salinas's main contender, Cuauhtémoc Cárdenas, denounced electoral fraud and did not accept the electoral outcomes. On election night, the computers of the Federal Electoral Commission had an unexplainable breakdown that delayed results for a almost week. Although the results remained disputed, Salinas's 50.4% of votes was the lowest ever for a PRI candidate. On the economic front, the 1988 fiscal deficit was more than 9% of GDP, and the annual inflation rate reached 114% (Table 5.1). Predictably, Salinas stayed the course of structural adjustment, and continued searching for

---

[7] This analysis is based on field research done in Mexico in 1993 and 1995. Fifty-seven people were interviewed, including policy makers, managers, politicians, union leaders, and scholars. Other primary sources include union and official documents, collective-bargaining contracts, and a press chronology (elaborated by my research assistant, Antonieta Mercado, based on the archives of *Entorno Laboral*).

Table 5.1. *Selected Macroeconomic Indicators for Mexico*

Year	Real GDP Growth (%)	Open Unemployment	Under-employment	Minimum Real Salary	Inflation (% Δ CPI)	Fiscal Balance (% of GDP)	Current Account Balance
1982	−1.9	4.3	n.d.	104.7	58.92	−11.98	−5,889
1983	−4.2	5.3	n.d.	84.8	101.76	−8.15	5,886
1984	3.5	5.7	n.d.	71.8	65.54	−7.25	4,183
1985	2.5	3.7	n.d.	70.9	57.75	−7.59	800
1986	−3.6	4.4	n.d.	63.2	86.23	−13.13	−1,377
1987	1.8	3.9	4.0	60.3	131.83	−14.22	4,247
1988	1.3	3.6	3.9	67.4	114.16	−9.61	−2,374
1989	3.3	3.0	3.8	73.6	20.01	−4.99	−5,825
1990	4.5	2.8	3.3	75.1	26.65	−2.8	−7,451
1991	3.6	2.6	3.5	80.1	22.66	−0.23	−14,888
1992	2.8	2.8	3.7	87.8	15.51	1.54	−24,442
1993	0.7	3.4	4.3	94.6	9.75	0.36	−23,400
1994	3.3	3.6	4.4	98.0	6.97	−0.78	−29,418

Sources: Inflation, fiscal balance, and current account balance figures are IMF statistics (IMF, 1996); real GDP growth has been calculated using IMF figures. Open unemployment and underemployment (those who work less than 15 hours per week) are rates of the economically active population and have been taken from Salinas (1992) for 1982 to 1987 and from Salinas (1994: 331) for 1987 to 1994. Real minimum salary is measured with base on 1980 and was taken from the Mexican Indicators of ECLAC for 1995.

consensus from business, peasants, and labor representatives through the PSE and its successor pacts. However, he was more far-reaching than his predecessor in his efforts to privatize state-owned enterprises and banks; deregulate economic activities; liberalize domestic prices, foreign trade, and investment; and reform social security. He even brought Mexico to join Canada and the United States in NAFTA. Salinas had made his career as a technocrat rather than a charismatic politician – in contrast to Pérez and Menem. Hence, he was less pragmatic than the two of them, although he did not recognize himself as a neoliberal. He claimed that economic constraints resulting from new international conditions and the failures of previous development strategy informed his "social liberalism," which he traced to the liberal reforms of Benito Juárez and the social quest of Emiliano Zapata.[8]

Salinas used economic performance as a tool to cope with the crisis of political legitimacy and increase his popularity. Macroeconomic indicators improved rapidly. Within a year inflation dropped to 20% and economic growth picked up, whereas the huge fiscal deficit turned into a surplus by 1992 (Table 5.1). In contrast to De La Madrid, Salinas proved to be a skillful politician. In 1991, over 60% of the population approved his performance and the PRI staged a dramatic comeback in mid-term elections. In elections reported by observers as fairer than any previous one, the PRI obtained more than 61% of the nationwide vote (Centeno 1994: 19). He also used market reforms as an instrument for coalition building both for policy implementation and electoral success. Heredia (1994) argues that he also imposed the powers of the president to business sectors by favoring those who supported him and also hindering their horizontal solidarity to implement his economic policies. Kessler (1998) and Schamis (1999) show how big business received a privileged access to privatized assets and were later expected to reciprocate by contributing to PRI electoral campaigns. Salinas also used the revenue obtained from privatization to gain electoral support through the National Program of Solidarity (PRONASOL). This social program served as a patronage machine that

---

[8] In a series of interviews (Cordera and Rocha 1994), Salinas associated the previous growth of the state with the high inflation and enormous external debt that constrained his policy making (p. 38). He argued that the neoliberal thesis provoked more "injustice and inequality" (p. 16) and claimed that "social liberalism" was rooted in Mexican history going back to the Liberal Reform of the nineteenth century under President Juárez and the Mexican Revolution, the first social revolution of the twentieth century (p. 19). State reform, thus, was necessary to pay the foreign debt and provide revenue for social programs (p. 15).

delivered benefits to poor PRI constituencies and was targeted to recover the allegiance of voters in the areas where Cárdenas had a stronger appeal in the 1988 elections (Centeno 1994, Kessler 1998). Salinas also benefited the middle class – the bulk of independent voters – with cheap access to credit and the boost in purchasing power provided by an appreciating currency.

Salinas not only built a support coalition but also weakened the alternatives through a policy of implicit alliances with the PAN, which appealed to business and the middle classes. The PAN had more ideological coincidences with Salinas in the economic policies than the PRD – weakened by its own process of institutionalization – and provided policy coalitions that eased legislative approval of Salinas's policies. Its growth also contributed to divide the electorate into three camps, thus enhancing the PRI possibilities to capture the single prize of presidential elections by dividing the anti-PRI vote (Elizondo and Heredia 1999). Finally, unlike Pérez, Salinas was successful in controlling labor opposition and even winning the support of labor unions for his market reforms. All PRI-associated confederations, including a new one formed with his support – the Federation of Goods and Services Unions (FESEBES) – supported his policies in corporatist annual pacts throughout his administration. Only a minority of unions unaffiliated with the governing party rejected market reforms and chose to approach the PRD. The next section analyzes the stimulus created by market reforms and the consequences of labor reactions to these policies for understanding why the interaction between Salinas and Mexican organized labor was different from the relationship between Pérez and the CTV in Venezuela.

The Policy Stimulus: Market Reforms

This section analyzes the policy stimulus created by Salinas's policies and their impact on labor at the national level and the concessions granted or denied by the government to its allied labor confederations to gain their support for market reforms. The government took the initiative by choosing a set of policies that changed the status quo for labor and also has the opportunity to buy off labor support if necessary. This first part of this section provides the information necessary to assess the government moves regarding labor. The second part of this section explains labor reaction and capacity to obtain concessions.

Salinas inherited a huge fiscal deficit and high inflation and focused on stabilizing prices through trade liberalization, wage restraint, and a balanced fiscal budget. Workers benefited by recovering purchasing power, even though they were hurt by wage restraint. Increasing exposure to international competition and privatization provoked job losses and industrial restructuring while curtailing union prerogatives in the most unionized sectors of the economy. Meanwhile, labor reforms and changes in the pension and the housing systems challenged the corporatist structure upon which the CTM had built its political influence.

Stabilization. Salinas's stabilization policies included price negotiations and wage caps equal to the approved hikes on the minimum wage approved by business and labor in annual corporatist pacts. He also implemented restrictive monetary and fiscal policies while committing to a stable peso. He cut subsidies, raised public-sector prices, reformed the tax system, and privatized large state-owned companies to achieve fiscal balance. Trade liberalization was also aimed at controlling the price of tradable goods while the exchange rate served as an anchor against inflation – fixed in 1988 and with a limited crawling peg since 1989 (Aspe 1993: 29–33). As a result, the reduction of the fiscal deficit and inflation was accompanied by an appreciation of the Mexican peso that fed a huge current account deficit (Table 5.1) creating the conditions for the financial collapse of 1995 (Lustig 1995, Pastor and Wise 1997: 422–3).

The impact of stabilization on the CTM and its constituencies was mixed. The reduction of inflation benefited wage earners, but real wages in manufacturing never recovered their precrisis level, real minimum wages continued to fall, and industrial employment dropped more than 15% between 1990 and 1994 (Pastor and Wise 1997: 432). Although unemployment and underemployment remained stable (Table 5.1), the informal sector continued to grow and employment in the manufacturing sector dropped from 1990 onward (Pastor and Wise 1997: 432, Cortés 1999: 22). In addition, wage ceilings restricted wage bargaining. Although the CTM unsuccessfully protested against them and continued demanding higher minimum wages, it signed all the corporatist pacts of Salinas's administration and even preached their benefits for real salaries.[9] In

---

[9] See CTM (1990, 1991, 1992, 1994a). The CTM denounced wage ceilings in Mexican courts in 1992 (*Uno más Uno*, December 15, 1992).

contrast, the CROM, the CROC, and the FTSTE did not qualify their support for the stabilizing policies and even boycotted the CTM demands for wage hikes in the CT.[10]

Trade Liberalization. Salinas reduced tariffs from an average of 34% in 1988 to 4% in 1993 (World Bank 1995). In addition to trade liberalization, Mexican integration into the NAFTA sought to make the Mexican economy more competitive. As a result, nonoil exports jumped 38% between 1988 and 1992 – with the *maquila* sector accounting for more than 50% of the expansion in industrial exports.[11] However, trade liberalization and export promotion benefited large firms at the expense of small and medium enterprises in the manufacturing sector, which dropped from 871 in 1988 to 401 in 1993.[12] This decline produced approximately 43,000 job losses, thus contributing to job destruction in the primary and secondary sectors in contrast to the less unionized service sector where employment grew between 1988 and 1993 (Pastor and Wise 1997: 430–4, Meza González 1999: 216).

Even though the CTM leaders thought that it hurt their constituencies, they accepted trade liberalization (Bensusán 1997: 24). They also promoted the NAFTA arguing that it would create employment despite the pressures of their American counterparts to reject the agreement.[13] The other PRI-affiliated confederations also accepted trade liberalization and supported NAFTA (Bensusán 1994b: 119). The CTM, the CROC, and the CROM all affiliated unions in most sectors of the economy and regions of the country and even competed for recruitment in the *maquila* sector (Quinteros 1990, Carrillo 1993). Thus, these confederations include losers from trade liberalization and winners of trade integration, but they chose

---

[10] Unless noted otherwise, the analysis of labor reaction to this policy and the following ones relies on press accounts and personal interviews with Hector Miranda, secretary of national relations of the FTSTE; Cuautemoc Paleta, secretary general of the CROM; Mario Martínez D'ector, leader of the CROC in the state of Mexico; Joel López Mayrén, secretary general of the COR; Francisco Hernández Juárez, secretary-general of FESEBES; and Juan Millán, secretary of education of the CTM, in 1995.

[11] Mexican exports (f.o.b.) grew from $30 billion dollars (U.S. billion) in 1988 to $ 79.4 billion dollars (U.S. billion) in 1994 (IMF 1996).

[12] Mexico's top-ten industrial conglomerates still produced 20% of total manufacturing output by the end of the 1980s, and their sectors were those where export growth was the strongest (Pastor and Wise 1997: 435, Calvo 1999).

[13] CTM (1990, 1991, 1993, and 1994), Góngora and Vázquez (1991), Bensusán and García (1993), and Pastor and Wise (1997: 434). American labor organizations were afraid of losing jobs to cheaper wages in Mexico.

not to give voice to losers. As their Venezuelan counterparts, all PRI-associated confederations supported the trade policies of President Salinas.

Privatization. In the 1930s, President Cárdenas had nationalized oil, electricity, and railroads to promote development. His successors continued expanding the state so that by 1983, the Mexican state owned 1,155 enterprises, accounting for 17.4% of GDP and 4.8% of total employment. However, by 1982, the deficit of state-owned enterprises had reached 4.2% of GDP and accounted for 73.5% of the public sector debt (Teichman 1995: 41, Rogozinski 1997: 93, 96, 102). Hence, Salinas tried to balance the fiscal budget by privatizing important economic assets, such as the national telecommunications company, the formerly nationalized commercial banking system, airlines, steel and copper mills, copper mines, TV channels, fertilizer companies, and part of the petrochemical industry (Aspe 1993: 37). His privatization program raised $24.3 billion dollars (U.S. billion) between 1990 and 1994, making it the largest in Latin America (IADB 1996: 171).

The federal law of state-owned enterprises passed in 1986, and its regulatory decree of 1990 established the rules of privatization by granting discretion to the executive power for the implementation of the process (Rogozinski 1997: 129). Executive discretion – coupled with ability to resort to repression – facilitated rapid privatization despite its tremendous impact on employment and work conditions.[14] For instance, twenty-five companies sold between 1989 and 1991 – excluding Mexican Telephones – (TELMEX) downsized 8,289 employees in two years (Rogozinski 1997: 172). Industrial restructuring and labor flexibility in firms targeted for privatization were drastic because they were viewed as prerequisites for divestiture to prevent overly onerous collective contracts from inhibiting the successful sale of the firms (Ramirez 1993: 20, Teichman 1997: 131).[15]

---

[14] According to a high-ranking policy maker (confidential interview 1995), the administration threatened union leaders with firm bankruptcy and the extinction of collective-bargaining clauses to persuade them of the need to introduce labor flexibility and restructure work conditions in the firms designated for privatization.

[15] Finance Ministry officials view labor union involvement in administrative decisions, such as promotions, state contributions to union companies, and the absence of competitive tendering to favor union companies, as contributing to the inefficiency and high cost of public firms. New collective contracts eliminated their exclusive access to government contracts, the right to distribute benefits to rank-and-file, and state financial contributions (Teichman 1995: 199–200).

Privatization especially hurt nationwide industrial unions that organized workers in large state-owned enterprises, which had higher unionization rates than other unions and collective contracts generous in fringe benefits and union privileges (Bensusán 1990). Although the CTM demanded worker ownership in its 1979 economic program, its unions were not included in the privatization schemes.[16] Even after the CTM had accepted the privatization of nonstrategic sectors, it could not obtain these concessions, which had paved the way for privatization in Argentina (CTM advisor José Domínguez, personal interview 1995, Teichman 1995: 166). Whereas most PRI-associated confederations also accepted privatization without compensation, unions in the new FESEBES were more successful in obtaining concessions that included workers' ownership and job stability in the case of telephone workers (see following text).

Pension Reform. President Manuel Avila Camacho established the IMSS in 1943. The IMSS was a tripartite institution that included labor unions on its board and provided medical care and pensions based on payroll taxes. Although the social security system originally covered only 2% of the population, by 1990 that proportion had risen to 59.4% (Madrid 1999: 125). The aging of the population, raising life expectancy, the economic crisis, and evasion of payments further contributed to its financial crisis. By 1990, real pensions had eroded, and pension spending had risen to 0.57% of GDP (Madrid 1999: 130–4). Salinas passed legislation to increase pensions and pension contributions as he sought to make the IMSS invest its reserves in financial assets. At the end of 1990, the finance secretariat and the Central Bank established the Project on the Stabilization of Pensions that proposed a private system based on individual retirement accounts that would be complementary to the existing public system with the aim of increasing domestic savings. In February 1992, the Congress reformed the Law of Social Security by approving the proposal and creating the System of Savings for Retirement (SAR). The SAR was a privately administered pension system of individual capitalization based on an employer

---

[16] In a few other cases, private buyers established worker ownership (personal communication from Jacques Rogozinsky, head of the Privatization Unit in the Finance Secretariat during the Salinas administration, 1998). He also wrote "the sale of state-owned enterprises to the unions that had preferential right could have reduced the efficiency of the privatized companies due to their lack of entrepreneurial skills and access to the capital markets . . ." (Rogozinski 1997: 127).

contribution equal to 2% of the payroll. The SAR complemented the IMSS but did not affect its structure (Presidencia de la República 1994: 89, Bertranou 1995). However, it did not include union representation in management as the IMSS did. Moreover, the SAR confirmed union fears that the government would use it as a beachhead for the privatization of the public system that would take place under President Ernesto Zedillo in 1996 (Domínguez, personal interview, 1995).

The "official" union movement was divided again, making it difficult for the CTM to mount a challenge against the SAR. If the SAR were to be implemented, the CTM demanded that its funds provide unemployment insurance or be managed by the union-run Workers' Bank (Bertranou 1994: 20). However, the CROC, the CROM, and the FESEBES contradicted the CTM and supported the SAR. Consequently, the government ignored CTM demands and included it only in a symbolic advisory committee. Unable to achieve policy input, CTM legislators voted for the bill in Congress, again showing the willingness of the CTM to comply with government policies even without concessions.

Reforming Social Security for Housing. President Luis Echeverría established the INFONAVIT in 1972.[17] INFONAVIT administered a 5% payroll contribution from workers. It used this fund to build public social housing for the poorest workers who earned a salary equal to five times the minimum wage at most. The highest priority in housing, however, was given to those earning a salary equal to two times the minimum wage at most (Robinson 1980: 57). The institute intervened in financing, planning, contracting, building, and distributing housing. Similar to the IMSS, it had a tripartite management, although labor had a dominant role – particularly with regards to housing distribution. As a result, clientelism and union competition replaced efficiency and solidarity principles in the distribution of housing, and the INFONAVIT became an important source of union financial resources and patronage (Robinson 1980: 157). In 1992, however, President Salinas replaced the union-controlled

---

[17] The presidency of Echeverría (1970–76) was the most populist after Cárdenas. Echeverría also extended the coverage of the IMSS, expanded the National Company for the Provision of Basic Staples (CONASUPO), created the National Fund for the Development of Workers' Consumption (FONACOT), and enlarged the public sector vigorously (Aziz Nassif 1989: 160).

management with individual accounts and transferred the management and administration of these funds to the SAR while ending INFONAVIT's direct involvement in housing construction.[18]

This reform excluded unions from the administration of funds, the intermediation for housing construction, and the assignation of housing credits that had previously been distributed among PRI-related national confederations (*El Economista*, February 10, 1992). Thus, it curtailed resources that had traditionally provided labor unions with selective incentives for membership and discipline, similar to the role of union-run welfare funds in Argentina. The CTM rejected this reform vigorously (Bertranou 1995: 22). Instead, it proposed to increase employer contributions to the fund, police the evasion of payments, and to improve their administration (*La Jornada*, October 11 and 12, 1991). Once again the CROC, the CROM, the COR, and some FESEBES's unions contradicted the CTM and supported the reform thus allowing the government to disregard CTM's demands and implement the reform (Bertranú 1995: 27).[19] Thus, even in a policy area with direct and significant impact on the organizational resources of labor, the CTM had weak bargaining power.

Labor Flexibility. Similar to the Venezuelan labor code, the Mexican Federal Labor Law regulated both work conditions and labor organization. Yet, whereas in Venezuela both areas became more rigid with the new law passed during Pérez's administration, the Salinas administration increased labor flexibility without undertaking legal changes. Labor flexibility in collective bargaining advanced under the discretion of the labor secretariat and the Conciliation and Arbitration Boards. They approved collective-bargaining contracts that, contrary to the spirit of the law, reduced fringe benefits and union prerogatives and increased the flexibility of work conditions.[20] This de facto reform reduced union influence and

---

[18] Personal interview with the Presidencia de la República (1994: 88), the leader of the INFONAVIT union and former INFONAVIT president Rafael Rivapalacios (1995), and Middlebrook (1995: 297).

[19] Of these organizations, only the FESEBES had good reasons to prefer the reform because their better-paid workers were unlikely to receive social housing. In October 1993, however, the CTM obtained a minor concession when the INFONAVIT's administrative council restored the old system of union mediation in credit assignation as a supplement to the new private system (Burgess 1996: 27).

[20] Cf. De La Garza (1993) and Middlebrook (1995). This de facto labor flexibility resulted from the government's attempt to divide the reform of work conditions from the reform of labor organization conditions, both of which were regulated by the Federal Labor Law.

increased flexibility in labor relations. In 1992, the government furthered its commitment to industrial restructuring by launching the National Agreement for the Promotion of Quality and Productivity (ANECP). This agreement sought to increase productivity and international competitiveness, solidifying a trend that had already seen labor productivity in manufacturing rise by 20.2% between 1988 and 1992. Thus, Mexico could retain a lower labor cost than the United States despite the appreciation of its currency (Salinas 1994: 234).

The flexibility of work conditions and the decline of collective benefits hurt CTM constituencies, and the CTM complained bitterly about this trend. CTM protests included delaying its endorsement of the ANECP for nearly two years and threats of solidarity strikes in the textile industry (Middlebrook 1995: 298). The CROC and the FESEBES contradicted the CTM again. These confederations were more favorable to labor flexibility and competitive concerns – although the FESEBES stressed union participation in these changes – and the division of organized labor allowed the government to ignore CTM demands.

Labor Organization Regulations. The Federal Labor Law also regulated labor organization. The CTM had pressed for changes in labor regulations to facilitate labor organization, especially in the public sector. In his campaign, Salinas had promised to reform the labor code and, beginning in 1989, the Employers Confederation of Mexico (COPARMEX) started to demand labor market deregulation and a reduction in union power in collective bargaining. In 1991, COPARMEX presented a proposal including the abolition of closed shops, limits to strike activity, the individualization of wage bargaining, and a reduction of union influence in work organization (Bensusán 1994a: 58–9).

The proposed reform would have affected the "inducements" for labor organization that had sustained the alliance between labor unions and the PRI, as well as the main instruments of union influence in collective bargaining (Chapter 2). In particular, the abolition of closed shops would have facilitated leadership competition within the PRI unions and even the emergence of partisan competition. Such institutional changes could have eased replacement of the leadership of the CTM and other PRI-affiliated confederations. Hence, in contrast to what happened in other policy areas,

---

Although the discretionary power of the Mexican executive permitted a reform that was not enacted as a law, this tactic created juridical insecurity.

105

all PRI-affiliated confederations joined the CTM to unanimously reject the reform of the labor code, complaining that it was too favorable to business. In this isolated case, the CTM obtained the support of all unions in the Congress of Labor and was able to organize a common front against the reform.[21] After this reaction, the government put off its reformist intentions in this area.

Summary. The CTM had to accept wage restraint, privatization, labor flexibility, the reforms of the IMSS and the INFONAVIT, and trade liberalization. Privatization affected public rather than private sector workers, whereas trade liberalization impacted differently on workers in tradable rather than nontradable sectors. Due to the predominance of cross-sectoral preferences of state federations over industry-wide national unions, the CTM did not actively seek compensation for the workers involved in privatization as non-CTM unions did. Nor did the CTM defend unions in import-competing sectors from trade liberalization. Additionally, the CTM could not prevent the challenges to its constituencies and union organization resources created by the reforms of the IMSS and INFONAVIT and labor flexibility. The exception in terms of its policy input was the reform of the labor law. In this case, the CTM built a unified front with other PRI-related confederations that reduced union competition and strengthened their bargaining power. The next section explains the CTM compliance with Salinas's market reforms despite the few concessions received in exchange (subordination).

Union Competition and PRI Monopoly

The interaction between the CTM and Salinas provides a nice contrast with that between Pérez and the CTV analyzed in the previous chapter and is an interesting case study for the theory presented in Chapter 2. That is, partisan loyalty promoted union-government collaboration, but partisan competition increased the incentives for labor militancy even for allied union leaders because they feared replacement. However, the capacity of unions to obtain concessions is related to whether the union is competing with others for the representation of workers. Union competition makes coordination for collective action more difficult and weakens every union, which can only control a share of the involved workers. In Mexico,

---

[21] Cf. Bensusán and Garcia (1993), CTM (1993), and Bensusán (1994a: 56–70).

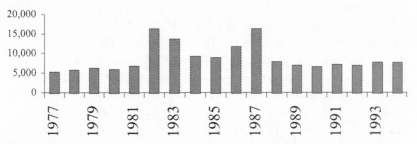

Figure 5.1 Strike petitions filled in the labor secretariat, 1977–94.
Source: Annual records of the labor secretariat.

not only did the CTM accept Salinas's reforms, but with other PRI-affiliated confederations also restrained its militancy with few concessions in return (subordination). According to the theory, subordination of a loyal union should be explained by union competition without partisan competition.

In Mexico, several national confederations all affiliated with the PRI competed for both members and for government favors. The alliance with the governing party granted them the label of official labor movement and a seat in the CT although the CTM was recognized as the largest and politically most important of all under the fifty-year leadership of Fidel Velázquez (Chapter 2). The CTM and other PRI-associated confederations reduced their militancy during the Salinas administration. As a result, the yearly average of strike petitions dropped from 9,818 during the De La Madrid administration to 7,007 during the Salinas administration. That is, contrary to industrial-relations theories, militancy was higher in the years of recession during De La Madrid's administration as measured by the number of strike petitions filed with the Labor Secretariat (Figure 5.1).[22] More significantly, Salinas's average was even lower than the yearly average of 7,511 experienced by López Portillo during a period of high growth and low unemployment (Labor Secretariat 1995).

The 1988 election was a wake-up call for PRI union leaders because it created the first legitimate challenge to the long-term incumbent PRI. PRI unions closed ranks with the party and restrained their militancy in support of governability, because if the PRI lost power, they would face worse challenges to their leadership survival. CTM's Fidel Velázquez even called for

---

[22] Strike petitions are a better measurement of militancy than legal strikes because of the multiple requirements needed to have a strike approved (explained on p. 67).

the expulsion of Cuauhtémoc Cárdenas when the latter questioned the nomination of Salinas before breaking with the PRI. PRI union leaders have been so closely tied to the PRI that they alienated themselves from other political parties like the PAN and the PRD, which explicitly rejected the corporatist arrangement, and in some cases, supported internal opposition to PRI union leaders (Murillo 1997b). This attitude is confirmed by CTM's distrust of political liberalization for fear of another political party gaining power and is equivalent to the CTV's defense of democratic stability after the failed 1992 coup attempt in Venezuela. At the same time, Salinas used repression to curtail partisan competition in the unions and punish the few defectors, thus reinforcing his monopolistic control of the official labor movement and further curtailing partisan competition for most PRI union leaders.[23] Hence, partisan loyalty reduced labor incentives for militancy due to the threat created by the 1988 elections, because most labor leaders feared a future with no access to the state if the PRI turned power over to another political party as it happened in 2000. The CTM, however, had more demands than other PRI-affiliated confederations. Its affiliated unions had a larger share of the legal strikes called by unions in the official labor movement from 1989 to 1992 although the share dropped in the two following years without significant concessions from the government (Labor Secretariat 1995).[24]

The government manipulated union competition for membership and dwindling state-distributed resources among PRI-affiliated labor confederations. Salinas's policies sharply affected the distribution of material and symbolic resources. Government officials rewarded compliant confederations by shifting scarce resources away from those that demanded the most. This induced the exit of affiliated unions from the CTM to the PRI-related confederations, such as the CROC and the CROM, which boycotted CTM policy demands. Simultaneously, Salinas fostered union competition by supporting the emergence of a "new unionism" concerned with work productivity and expressed in the newly organized FESEBES whose leaders had a close relationship with the president (Collier and Samstad 1995). After the Labor Secretariat ignored CTM complaints and

---

[23] For example, early in his administration, Salinas punished some PRI union leaders who supported Cuauhtémoc Cárdenas in the 1988 elections, such as Joaquín Hernández Galicia of the oil workers' union (see following text).

[24] A comparison of strike petitions would have been more appropriate, but the Labor Secretariat provides data only on legal strikes for national confederations.

granted the FESEBES its official registration in 1992, the FESEBES and the CROC launched a common front within the CT, which appeared as an alternative to the CTM (*Uno más Uno*, December 16, 1992). In addition, in February 1993, PRONASOL incorporated them into a program for the modernization of unionism that had previously been rejected by the CTM (*El Financiero*, February 24, 1993).

Salinas also curtailed CTM political resources, which had traditionally been the most effective in compensating for the industrial weakness of the majority of small and local CTM unions. In 1990, the fourteenth conference of the PRI introduced individual affiliation and established equal representation for the corporatist sectors as well as a new territorial structure. The following year, its fifteenth conference merged the labor and peasant sectors (Mendez Berrueta and Quiroz Trejo 1994: 293). As a result, the percentage of legislative PRI candidates from the labor sector dropped from seventy-five or 21.4% of PRI slates in 1988 to fifty-six or 15% in 1994 (Reyes del Campillo 1990 and personal communication). However, by 1993, the XVI Assembly of the PRI returned the corporatist structure to the National Executive Committee (Marbrán, personal interview, 1995). Therefore, the political changes may have served as warning signals for the CTM because it still held majorities on the boards of tripartite institutions, such as the IMSS and the Minimum Wage Commission.[25]

Salinas's manipulation of union competition made the CTM lose affiliates to other national confederations that had a better relationship with the government and hindered collective action of all PRI confederations.[26] Just as urban riots signaled increasing leadership competition for the Venezuelan CTV, the government's favoring of the competing CROC and FESEBES and the transfer of unions from the CTM to the CROC and the CROM signaled increasing union competition for the CTM. The CTM was forced to bring its "price" down and to close a "bad deal" with the government due to the competition with other PRI-related national labor confederations that could also provide labor support.[27] The Salinas

---

[25] As the CTV in Venezuela, the CTM was strengthened within the PRI by its alliance with other groups within the party who also felt challenged by the changes in the party structure. These allies took advantage of the upcoming presidential elections of 1994, when the reformers would most need their support.

[26] The exit of CTM-affiliated unions was reported by several newspapers, in particular in the period between 1990 and 1992.

[27] Domínguez (personal interview, 1995) complained that the government favored other confederations to put down CTM's protests. A high-ranking official of the administration

administration was successful in manipulating this competition among PRI-related confederations using state-distributed resources because it did not have to risk losing their allegiance to another political party. That is, the CTM and particularly Fidel Velázquez had alienated other political parties, and Salinas was effective in weakening the PRD as an alternative to neoliberalism. Furthermore, the CTM could not impose its majority in the CT whereas the Mexican presidency had discretionary powers over resource distribution – including the PRI structure – further hindering the articulation of horizontal solidarity among PRI-affiliated confederations. Therefore, union competition in the context of a monopolistic party that curtailed partisan competition made subordination (ineffective restraint) the union-government interaction.

There was an exception, however. The CTM did build a common front with all PRI-related confederations in the CT to reject the reform of the labor code, thereby reducing union competition. In this single instance, the absence of union competition and partisan competition shifted the union-government interaction from subordination to cooperation by making CTM restraint effective in halting this reform. Finally, a minority of independent unions vociferously denounced Salinas's market reforms, and some even approached the PRD. Salinas's response to them ranged from ignorance to repression because he did not want to give in to unions associated with the political opposition. This was especially true after the PRD emerged as a credible challenger and appealed to these unions for electoral support because Salinas had tried to weaken its viability as an alternative to market reforms to recover the votes lost in the 1988 election.

Sector-level Analysis: Introducing Variation within the Same Country

As in the previous chapter, this section shows that not every Mexican union interacted with the government in the same fashion as the CTM. This section analyzes five case studies in different sectors of the economy. The comparison across case studies within the same country allows to hold national variables constant to test the effects of partisan loyalty, partisan or leadership competition, and union competition in different economic

confirmed that competition was used to control CTM demands (confidential interview, 1995).

contexts. The sectors studied included oil, automobile, telecommunications, electricity, and public education.

Interest-based theories provide an account of subnational variation, which national-level theories do not explain. However, Mexican industry-specific case studies differ from those in Argentina and Venezuela, because only two of the five studied unions were affiliated with the CTM. This fact is important because the CTM was more centralized than the CTV and the CGT, making it a more important actor at the level of individual unions when the unions were affiliated with the confederation. The analysis of the case studies, however, follows the same patterns as in the previous chapter. It starts with oil and automobile industries that suffered the effect of increasing exposure and whose unions were affiliated to the CTM and organized workers in tradable sectors. It continues with the telecommunications, electricity, and education sectors, which were under state control organized by non-CTM unions. Whereas both telecommunications and electricity went through industrial restructuring, only the former was privatized; electricity privatization was on the agenda. Teachers, instead, had to deal with the decentralization of education.

Oil. After President Cárdenas nationalized the oil industry in 1938, the state-owned company, PEMEX (Mexican Oil), had monopolized oil production. Mexico found new oil reserves in the mid-seventies that doubled its previous holdings, and benefited greatly from the concurrent surge in oil prices. After the debt crisis, oil revenue, which accounted for 8.7% of GDP in 1983, became even more crucial for the Treasury (Hierro and Sanginés 1991: 153–5, 174). Therefore, Salinas implemented policies aimed at making the industry more productive by opening parts of the industry to private investment and replacing political criteria for efficiency in management.[28] PEMEX also changed investment strategies, established public bidding for supplying contracts, and restructured work organization through collective bargaining in 1989, 1991, and 1993 (Barbosa 1992: 21, Loyola and Martínez 1994: 287, and Pérez Pérez 1995: 73).

The new collective-bargaining contracts created deep challenges for labor by introducing internal and external flexibility, reducing fringe

---

[28] By 1989, PEMEX still accounted for 6.9% of GDP and almost one-quarter of public sector income, and by 1991, one-third of Mexican exports were oil products (ECLAC 1993: 280, 287).

benefits, and curtailing union prerogatives on hiring and promotion. The unions also forfeited a 2% union fee for social welfare applied to suppliers' contracts. This curtailed its financial resources, subsidies for union stores, the obligation of contracting companies to employ union personnel, and the exclusive right to perform contract work in land drilling, plant maintenance, industrial installations, and infrastructure.[29] The 1991 collective contract eliminated union participation in job allocation, promotions, and work organization. Moreover, between 1989 and 1993, PEMEX cut its personnel from 210,000 to 106,939 and expanded workers in nonunionized categories, thus curtailing the ranks of the union.[30] Finally, in 1993, the government divided PEMEX into four divisions: refining; exploration and production; gas and basic petrochemicals; and nonbasic petrochemicals. These divisions, which did not coincide with the organization of the union into sections, made it harder for the union to respond to the changes and further weakened its national strength (Loyola and Martínez 1994: 310, Teichman 1995: 126). Although labor flexibility and the drop in fringe benefits affected union constituencies, and despite previous protest to reforms in the industry under De La Madrid, the union passively accepted the changes to collective contracts without compensation.[31]

The subordination of the STPRM was surprising given its historical political power. The monopolistic union had originated as the merger of several unions before it organized the strike that allowed Lázaro Cárdenas to nationalize the industry (Bizberg 1990: 39).[32] This monopolistic union benefited from the prosperity of the industry and the financial resources obtained through its fees on contracts, which along with

---

[29] The 2% fee on contracting had the double consequence of developing a welfare fund similar to those in Argentina and increasing the incentives for the union to press for subcontracting of PEMEX activities (Loyola 1990b: 163). The union also used those resources in shops, farms, and companies to supply PEMEX, which employed transitory workers who wanted to obtain a permanent position in the company (Novelo 1991: 107–8).

[30] Cf. PEMEX (1987, 1989, 1991, and 1993). On a description of the process of personnel reduction, see Barbosa (1995: 28); on other modifications through collective bargaining see Barbosa (1992: 23) and Loyola and Martínez (1994: 288); and on the loss of union prerogatives, see Loyola and Martínez (1994: 299–301) and Teichman (1995: 126).

[31] Cf. Novelo (1989), Cruz Bencomo (1989: 28), Barbosa (1992), Loyola and Martínez (1994: 295–7), Pérez Pérez (1995: 73), and García Solís (personal interview, 1995).

[32] Referring to the STPRM, Cook (1995: 86) writes "once probably the most powerful union in the country, the new union leadership did nothing to resist the extensive reforms that caused thousands of layoffs, eliminated benefits and seniority, and radically altered the collective bargaining agreement."

closed-shop clauses were used to curtail leadership competition.[33] The absence of union competition or leadership competition should have led to cooperation (effective restraint) as the union-government interaction rather than compliance without any compensation in return (subordination). In fact, when De La Madrid introduced a public bidding system for public sector contracts that explicitly excluded unions, the STPRM obtained an exemption from the government, taking advantage of its strong bargaining power as a monopolistic union in a strategic sector (Novelo 1989: 16). In 1987, the union also forced the resignation of PEMEX Director General Ramón Beteta and obtained a reduction in the number of nonunionized "managerial" employees in the collective contract. The contract also put more funds into maintenance, stipulated that 30% of PEMEX tanker requirements were to be rented from the union companies, and increased benefits and salaries giving further proof of the strength of the union (Teichman 1995: 124).

However, the demise of this powerful union resulted from the nondemocratic nature of the Mexican regime and Salinas's attempt to weaken the PRD as a viable option to neoliberalism. During the 1988 election, the leader of the union, Joaquín Hernández Galicia (La Quina), had supported Cuauhtémoc Cárdenas against Salinas and threatened to strike to protest the opening of basic petrochemicals to private investment immediately afterward.[34] Salinas reacted immediately. In January 1989, he sent the military to put Hernández Galicia in prison on charges of murder and illegal arms possession. When the union elected a transitory leadership, the Labor Secretariat refused to recognize it and instead imposed an acquiescent leader controlled by the CTM, Sebastián Guzmán Cabrera (personal interviews with union leaders Cruz Bencomo and Vázquez, 1995). This new leader accepted the changes in the collective contracts of 1989, 1991, and 1993 and even repressed those who protested them.[35] This

---

[33] Union leader Cruz Bencomo (personal interview, 1995) confirmed the account of Aldana (1988: 182), Cruz Bencomo (1989: 26), and Novelo (1989: 19) on the political value of access to employment and financial resources.

[34] In 1985, Hernández Galicia allowed union leaders affiliated with the Socialist Workers' Party (PST) to hold leadership positions in certain sections. In 1988, in most electoral districts dominated by oil workers, Salinas lost the presidential election to Cárdenas while PRI-union candidates for representatives and senators were elected (Cruz Bencomo 1989: 27–8, Reyes del Campillo, personal communication, 1995).

[35] For example, in a General Assembly of July 14, 1992, the new secretary general, Sebastián Guzmán Cabrera, defended the restructuring plan implemented by PEMEX while acknowledging the job losses implied by the plan. Simultaneously, one of his union allies

repressive imposition explains why the union-government interaction was subordination rather than cooperation. The nondemocratic nature of the Mexican regime allowed the president to repress partisan competition in the union movement to prevent loyal union leaders from exiting to other political parties and forcing their compliance instead.

Automobile. A 1962 Decree of National Integration marked the first government attempt to organize the automobile industry around national priorities. Because the government had to approve the construction of plants, the number of producers was limited. Price controls, production quotas for assemblers, and a 60% locally manufactured content requirement fostered import substitution industrialization. Within the following decade, sales tripled, and employment grew almost fourfold. In the 1970s, further decrees also added export promotion regulations and continued the expansion of the industry. Production reached more than half a million units, and the industry employed more than 90,000 people (Morris 1998a: 115–18).

However, the debt crisis took a toll in the industry. The production of motor vehicles plunged 50% between 1981 and 1983 and it had not recovered its 1981 levels by 1988 despite vigorous export promotion during the De La Madrid administration (Morris 1998a: 125–6). In the belief that domestic markets promoted inefficiency and hindered exports, Salinas enacted the decree for the promotion and the modernization of the automobile and autotransport industry to put an end to import substitution industrialization in 1989. The decree allowed the importation of complete vehicles, lowered the domestic content requirement, and eliminated the obligation to produce parts domestically and the limits on the makes and models. Additionally, price deregulation, fiscal incentives, Mexican integration into North American markets, and labor flexibility in the new export-oriented plants of northern Mexico were expected to promote the growth of exports (Arteaga 1990: 142, Von Bulow 1994: 23, Morris 1998a: 121).[36] Therefore, industrial restructuring concentrated its impact on the

proposed to apply the closed-shop separation clause to "professional agitators" who rejected restructuring (*La Jornada*, July 23, p. 13 quoted in Melgoza 1992: 184).

[36] Motor vehicle and passenger vehicle production more than doubled between 1988 and 1994, as did the value and number of automotive exports between 1988 and 1993. They grew from 173,147 units in 1988 to 471,912 units in 1993 (Morris 1998a: 126, 127, 130, 136). In 1993, 85% of automotive exports were directed to North American markets (Von Bulow 1994: 15).

old plants of central Mexico. These had been established during the period of import substitution industrialization, and had more rigid collective-bargaining conditions, better wages, and stronger unions than those in the north (Herrera 1992, Carrillo 1993).

Because collective bargaining was defined at the plant level and the Ford Motors Company was studied in the previous chapter, this section relies on the experience of a single plant of the Ford Motors Company left in central Mexico. The Ford Motors Company had already closed two of its three domestically oriented plants in central Mexico and opened two export-oriented plants in the north during the 1980s (Carrillo 1993: 381). Collective bargaining in the three plants was decentralized to the plant level, although in all cases it involved approval by the national company union and the CTM (Von Bulow 1995: 11). However, the remaining plant in central Mexico – situated in Cuautitlán – inherited higher labor costs and more rigid work conditions than the new ones and was controlled by a more powerful local union committee.[37] Thus, this plant suffered a much stronger shock from the policy changes in the automobile sector.

The company wanted to change this disparity, which reduced labor productivity in this plant and could promote labor unrest in the northern plants (Arteaga 1990: 148). In 1987, the Ford Motors Company fired all Cuautitlán workers and rehired them under a more flexible collective contract. The new contract also increased the authority of the national leadership of the union in collective bargaining at the expense of the local executive committee in Cuautitlán (Arteaga 1990: 153–5, Von Bulow 1995: 13–14). The 1989 and 1991 contracts further increased labor flexibility (Ford 1989, 1991). As a result, a comparison between this plant and the other five domestically oriented plants in the central region shows the costs paid by Cuautitlán workers. Although their average wage was higher than that of the other five in 1984, it had become lower ten years later because this plant had the lowest increase in nominal wages and the most substantial drop in real wages during this period (Morris 1998b: 165, 168).

Due to the high visibility of the industry in the process of trade integration and the nondemocratic nature of the Mexican regime, as in

---

[37] In 1987, the average wages in Cuautitlán were more than double those of the northern plants of Chihuahua and Hermosillo (Arteaga 1990: 150, Carrillo 1993: 371). Collective-bargaining conditions established seniority as the main promotion criterion, limited internal flexibility, and granted the union important management prerogatives. These were exercised by the elected local union executive committees that had replaced CTM-appointed delegates in 1977 (Carrillo 1993: 386–7, Middlebrook 1995: 273).

the previous case study, repression and CTM meddling shaped the union dynamics. The National Union of the Ford Motor Company (SITRAFORD) organized the three Ford Motors' plants. The union was affiliated with the CTM, which was predominant in the automobile sector where non-PRI unions had been influential in the 1970s.[38] The national leadership of the union approved collective contracts and strikes, and was accountable to the executive committee of the CTM (Morris 1998b: 157). The Ford-Cuautitlán section had a two-tiered structure of union governance, in which democratically elected local executive committees co-existed with the national leadership. The Cuatitlán plant also experienced more leadership competition than other CTM plants in the central region (although not as much as the two non-CTM plants). Three of four elections in the period from 1981 to 1995 were contested, and the local union experienced turnovers in their authorities (Morris 1998b: 158).

When the company tried to level Cuautitlán's work conditions with those of northern plants in 1987, it created a conflict between the local and the national leadership of the union. However, workers in the northern plants did not show solidarity with those in Cuatitlán, preventing the expansion of the conflict (Carrillo 1993: 383, Von Bulow 1995: 14). Cuautitlán workers reacted militantly with work stoppages and violent incidents despite a previous history of labor peace in the plant (Von Bulow 1995: 31).[39] As in the previous case, the CTM took over the union and replaced the local executive committee and imposed subordination to permit labor restructuring. However, the discontented workers elected a new local executive committee in 1988 that was linked to left-wing parties and hostile to the CTM (Von Bulow 1995: 30–1).

This election signaled partisan competition and a break with partisan loyalties. Under the new local leadership, Cuautitlán's workers militantly rejected the policies of the company and questioned the national leadership of the union. In 1990, to escape CTM intimidation, the local executive committee applied for affiliation with the COR in search of an umbrella organization to second their leadership challenge (union leader P.B. Díaz, personal interview, 1995). The CTM reacted to this attempt to

---

[38] The CTM controlled only six of the eleven unionized plants in 1976 and eighteen of the twenty-one unionized plants in 1987. Its predominance was the largest in export-oriented plants, which gathered 85.5% of CTM members, including those in Ford Motors' two northern plants of Hermosillo and Chihuahua (Carrillo 1993: 375–6).

[39] Only thirty-five work days were lost between 1943 and 1987 (Von Bulow 1995: 13).

exit the CTM with a violent takeover of the union. Ford management and the government sided with the CTM because this confederation was fostering labor restructuring in all its affiliated automobile plants (Von Bulow 1994: 15).[40] The Labor Secretariat allowed a public ballot procedure supervised by company personnel within Ford Motors' premises to decide the union affiliation to the COR. This procedure intimidated workers and resulted in a close victory of the CTM. Afterward, the government backed a violent CTM intervention into the union to limit leadership competition when another non-PRI local executive committee was elected again in 1992 (P.B. Díaz, personal interview, 1995).[41] On both occasions, subordination was imposed onto the local union.

All in all, leadership competition and a break in partisan loyalties increased the militancy of this plant relative to other CTM plants in the region and other Ford plants in the north (Morris 1998b). The national leadership and the CTM reacted with repression. The lack of solidarity from the new and already flexible plants in the north provided some cushion for the national leadership by reducing the risk of a rebellion that was spreading to the rest of the union. As argued by Morris (1998b) and Von Bulow (1995), in this case study the limitation for union democracy coupled with the authoritarian nature of the Mexican regime allowed the CTM to impose subordination as the union-government interaction thereby ignoring the preferences of Cuautitlán's workers.

Telecommunications. Even before its nationalization in the 1970s, TELMEX had turned into a monopoly due to the merger of Ericsson and Mexicana in 1950. The fiscal crisis made this privatization a priority because it would not only provide revenues to the state but also allow the necessary investment in a sector that was crucial for a competitive open economy. In September 1989, Salinas announced the privatization of state-owned TELMEX at a union meeting. The tender terms granted a six-year exclusive license, which included investment and improvement targets and established a new regulatory framework that would reduce cross-subsidies

---

[40] Middlebrook (1995: 290–1) argues that because labor flexibility was easier to achieve in CTM-affiliated than in independent unions, the CTM increased its influence on the automotive industry during the 1980s.

[41] A worker died and several were hurt as a result of CTM-directed violence. Furthermore, the company contributed to the restriction on leadership competition by dismissing non-PRI union leaders after the 1992 election. Thus, both the PRI government and the company were interested in restricting leadership competition.

during the same period. To make TELMEX more attractive, the government also raised prices and reduced taxes on telecommunications, concentrated voting power in 40% of shares, and ruled that foreign investors could own up to 49% of the holding purchasing the controlling shares. Three bids were received in November 1990, and the Grupo Carso in association with Southwestern Bell and France Telecom was selected as the winner (Rammamurti 1996: 79–86).

The STRM restrained and supported the privatization.[42] It also agreed to change the fifty-seven-year-old collective contracts with a single contract for all unionized workers, reduce labor classifications from more than 500 to 50, and introduce new technologies of labor organization.[43] The union not only recognized the need for privatization to make the company efficient due to the fiscal crisis, but also received concessions in return for its support. Concessions included the maintenance of collective rights, job stability, and the permanent hiring of 4,636 workers with short-term contracts and 467 new workers. The union also received generous contributions to social and training funds. Workers received wage hikes of 15% and benefit raises of 16% and worker ownership – which was raised from 3% to 4.4% of capital in the negotiations with the union.[44]

The STRM was not affiliated with the CTM and had emerged in 1950 from the merger of the two unions of private telephone companies Ericsson and Mexicana (Xelhuantzi López 1989: 11). It was a monopolistic union with closed-shop arrangements. In 1976, a rank-and-file rebellion replaced a corrupt PRI leader with a younger leader, Francisco Hernández Juárez. Although Hernández Juárez was affiliated with the PRI, he reformed the union constitution to increase democratic participation. He also introduced voting procedures for the collective approval of collective contracts and strike actions and rules forbidding reelection (Xelhuantzi López 1989: 33–50). However, successive modification of the

---

[42] Following the general trend in labor militancy under De La Madrid, this union had called strikes in 1984 and 1987.

[43] Cf. STRM (1988), TELMEX (1988, 1990, 1992 and 1994), Rammamurti (1996: 80), and De La Garza and Melgoza (1998: 203–12).

[44] This account is derived from personal interviews with union leaders Francisco Hernández Juárez and Mateo Lejarza, labor relations' manager Javier Elguea, a confidential interview with a high-government official in 1995, and from the analysis of collective contracts by Vázquez Rubio (1989: 60 and 66) and De La Garza (1989: 51–5). Although workers paid the prevailing market prices for their shares, the union organized a trust fund that obtained $325 million (U.S. million) dollars in soft credit from a public bank to buy the stocks that would be paid with the dividends (Rammamurti 1996: 80).

union constitution permitted Hernández Juárez's reelection while he reduced leadership competition by centralizing resources, promoting unity lists in assemblies, and maintaining his responsiveness to rank-and-file demands. Pilar Marmolejo, training director at TELMEX, said, "After we reached an agreement with the union, Hernández Juárez calls his constituencies for their approval or rejection of the commitment reached by the union. . . . I do not recall a negative vote" (personal interview, 1995). Rosario Ortíz, a dissident activist associated with the PRD and opposed to Hernández Juárez and to privatization, denounced a "subtle repression" of dissidents. However, she admitted that Hérnandez Juárez co-opted the rank-and-file and dissident activists using the resources he obtained from collective bargaining (personal interview, 1995).[45]

The strength of this monopolistic union and the uncontested leadership of Hernández Juárez made him a political asset for Salinas, who established a close personal relationship with him. This personal relationship facilitated bargaining during privatization (Hernández Juárez, personal interview, 1995). In this case, the absence of union competition or leadership competition made cooperation (effective restraint) the union-government interaction. However, after privatization, the union continued to collaborate with the new management in return for union participation in the programs for quality, productivity, and training – including a union-management committee measuring productivity – and compensation for additional efforts and generous benefits for workers – such as new welfare programs.[46]

Electricity. Two state-owned enterprises monopolized the electricity sector. The Light and Power Company of Center Mexico (CLFC) had been established in 1903, and the government bought 95.6% of its stocks in 1960. The Federal Commission of Electricity (CFE), founded in 1933, bought the rest of the electricity companies at the time of nationalization

---

[45] Clifton (1995) analyzes the rules and practices of this union and emphasizes the control of most technical decisions by a group of advisors under the direct supervision of Hernández Juárez. Both the official leaders and the opposition present a similar view of his leadership (personal interviews with STRM's Mateo Lejarza and Rosario Ortíz, in 1995).

[46] Cf. De La Garza and Melgoza (1998). The cooperation between management and the union was established in the letter of agreements, and reinforced in personal interviews with STRM's Hernández Juárez and Lejarza, and TELMEX's Elguea and Marmolejo in 1995.

in 1960 (De La Garza et al. 1994: 21, 306). The SME organized the CLFC, whereas the Single Union of Electricity Workers of the Mexican Republic (SUTERM) affiliated the personnel of the CFE. SUTERM was affiliated with the CTM, but the SME was not.

As in telecommunications, the fiscal deficit and the demands of an open economy made electricity infrastructure crucial. Salinas's national program for the modernization of energy industries sought to improve productivity, quality, and efficiency in the energy sector, diversify energy sources, and increase investment. Salinas also raised electricity fees and opened energy investment to foreign capital. This program created a more serious challenge for the CFLC than for the CFE and, therefore, this section analyzes the SME-government interaction. The CFLC was an obvious target for privatizing and restructuring because it had been in bankruptcy status for many years, produced only 5% of the electricity it distributed, and had accumulated large debts by buying overpriced electricity from the CFE. The CLFC had a very generous collective bargaining contract that reduced management discretion with a very detailed specification of industrial relations (Melgoza 1992: 69–74; 1994: 161). As a result, the private sector demanded its privatization, and the government proposed to dissolve the company and merge it with the CFE (Melgoza 1994: 165).

The SME rejected this proposal that risked the jobs of its constituencies and threatened its survival by forcing its merger with the larger SUTERM, thus ending its independence from the CTM. The SME had a monopoly of representation, and its constitution facilitated leadership competition because it established a secret and universal vote, a system of first-past-the-post for each leadership position, and the renovation by halves of two-year term executive-committee positions (SME 1992: art. 23 and 34). Workers' committees with minority representation controlled the implementation of the collective contracts on the shop floor (Melgoza 1994: 159). These multiple opportunities for leadership competition made union leaders more responsive to their constituencies and provoked the emergence of two competing factions within the union: one militant and one moderate.[47]

---

[47] This account is derived from personal interviews with union leaders Jorge Sánchez and Jorge Durán, from the moderate faction, and Horacio Romo, from the more militant faction in 1995.

Because the government had repressed a strike organized by the militant faction against the market reforms of De La Madrid in 1987, the moderate faction won the elections that year (Melgoza 1992: 175). In February 1988, the new union leader Jorge Sánchez obtained the union endorsement for the Salinas nomination despite SME's historic independence from the PRI. In return for restraining a formerly militant union, Salinas granted Sánchez assurance of the company's survival. In 1989, Salinas also agreed to rescue the firm by buying a small portion of shares still in private ownership to make it a state-owned company but different from the CFE. The union also secured job stability and the maintenance of work conditions for workers through the process of industrial restructuring. A new collective contract established two management-union commissions in charge of increasing productivity and achieving financial viability, which enhanced union participation in industrial restructuring building upon the traditional SME culture of participation.[48] It also granted new fringe benefits, such as earlier retirement for risky jobs, and bonuses to pay for housing, education, and household expenses for workers.[49]

However, in 1993, after two reelections Sánchez lost a close union election to militant union leader Pedro Carrillo, who denounced him for having sold out to Salinas. Leadership competition led to a break in partisan loyalty, which increased SME militancy. In 1994, SME refused to sign the corporatist pacts, organized street demonstrations, and even threatened to strike during collective bargaining. Because it was still a monopolistic union, it achieved a reduction in the productivity targets for workers. Summing up, President Salinas supported Sánchez – who had been twice reelected – to prevent more militant leaders from turning the union hostile again. Sánchez was, like Hernández Juárez, a political asset for a president with few union allies. Union monopoly and little leadership competition made cooperation the union-government interaction. Once leadership competition emerged again and broke with the loyalty of the union to the governing party, the union increased its militancy and shifted its interaction with the government from cooperation to opposition.

---

[48] The account derived from interviews with Jorge Sanchez and a high government official under Salinas (confidential) in 1995 was confirmed by Pérez Pérez (1993). Melgoza (1992: 80) analyzes SME's culture of participation in the industrial organization of the company since 1966.

[49] Cf. Melgoza (1992: 178–80 and 1994: 165–6), SME (1994), and personal interview with J. Sánchez (1995).

Education. The Mexican Constitution put primary education under the jurisdiction of municipalities and secondary education and teacher training under the jurisdiction of the states. However, beginning in 1921, the Public Education Secretariat (SEP) expanded and centralized the education system at every level.[50] Centralization, politicization, and bureaucratization were blamed for the increasing inefficiency of the education system, in particular through the power of the union in the assignment, administration, and promotion of personnel (Street 1983: 243, Arnaut 1992a: 9). Between 1970 and 1980, personnel grew from 400,000 to 900,000 with a disproportionate portion of the budget spent on administrative expenditures (Ornelas 1995). Fiscal deficit and concerns with the quality of education prompted Salinas to announce decentralization in his program for the modernization of education in October 1989. In three years he had transferred 513,374 teachers, 116,054 administrative employees, 9.2 million elementary students, and 2.4 million secondary students from national- to state-level jurisdiction (Arnaut 1994: 258). The union rejected decentralization claiming that the national state was relinquishing its budgetary responsibilities. It became particularly adamant against the state after a leak from the SEP in 1991 mentioned the intention to divide the union into 32 parts to coincide with the new state-level districts (Arnaud 1994, SNTE 1995: 29).[51]

The Federal Labor Law for State Employees restricted strike activity in public education and granted federal agencies the right to define wages "taking into consideration the opinion of unions" (art. 87). In spite of these limitations, teachers had engaged in illegal strikes, and the SNTE had exercised great influence in work conditions in the sector (López Cárdenas 1989: 256). The SNTE emerged as a monopolistic and centralized union in December 1943 from the merger of four education unions and several small groups (Avila Carrizo and Martínez Brizuela 1990: 23). The SNTE was affiliated with the FSTSE but, as its largest union, retained

[50] In 1928, the SEP controlled only 20% of the students and the federal government paid for only 6.1% of education expenditures. By 1991, however, the SEP controlled 65% of students and the federal government paid for 80% of education expenditures (Ornelas 1995).
[51] High-ranking policy makers in the SEP and Finance Secretariat admitted in a confidential interview (1995) that the division of the nationwide union into thirty-two state unions was one of the unachieved objectives of the reform. This objective was perceived by PRI and dissident union leaders as well (personal interviews with SNTE advisor, J. Rodríguez, and CNTE leader, J.M. Del Campo, 1995).

great autonomy. The SEP backed the merger to reduce interunion conflicts and control the influence of communism among teachers (Arnaut 1993). After that, the PRI controlled the nationwide union that served as a political machine and played a key role in elections due to its territorial dispersion. In return, union leaders were appointed positions at the legislative and executive levels (Arnaud 1992b). Furthermore, the expansion of education enlarged union ranks and provided administrative appointments for union leaders. Yet, because supervisors knew that they owed their position to their union careers, they paid more attention to the political control of members than to the monitoring of their performance (Cook 1996: 79, 85, Street 1992: 116). Centralization strengthened the national leadership who restricted leadership competition (Arnaud 1992b: 19–30, Cook 1996: 80).

Rank-and-file discontent fostered a regional dissident movement that took advantage of the conflict between the union leadership and the SEP created by a regional deconcentration of the administration of school procedures in 1978. The following year, the dissidents created the National Coordinating Committee of Education Workers (CNTE) to coordinate different regional demands for union democratization and economic grievances. The CNTE gained control of local unions in Oaxaca and Chiapas (Foewaker 1993, Cook 1996). In the 1980s, the erosion of teachers' salaries and union control over administrative positions furthered discontent. In 1989, CNTE's mobilization reached its zenith and toppled Jongitud Barrios from the leadership of the SNTE.[52] The new PRI union leader Elba Esther Gordillo had a weak political base. Thus, to avoid losing control of the union and enhance her internal legitimacy, she abolished the automatic affiliation with the PRI and included the internal opposition within the national leadership through proportional representation. The changes institutionalized leadership competition that had previously been restricted.[53]

---

[52] According to Cook (1996: 270), "Teachers from throughout the country engaged in work stoppages, marches, hunger strikes, and *plantones* in Mexico City and regional capitals from February to May 1989." Indeed, the largest demonstration of teachers' dissent occurred in 1989, with more than 500,000 union members joining the work stoppages scheduled in April – more than half of the country's largest union (269). Only in Mexico City, "in ninety days . . . there were forty-one demonstrations, eighteen meetings, more than sixty local assemblies, six national assemblies, four forums, two sit-ins, six strikes, and thirty-two negotiations sessions" in 1989 (Arnaud 1992b: 51).

[53] Cf. Gordillo (1992: 21), J.M. Del Campo (personal interview, 1995), SNTE (1995: 13), and Cook (1996: 272). According to Cook (p. 279), dissident "members enjoyed full

With this background, the SNTE had become a monopolistic union that institutionalized leadership competition through proportional representation (SNTE 1992). The new leaders, in particular, did not want to appear passive vis-à-vis their internal rivals who had created a replacement threat, thus they increased SNTE militancy. In 1991, when decentralization was discussed in Congress, the SNTE called eight local strikes (in addition to another four called by the CNTE); three large marches; many sit-ins and meetings; and a national process of consultation with the rank-and-file. To obtain the support of the SNTE and reduce its mobilization, the government granted important concessions. These concessions included provisions for the central government to retain control of evaluation, curriculum, and funding of training. They also included a teacher statute setting forth rules for career development and minimum working conditions; teachers' salary hikes above the national wage ceilings; and new pension benefits and pay incentives.[54] The federal government would also earmark the states' education budget instead of decentralizing financial decisions on education expenditures. This was done to guarantee the uniformity of teachers' work conditions established in the new teachers' statute across the former federal and state jurisdictions (SNTE 1995: 68–77). These concessions facilitated the decentralization process, although they substantially modified its original design (Arnaud 1994: 257–60). In short, leadership competition and growth of dissident activists increased the militancy of the SNTE. The government placated this mobilization by granting concessions to their allied union leaders to avert their replacement by non-PRI-affiliated union leaders, leading to opposition (effective militancy) as the union-government interaction.

participation in the union's first congress after the 1989 mobilization . . . [many of their positions] . . . were incorporated into the documents and resolution of the 1990 congress. It was also important for Gordillo that the SNTE be able to demonstrate to the Salinas government that it could generate new ideas, 'modernize' itself, and do so while incorporating the strongest elements of the opposition."

[54] According to José Antonio Rodríguez (personal interview, 1995), advisor to secretary general of the SNTE and the SNTE (1995: 68), teachers' real incomes (including productivity incentives and benefits) increased from 1.3 minimum salaries to 3.4 minimum salaries from 1988 to 1994. In contrast, CNTE union leader Jesús Martín Del Campo (personal interview, 1995) claimed that basic real salaries grew 35% between 1988 and 1994. In any case, they fared better than most sectors of the economy that lost purchasing power and passed from having the lower average income in the public administration to having the second-best average income in the public sector (SNTE 1995: 112–13).

Summary. The union of PEMEX and the local section of Ford Motors in Cuautitlán were forced into subordination. The challenges created by industrial restructuring triggered the initial increase in leadership competition and militancy. The CTM, however, did not tolerate leadership competition and, allied with the government, repressed workers' preferences and forced subordination as the union-government interaction. In contrast, the union in TELMEX restrained its militancy in return for concessions regarding privatization and labor restructuring (cooperation). The loyal leader lacked leadership competition making partisan loyalty prevail while union monopoly increased labor bargaining power. Hence, the union cooperated with the government for privatization and with private management for labor restructuring. In electricity, the loyal leader of the SME also headed a monopolistic union. As a popular leader continuously reelected, he did not perceive leadership competition. He restrained labor militancy to show his loyalty to Salinas in return for the survival of the company and the union besides other concessions (cooperation). An unexpected electoral defeat made him lose the union. His successor broke partisan loyalty and increased labor militancy moving the union-government from interaction to opposition. Finally, in the teachers' union, leadership competition emerged from a rank-and-file rebellion that toppled a leader who would not accept democratic turnover. The emergence of leadership competition increased the incentives of the new PRI leader to become more militant whereas union monopoly strengthened labor bargaining power. To put down SNTE's protests against decentralization, the government had to grant sizeable concessions. In this case, leadership competition and union monopoly brought about opposition as the union-government interaction.

Conclusion

The single-party system that emerged from the Mexican Revolution reduced the possible allies for labor outside the dominant PRI. Because labor support was fundamental for sustaining this inclusive regime, the PRI curtailed partisan competition in the union movement, thus reinforcing the value of partisan loyalty for labor unions. Despite the predominance of the CTM, several labor confederations expressed alliance with the PRI. Although partisan loyalty without partisan competition induced labor restraint, union competition weakened all PRI-associated labor confederations, making them ineffective in achieving much in exchange for their collaboration (subordination). Partisan loyalty was reinforced by the threat of the 1988 elections, especially because the CTM had long feared the consequences of the PRI losing power. Salinas strengthened the monopoly of the PRI over unions by punishing defectors to other parties and used the powers of the Mexican presidency to manipulate union competition among PRI-affiliated confederations. Hence, the combination of union competition and no partisan competition resulted in subordination as the government-union interaction. Only in the case of the attempted reform of the Federal Labor Law did a common front of all PRI-related labor confederations reduce union competition and permit the CTM to exercise policy influence. For most market policies in the set, subordination (ineffective restraint) was the interaction between the CTM and Salinas. In turn, this subordination was fundamental for the success of Salinas's economic policies upon which he also built his political legitimacy.

Salinas's market reforms also triggered the process of industrial restructuring, privatization, and decentralization that challenged the status quo for individual unions. However, not even in Mexico, where democracy was more restricted and presidents were more powerful than in Venezuela and Argentina, did all unions studied follow the same path as the CTM. However, economic pluralism would have expected higher militancy in all service sectors rather than the variation provoked by leadership competition in education and electricity. Indeed, economic interest cannot explain short-term changes in union behavior, such as the one that followed the defeat of Sánchez in the SME.

Despite restrictions to democracy, union leaders still fear replacement by rebellion rather than election as in the SNTE. The public sector and non-CTM unions studied – STRM, SME, and SNTE – all had monopolies of representation that strengthened labor bargaining power and allowed them to obtain concessions from an allied administration. When the unions of telephone workers (STRM) and electricity workers (SME) were controlled by allied leaders and faced no leadership competition, they exercised restraint. As a result, cooperation (effective restraint) was the union-government interaction. However, although the leadership of Hernández Juarez in the STRM remained uncontested and cooperation continued from privatization to restructuring, the situation changed in the SME. When Sánchez lost control of the union, the new leadership broke the partisan loyalty and increased its militancy, thus moving the

Table 5.2. *Summary of Union-Government Interactions in Mexico*

Union	Union Competition	Partisan Competition	Observed Interaction
CTM t-1	yes	no	Subordination
CTM t-2	yes	no	Subordination
STPRM t-1	no	no	Subordination
STPRM t-2	no	no	Subordination
Cuautitlán t-1	yes	yes	Resistance (1988 and 1992)
Cuautitlán t-2	no	yes	Subordination (1990 and 1993)
STRM t-1	no	no	Cooperation
STRM t-2	no	no	Cooperation
SME t-1	no	no	Cooperation
SME t-2	no	yes	Opposition
SNTE t-1	no	yes	Opposition
SNTE t-1	no	yes	Opposition

union-government interaction to opposition. Opposition (effective militancy) was also the union-government interaction regarding the decentralization of education (Table 5.2). In this case, leadership competition from the CNTE, which had toppled her predecessor, made the SNTE union leader more aware of the replacement threat and more prone to militantly demand concessions that were granted by an administration that did not want to lose control of a monopolistic union.

Economic pressures can explain workers' preferences against the erosion of gains acquired under import substitution industrialization due to economic liberalization in the cases of Ford Motors' workers in Cuautitlán and oil workers. However, the less democratic nature of the regime permitted the violent intervention in the cases of these CTM-affiliated unions against the economic preferences of workers. The CTM was ruthless because its leaders perceived such behavior as a price to be paid to reduce leadership competition, which could threaten their own replacement. This imposition of union strategies was only possible because of the centralized authority of the CTM and the nondemocratic nature of the Mexican state. These institutional characteristics mediated the effect of economic interest in generating leadership competition and explain the emergence of subordination as the union-government interaction. These cases, however, do not contradict the theory but highlight its limitations and the importance of national institutions. In both cases, the government

127

and the CTM violently imposed subordination as the union-government interaction. These exceptions could be explained by the nondemocratic nature of the regime and the CTM (Cook 1995, Middlebrook 1995) or by the sanction power of the party over union leaders (Burgess 1998a). Explanations based on internal democracy, such as Von Bulow (1995) and Morris (1998b), however, do not account for the fact that a democratic union (the local Cuautitlán union) shares this category with a highly undemocratic one (STPRM).

The centralized authority of the CTM forced subordination onto these cases and its absence provided the non-CTM case studies with the opportunity to develop a new role in industrial organization and provide services for workers. For instance, STRM used workers' stock to build a savings fund providing soft credits for housing and consumer durable goods. Both the STRM and SME represented workers in committees to deal with ways to increase productivity. The SNTE began to provide funds for housing and subsidized consumer durables as well as teacher training. It also funded a research institute and a forum open to different political parties as part of a strategy to support SNTE candidates regardless of party to promote union interests (J. Rodríguez, personal interview, 1995, SNTE 1995: 14–15). These strategies reduced dependency on political resources in preparation for political liberalization and the possibility that the PRI would lose power as it happened in 2000.

The success of Salinas's economic policies allowed the PRI to win the 1994 presidential elections, which were considered relatively fair. This is no minor accomplishment considering that the original PRI presidential candidate, Luis Colosio, was shot during the campaign, and a guerrilla movement emerged in the state of Chiapas in the last year of his administration. To win that election, however, Salinas refused to devalue the peso despite its appreciation. Upon his inauguration, President Ernesto Zedillo (1994–2000) devalued the peso and suffered a harsh recession the following year. He tried to build his political legitimacy with a quick economic recovery and the acceleration of political liberalization to the point that the opposition won the 1997 mid-term elections, the PRI held its first primaries ever in 1999, and the PRI lost the 2000 presidential elections. Continued democratization should make my theory more appropriate for Mexico by providing unions with new partisan allies and increasing the public avenues for voicing union dissidence, thus, increasing opportunities for leadership and partisan competition in the union movement. In fact, taking advantage of political liberalization, some formerly allied labor unions adopted a more autonomous stance. This process culminated with the organization of the National Union of Workers (UNT) that joined unions formerly in the official labor movement – such as the STRM – and independent ones. It accelerated after the PRI lost the presidency to Vicente Fox, from the PAN, in July 2000. The UNT demanded, along with employers, the elimination of corporatist controls, such as closed shops, while some PRI unions tried to increase their autonomy from the party.

The corporatist literature could have explained the restraint of the CTM based on partisan loyalty in its neocorporatist version and the state's capacity to control organized labor in the state corporatist tradition. However, these national-level theories cannot account for the variation in union-government interaction across economic sectors, with the exception perhaps of the subordination of the oil workers and Ford Motors' workers in the version of state corporatism. Additionally, industrial-relations theories fail to account for a drop in militancy that does not take advantage of declining unemployment and improving economic growth. Without denying the importance of economic interests, macroeconomic conditions, and political institutions on labor behavior, this chapter shows that partisan loyalty and leadership or partisan competition account for labor reaction in terms of militancy or restraint. At the same time, union competition explains the strength of the union and its capacity to make this reaction into an effective strategy to obtain concessions.

In short, this theory takes into consideration the economic incentives created by the policy shift on organized labor to explain its interaction with Salinas. It accounts for the CTM support of Salinas although it had preferred another PRI "pre-candidate" – Alfredo Del Mazo – for the 1988 election and did not receive sufficient compensations for swallowing the bitter pill. It also explains the variation in union-government interaction for the individual unions studied, although qualifications to tolerance for the replacement threat must be added in the cases of the oil workers and Ford Motors' workers at Cuautitlán. Partisan loyalty without partisan competition and union competition weakened the bargaining power of the CTM, thus explaining that subordination was the union-government interaction. The same was true, although transitory, of the Argentine CGT that was divided into three factions between 1989 and 1992 but retained its partisan loyalty to Peronism. In contrast to Mexican unions, however, Peronist unions reunified to recover bargaining power vis-à-vis an allied administration and obtain concessions in return for their restraint (cooperation). In Venezuela, instead, the CTV had a near monopoly of representation that reinforced its bargaining power, whereas partisan competition made allied union leaders become more militant (opposition). Labor restraint, however, enhanced the success of Salinas and Menem in implementing market reforms, whereas labor militancy contributed to Pérez's demise.

6

From Pickets to Prices: Labor Unions and
Market Reforms in Argentina

The conversion of Peronism from populism to neoliberalism and the 1983 democratic transition closed half a century of political and economic instability in Argentina. After the overthrow of Perón in 1955, presidents did not complete their terms in office, and military coups marked their turnovers. Multiple devaluations of the exchange rate, mounting inflation, and erratic economic growth accompanied political instability, which turned toward violence with the emergence of guerrilla groups in the late 1960s. To halt this violence, Perón was permitted to return from exile and be elected president in 1973. He followed expansionary economic policies and further enlarged the public sector (Di Tella 1983, Sturzenegger 1991). After his death the following year, battles over economic policy – including a general strike called by the CGT – and urban violence escalated (Torre 1983). By 1976, the economy was in recession, the fiscal deficit had reached 15.1% of GDP, and the wholesale price inflation peaked at 499% (Frieden 1991: 189).

The military took power again in March of 1976, imposing a very repressive authoritarian regime, banning union and political activities, and implementing neoliberal policies. Its financial liberalization increased interest-rate differentials between Argentina and the rest of the world.[1] High interest rates and an exchange rate that lagged behind inflation provoked an appreciation of the domestic currency, which with trade liberalization put pressure on manufacturing firms in the consumer-oriented import-competing sector and generated massive inflows of capital. Firms

---

[1] The following analysis of the economic policies of the military is derived from Canitrot (1980, 1981), Schvarzer (1983), Azpiazu, Basualdo and Khavisse (1987), Basualdo (1987), Smith (1989), and Schamis (1999).

acquired dollar-denominated debt to keep their operations afloat or went bankrupt. The foreign debt grew three times between 1978 and 1981. Most of the private debt was concentrated in a few large banks and industrial firms, which benefited from access to industrial promotion and public contracts.[2] As a result, only 5% of all private debtors were responsible for 79% of the total private external debt, the fiscal accounts remained in the red, and state-owned enterprises accounted for more than half of the foreign public debt by 1981 (Schamis 1999: 260, Pirker 1991: 81).[3] Even before the Mexican unilateral moratorium triggered the debt crisis in 1982, many banks had collapsed and been taken over by a government whose reserves dwindled as it tried to sustain the financial system. To avert mounting social unrest, the military rulers decided to launch an invasion of the Malvinas/Falkland Islands in April 1982. As a result, they provoked a war against Great Britain. After their defeat, the military rulers were forced to accept a democratic transition, and elections were called for in October 1983.

Raúl Alfonsín, the Radical Party candidate, surprisingly won the presidency with 52% of votes, defeating for the first time a Peronist candidate in competitive elections. President Alfonsín had to undertake the delicate task of consolidating democracy following half a century of political instability. Like Lusinchi in Venezuela and De La Madrid in Mexico, President Alfonsín had to confront the dire effects of the debt crisis. In 1983, the Argentine external debt reached $46.5 billion, and capital flight in the previous two years amounted to $8.9 billion (U.S. billion). Although the GDP – which had dropped 6.1% in 1981 and 5.2% in 1982 – increased by 2.8% in 1983, inflation hit 343.82%, and unemployment grew to 4.2%.[4] Moreover, unlike Lusinchi's AD and De La Madrid's PRI, Alfonsín's party had no ties to labor. Instead, there was a history of distrust with Peronist unions that peaked during the 1983 electoral campaign when Alfonsín accused them of a secret pact with the military. After his inauguration, Alfonsín

---

[2] The military rulers implemented a policy labeled "peripheric privatization" that implied the subcontracting of services by state-owned enterprises. Bocco and Repetto (1991: 110) calculate that overcharges by suppliers to the state grew from 0.6% of GDP in 1976 to 2.12% of GDP in 1982/83.

[3] Gerchunoff and Llach (1998: 375) show that expenditures of the central government surpassed its revenue from 1976 to 1983. The fiscal deficit was 3.7% of GDP in 1977, 5.5% in 1980 and around 10% in 1982.

[4] The data on GDP, debt, and inflation are from IMF (1997), the data on unemployment are from ECLAC (1984), and on capital flight from Edwards (1995: 23).

tried to change the regulations on union elections to facilitate leadership competition, thus threatening incumbent Peronist labor leaders. This move unified the two factions within the CGT to organize a general strike as the bill was killed in the Senate (Gaudio and Thompson 1990: 41).[5] In such a context, Peronist unions lacked a political incentive to restrain their militancy, unlike their counterparts in Venezuela and Mexico. Indeed, Peronist electoral opposition to Alfonsín provided Argentine unions with an incentive to increase their militancy against his administration. The Peronist-controlled CGT organized thirteen general strikes against Alfonsín's economic policies.

In June 1985, Alfonsín launched the Austral Plan – an adjustment program based on income policies and fiscal austerity.[6] Labor opposition, business distrust, and the erosion of political credibility contributed to the failure of this program.[7] Alfonsín tried to cope with labor opposition and achieve wage restraint by reaching an agreement in 1987 with a group of large Peronist unions. He granted them a wage hike, the reenactment of the Peronist labor legislation, and the appointment of a union leader as minister of labor. However, the agreement was hard to enforce because other unions increased their wage militancy – especially during the 1987 campaign for congressional elections, which the Peronist party won by a landslide (Gaudio and Thompson 1990: 165–90). Peronist legislators killed Alfonsín's privatization initiatives in Congress.[8] Although he launched another stabilization plan based on price agreements, tighter monetary and fiscal policy, and a fixed exchange rate in 1988, he could not enforce wage or price restraint. By early 1989, the fiscal deficit had to be financed with short-term debt and seigniorage, thus generating an inflationary tax.[9]

---

[5] In a personal interview (1999), Alfonsín explained this bill as a preemptive move in the expectation of labor opposition to his policies.

[6] A freeze on prices and wages accompanied a new monetary sign, a complex de-indexation mechanism based on the difference between old expected inflation and new expected inflation, exchange rate controls (with a crawling-peg following the initial fixed exchange rate), and restrictive fiscal policies (Bouzas 1993: 10–12, Fernández 1991).

[7] Between 1987 and 1989 he also suffered several military rebellions as a result of his policy to bring the former military rulers to trial for human rights violations.

[8] In 1987, Minister of Public Works Rodolfo Terragno launched a proposal to privatize the national telephone and airline companies, but these projects generated criticisms from the unions, the Peronists, and left-wing parties (Margheritis 1997: 154–64).

[9] Seigniorage is the revenue raised through printing money, which increases the money supply thereby generating inflation. It can result in an inflation tax when the increase in prices generates losses for money holders.

The possibility of Peronist Carlos Menem winning the 1989 presidential election and returning to populist economic policies created uncertainty in the business sector.[10] High interest rates, recession, and a growing external debt added to political uncertainty. This situation was the catalyst for a run on the Argentine currency that depleted reserves, therefore forcing the central bank authorities to end their commitment to exchange rate stability in February. The large corporations responded with a run to the dollar that caused the collapse of the domestic price system. The price of the dollar grew twenty-five times in six months, and monthly inflation peaked at 200% in July 1989 (Gerchunoff and Torre 1996: 735, Schamis 1999: 262). This crisis forced a presidential turnover five months before schedule.

The First Menem Administration (1989–95): From Hyperinflation to Market Reforms[11]

The first administration of Carlos Saúl Menem lasted between July 1989 and July 1995 when he was inaugurated for his second term after a constitutional reform, in 1994, allowed presidential reelection. Menem had entered the Peronist primaries as an underdog against Antonio Cafiero, the president of the Peronist Party. Menem won the primaries with the support of most unions and ran for president with a vague populist campaign promising generalized wage hikes and a "productive revolution." Once inaugurated, Menem surprised foes and followers by launching a drastic program of stabilization and market-oriented reforms. Menem's conversion followed his realization of the costs of hyperinflation and the distrust of business. It was a strategy for political survival rather than ideological conviction (Palermo 1995).[12] His determination to win

[10] Carlos Menem ran a populist campaign and the last Peronist administration had left memories of expansionary policies leading to high inflation and economic instability.

[11] The primary sources for this section were collected in Buenos Aires between 1992 and 1995. They include more than seventy interviews with union leaders, government officials, and company decision makers; an extensive search of all the newspapers of the period between 1983 and 1995 in the archives of *Clarín*; and collective bargaining contracts, union documents and annual reports, company and official documents, government reform proposals, laws, and decrees of the period.

[12] This view is backed by Margheritis (1997: 137). She reports her interviews with union leaders Julio Guillán (FOETRA) and Antonio Cassia (SUPE) on a 1989 meeting with Menem, where he explained that the Central Bank had run out of reserves, the country was bankrupt, and there was no alternative to structural reforms to "save democracy."

credibility for his market reforms, despite his populist past, inspired his appointment of executives of the Bunge & Born corporation as his first two economy ministers and several members of a neoliberal party, the Union of the Democratic Center (UCEDE), into his administration.[13]

The laws of State Reform and Economic Emergency approved after Menem's inauguration, triggered the policy shift.[14] These laws cut public expenditures, started the privatization of public enterprises, launched trade liberalization, and reformed the tax system (Gerchunoff and Torre 1996, Pastor and Wise 1999). Deregulation of prices, trade, financial market, and other economic activities followed in 1990 (decree 2,476). However, macroeconomic instability persisted until a new economy minister, Domingo Cavallo, launched in the following year the Convertibility Plan, which successfully controlled inflation (Table 6.1). The fixed exchange rate anchored domestic prices, inflation fell, economic activity picked up, and external capital flowed in (Canitrot 1994: 88–9). Most analysts argue that the high social costs of hyperinflation enhanced popular support for economic policies that promised to control inflation. Thus, the success of the Convertibility Plan was key in explaining the 41% plurality obtained by the Peronist Party in the 1991 legislative elections.[15]

The Menem administration succeeded in stabilizing and reshaping the Argentine economy, a task in which previous administrations had repeatedly failed. The economic crisis not only forced his conversion into

[13] Bunge & Born was a multinational corporation and a long-term adversary of Peronism, to the point that Peronist guerrillas kidnapped its CEO in the 1970s. Alvaro Alsogaray, the leader of the right-wing party that joined the Menem administration, had long been a defender of economic liberalism and fierce critic of Peronism.

[14] To compensate for the time gap between presidential and congressional inauguration, Menem and Alfonsín reached an agreement by which the Radical Party promised a congressional quorum to pass Menem's emergency laws.

[15] Weyland (1996a) uses prospect theory to explain the effect of hyperinflation in gathering popular support for neoliberalism in Latin America. Palermo and Torre (1992), Palermo and Novaro (1996), and Torre (1998) claim that the crisis facilitated the popular acceptance of this conversion as a "fuite en avant." These arguments are supported by the evolution of public opinion among voters of Peronism in the 1989 election. According to Lynch Menéndez Nivel & Associates, in September 1989, 70% of Peronist voters had a positive view of the economic policies. By November, 47% held positive views and by December, only 26% did. The numbers kept falling as the government failed to control inflation. In September 1990, 19% of these voters had positive views and by March 1991, only 14% held those views of economic policies. Yet, after the March 1991 Convertibility Plan, the number climbed to almost 45% by May and to 58% by September of that year.

Table 6.1. *Selected Macroeconomic Indicators for Argentina*

Year	Δ% CPI	Fiscal Deficit[a]	% Δ GDP[b]	Trade Balance[c]	Unemployment Rate[d]
1985	672.15	−5.35	−6.61	4,878	6.3
1986	90.10	−2.40	7.32	2,446	5.9
1987	131.33	−2.69	2.58	1,017	6.0
1988	342.96	−1.34	−1.89	4,242	6.5
1989	3,079.81	−0.66	−6.36	5,709	8.1
1990	2,313.96	−0.33	0.65	8,628	8.6
1991	171.67	−0.53	8.9	4,419	6.9
1992	24.90	−0.03	8.65	−1,450	6.9
1993	10.61	−0.61	6.03	−2,428	9.9
1994	4.81	−0.67	7.42	−4,238	10.7
1995	3.38	−0.7	−4.4	2,238	18.6

[a] As a percentage of GDP.
[b] 1990 prices.
[c] In millions of U.S. dollars.
[d] As a percentage of the economically active population according to the Permanent Household Survey of INDEC for the month of May of each year except for 1987 when it was measured in April and 1991 when it was measured in June (the INDEC makes a second annual measurement in October).
Sources: International Financial Statistics of the IMF (1997), INDEC (1996, 1994).

neoliberalism but also provided an adequate context for his success.[16] However, the crisis was not sufficient for the success of reforms. To avoid a repetition of the obstacles faced by Alfonsín, Menem built a coalition that included most labor unions and provincial governors while retaining the electoral support of the traditional Peronist constituencies among the lower strata.[17] In building this coalition, his leadership skills doubtless played a key role.[18] However, analyses of the legislative processes, the

[16] Acuña (1994: 91) argues "hyperinflation was presented as the evidence of the irreparable failure of the state-centered economy – a failure that could only be overcome by freeing private initiative from state intervention and by reducing the size of the government sector to its bare minimum."

[17] The poor continued to support the Peronist Party even after the conversion of Menem toward neoliberalism. This support was based on long-term cultural identities (Ostiguy 1998: Chapter 5) or sheer clientelism (Levitsky 1999: Chapter 6). Provincial spending increased to reward supportive governors (Gibson 1997) and the Peronist Party helped him to build legislative support (Corrales 1996).

[18] O'Donnell (1994) crafted the concept of "delegative democracy" to describe the vertical accountability of presidents to the masses combined with the lack of horizontal account-

unified character of an administration in which the same party controlled the executive and the legislature, and his coalition politics show a leadership that included more crafting than imposition.[19] As a result, there was only a minor splinter in the Peronist Party with the defection of eight legislators who would eventually joined other parties in forming the FREPASO.

However, the conversion of Menem to neoliberalism divided the Peronist CGT in October 1989. A proreform CGT-San Martín and a populist CGT-Azopardo disputed over the CGT label while a group of independent unions did not take sides.[20] The CGT unified in March 1992. A small group of unions – led by a union of teachers and one of the public administration employees – broke ranks with the CGT and organized a new confederation: the Congress of Argentine Workers (CTA). The CTA resisted market-oriented reforms and eventually participated in the creation of FREPASO. Two years later, another spin-off of the CGT-Azopardo resulted in the truck drivers' and bus drivers' unions organizing the Movement of Argentine Workers (MTA) as a populist internal faction within the CGT. The next section provides a view of the effect of market reforms on labor at the national level. The first part focuses on government initiatives and concessions before shifting in the second part to an explanation for the restraint of the CGT and its ability to obtain concessions.

The Policy Stimulus: Market Reforms

Hyperinflation and fiscal deterioration forced the government into drastic policies. Stabilization efforts were thus accompanied with trade liberalization and a reform of the state (including privatization and a tax reform) to provide for sources of revenue alternative to printing money. The effect on workers was mixed. Although stabilization restored their purchasing

---

ability through checks and balances and applied it to Menem. Novaro (1994) and Margharetis (1997) analyze Menem's charismatic and unrestricted leadership, which was reinforced by his packing of the Supreme Court with partisan judges and the extensive use of decrees during his administration (Ferreira Rubio and Goretti 1996).

[19] Acuña (1994) and Jones (1997) point to the Peronist control of the Senate and the Lower Chamber in alliance with UCEDE, and to the party loyalty of Peronist legislators to explain Menem's legislative success.

[20] The CGT-San Martín was named after the site of the union conference where the division emerged and the CGT-Azopardo after the street where it had its headquarters.

power, trade liberalization and privatization increased job losses, and the unemployment grew dramatically to reach 18.6% of the economically active population in May 1995 (Table 6.1). The pension, social security, and labor reforms affected workers' social benefits and work conditions as well as business' labor costs and labor market flexibility. At the same time, these policies impinged the sources of financial and organizational power of labor unions that had emerged from their alliance with Peronism.

Stabilization. Argentina had a long history of high inflation, and Menem was inaugurated amidst a hyperinflationary crisis. In 1989, the annual rate of inflation surpassed 3,000% (Table 6.1). Menem's first three economy ministers attempted to restrain inflation with seven stabilization packages that failed to control the price race and the stampede to the dollar of money holders (Corrales 1998a: 629). The year 1990 started with a second hyperinflation and closed with another run on the dollar that forced Menem to name a new economy minister, Domingo Cavallo, soon afterward. Cavallo sent a bill that was passed by Congress as the Convertibility Law on March 27, 1991 (law 23,928). This law established full convertibility between the newly created peso and the U.S. dollar, with a parity of one to one. It also confirmed the independence of the central bank, and forced it to have reserves in hard currency equal to at least 100% of the monetary base. It cancelled the "indexation" of nominal values (to a preestablished index) for the cancellation of debts and the negotiation of salaries and permitted transactions in any currency (Llach 1997: 124–5, Starr 1997: 87).[21] This currency board halted inflationary expectations by fostering credibility on the stabilization commitment.[22] To further constrain inflation, the government forbade a wage hike unless accompanied by productivity increases (decree 1,334 of 1991).

The effect of these policies on workers was mixed, and so were labor reactions. Price stabilization dramatically improved the purchasing power of wages, and permitted a recovery of union finances (through fees and

---

[21] Previously, the Bonex Plan had compulsorily extended the maturity of domestic debt and converted deposits into bonds (decree 36/90), thus reducing the supply of money and recapitalizing the Central Bank with the necessary foreign reserves to launch the Convertibility Plan.

[22] Palermo (1995) and Starr (1997) argue that the currency board showed the commitment to fiscal self-restraint by placing monetary policy out of the government's hands. Business reacted very favorably, and the country risk of Argentina plummeted from over 70% in December 1989 to less than 15% in August 1991 (Llach 1997: 189).

contributions to union-run welfare funds).[23] However, decree 1,334 curtailed the ability of labor leaders to negotiate wages, and the real wages in the industry did not recover the levels of January 1989 (Figure 6.1).

The proreform CGT-San Martín supported stabilization, and the populist CGT-Azopardo rejected it, although without organizing any general strike. After 1992, a unified CGT adopted the positions of the proreform faction, accepting stabilization and rejecting wage restraint.[24] In 1993, the government conceded free wage bargaining although decentralized at the firm level. Yet, the unions that held monopolies of representation would be workers' representatives even at the firm level, thus reinforcing the authority of national leaders as demanded by the CGT (decree 470/93).[25]

Trade Liberalization. By 1989, protectionism was still very high. The average tariff was 39% – with a maximum of 65% – whereas tariff dispersion and the number of items subject to nontariff restrictions was very large (Agosín and Ffrench-Davis 1995). The Menem administration had originally planned a gradual reform to reach a maximum tariff of 20% within four years. However, in 1990 Menem accelerated trade liberalization, and by the end of the year nontariff restrictions to imports almost ceased to exist whereas the average tariff dropped to only 17%. The following year, the average tariff fell to 10% – ranging from 0% for raw materials to 11% for input goods to 22% for manufactured goods (Gerchunoff and Torre 1996: 741). The automobile and electronic industries, though, received a special tariff of 35%.[26]

---

[23] In personal interviews, CGT Secretary-General José Rodríguez argued that hyperinflation hurt workers the most, whereas commerce workers' union leader Armando Cavalieri said that hyperinflation made union leaders realize the depth of the crisis and become more pragmatic about economic policies (1992).

[24] In 1992, the CGT denounced decree 1,334 for imposing salary restrictions to control inflation and regulating collective bargaining despite the deregulation claims of the government. It also complained that because productivity was hard to measure, it was difficult to implement it effectively (CGT 1992: 3).

[25] Former Labor Minister Rodolfo Díaz argued that the terms of this decree had been discussed with unions. He said that the decree responded to the labor demand to permit a return to wage bargaining and business demand to decentralize collective bargaining (personal communication, 1997). This decree had resulted from secret negotiations among the CGT, employers, and the government (Matsushita 1999: 184) and was also linked to labor support for pension reform (*Clarín*, February 3, 1993).

[26] President Menem also continued the process of regional integration into Mercosur that had been started by President Alfonsín. In 1990, the presidents of Mercosur countries

139

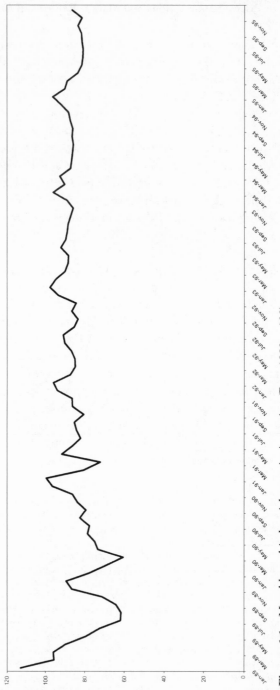

Figure 6.1 Monthly real industrial wage in Argentina (Base 1983 = 100).

Source: Consejo Técnico de Inversiones (1997: 65).

However, the fixed exchange rate and declining inflation provoked an appreciation of the peso that combined with trade liberalization to contribute to current account deficits and increasing unemployment (Table 6.1). By increasing the exposure of workers in tradable sectors, trade liberalization also threatened their work conditions and wage bargaining power while triggering processes of industrial restructuring that enlarged the heterogeneity of work conditions across sectors and firms. These processes could have created conflicts of interests within the CGT. However, political alignments prevailed at the peak level, although at the industry level there was variation in behavior as shown by the case of automobile workers described in the following text. Both the populist CGT-Azopardo and the proreform CGT-San Martín included unions in the tradable and nontradable sectors. Twelve of twenty unions in the leadership of the proreform CGT-San Martín were in the nontradable sector, and the same was true for fourteen of twenty unions in the leadership of the populist CGT-Azopardo.[27] Nonetheless, the CGT-Azopardo rejected trade opening whereas the CGT-San Martín and the independent faction ignored it. After 1992, the unified CGT demanded in a public statement a more gradual opening (CGT 1993) but did not pursue any action to support this goal. Despite the fact that the CTA mostly organized public-sector employees who were not affected by trade liberalization, it harshly criticized the drastic economic opening and its effects on employment (CTA's Secretary-General V. De Gennaro, personal interview, 1995).

Privatization. Although Perón had championed nationalization, the fiscal deficit had brought about the deterioration of publicly provided services to the point that privatization gained popular consensus as a solution to poor performance (Gerchunoff and Cánovas 1996: 192, Palermo and Novaro 1996: 244–5).[28] Menem privatized the property and

---

scheduled a reduction of tariffs until the customs union five years later. Regional integration increased demand for tradable products, and Brazil was the main trade partner of Argentina. The CGT denounced Mercosur to the ILO as an attack against labor rights as late as 1994 (Cassia 1994b).

[27] These figures are based on my own calculation from the report on the executive committees of both CGTs in *Clarín* (October 28, 1989).

[28] Perón nationalized the railroads, telephones, and ports announcing Argentina's economic sovereignty. By 1989, the Argentine state controlled the full production and distribution of gas and electricity; two-thirds of oil production and 80% of its refining; most telecommunications' infrastructure; all ports and railroads; and around half of air and sea

administration of more than a hundred state-owned companies in oil, petrochemicals, coal, gas, water, electricity, telecommunications, transportation, ports, railroads, highways, banks, and hotels (Indec 1996: 504–22). Argentina was second only to Mexico in terms of privatization revenue, earning $18,446 million (U.S. million) between 1990 and 1995 (IADB 1996: 171).

The privatization program challenged the unions and workers in state-owned enterprises and brought job losses and reductions in union ranks as well as industrial restructuring that curtailed many benefits in their generous collective contracts.[29] The populist CGT-Azopardo rejected privatization whereas the proreform CGT-San Martín and subsequently the unified CGT supported it in return for employee-owned stock programs administered by unions and generous packages of voluntary retirement for workers.[30] Moreover, some unions and union-organized cooperatives also participated in the privatization of their sectors and absorbed part of the workers who had lost their jobs in this process (CGT 1995: 35–6, CGT advisor C. Tomada, personal interview, 1993). The exceptions were some of the unions in the populist CGT-Azopardo, in particular the Association of State Employees (ATE) that would become part of the CTA.[31] Other union groups in the populist CGT-Azopardo protested privatization and even organized strikes against it, such as those in the telephone workers'

---

transport. It also controlled an important part of steel, chemical, and military-related production as well as several important financial institutions (Margheritis 1997: 154–64).

[29] Workers and unions in state-owned enterprises had traditionally enjoyed a privileged position. Despite the huge deficits of public companies, they had obtained wage increases above inflation as late as 1988 (Llach 1997: 214). In 1990, the government issued a decree canceling collective contracts in state-owned enterprises to force their renegotiation to unions (personal interview with Labor Minister E. Rodriguez, 1993 and CGT advisor H. Recalde, 1993). Gonda (1995a) shows that 61.6% of the jobs lost between 1991 and 1995 were in the public sector, which had included 18% of the workforce by 1985 (Schenone 1991:19).

[30] The privatization law that established the programs of employee-owned stock did not specify the proportion of shares. The number of shares included in the program was bargained with unions on a case-by-case basis providing an instance in which the government could make differences between loyal and disloyal unions. Although the law did not establish union administration, this was a widespread practice that evolved from the need to create a trust for the stocks until their full payment out of the dividends of companies (personal interviews with labor ministers R. Díaz, 1992, and E. Rodríguez, 1993).

[31] According to ATE's secretary general, the government excluded it from the employee-owned program in the privatization of military factories in Córdoba (De Gennaro, personal interview, 1995). Former Labor Minister E. Rodríguez said that they did not participate for ideological reasons (personal interview, 1995).

union of Capital Federal (see the following text). The CTA denounced privatization as a loss of valuable assets and jobs (De Gennaro, personal interview, 1995).

Reform of the Pension System. Perón had been responsible for the development of the Argentine pension system, which covered 69% of the economically active population in 1980 giving Argentina one of the highest rates of coverage in the region (Madrid 1999: 184–5).[32] However, reductions in employer contributions during the military rule, problems of tax evasion, the growth of the informal sector, and the aging of the population provoked a crisis of the pay-as-you-go system. By 1990, its level of self-financing reached 65.8%, the ratio of contributors to beneficiaries was 1.8 to 1, pension spending was more than a third of total government expenditures, and pensions were a mere 40% of average wages (Madrid 1999: 189). The government introduced a bill to privatize the pension system in June 1992 with the goal of dealing with the crisis and fostering internal savings (Ministry of the Economy 1993: 67). The original government proposal called for a mixed public and private system in which all workers who contributed at least thirty years would be offered a basic universal pension – funded by employer contributions and earmarked taxes. It included a mandatory individual capitalization scheme for all workers under the age of forty-five. Workers above that age would either remain in the public system or choose a private fund (Brooks 1998: 12).

The CGT rejected the proposal because the state did not recognize contributions of those under forty-five and did not organize a public pension fund. Labor unions also demanded the right to participate as administrators of pension funds. To avoid the threat of a general strike, a new government project recognized contributions for those younger than forty-five years and created an additional pension benefit to compensate workers for their past contributions to the pension system. It explicitly included a provision for unions to create pension funds (with a special clause that permitted union employees to work at the same time as brokers of their pension funds) and made the new system optional. The government also created a pension fund run by the publicly owned Banco

---

[32] During Perón's tenure, pension benefits were extended to commercial employees, industrial workers, police and penitentiary personnel, rural workers, the self-employed, and professionals.

de la Nación and included workers, employers, and beneficiaries into the National Committee of Social Security that would oversee the system (E. Rodríguez, personal interview, 1995, Schulthess and Demarco 1994, Isuani and San Martino 1993: 85–121, and Madrid 1999: 221–5). After these concessions, the CGT sent its Congress representatives to vote for the reform (Llanos 1997: 20).[33] In return for these concessions, the unified CGT supported the new bill that became law 24,241 in early 1993. In addition, some CGT unions associated to establish pension funds, others charged fees for advising their members on their choice of pension fund with the possibility of future capitalization of cumulated fees, and some planned to offer life insurance to pension funds.[34] In contrast, the CTA rejected the reform and advised its members to remain in the public system (De Gennaro, personal interview, 1995).

Reform of Social Security Administered by Unions. As secretary of labor, Perón issued decree 30,655 that created the commission of social services and gave a boost to union-provided social security through health or welfare funds (*obras sociales*) in 1944 (Danani 1994: 15).[35] In 1970, welfare funds were universalized as health insurance for salary earners by a law that formally separated their administration from unions but made them compulsory by applying monopolies of representation for affiliation.[36] This law also established lax controls and assigned 10% of total contributions to a compensatory fund that would redistribute subsidies to the neediest funds. By 1995, 216 of 281 welfare funds were union run and they affiliated more than nine million people including family members. Another six union-employer–administered welfare funds covered more than five million beneficiaries including family members (INDEC 1996:

[33] At the last minute, the Menem administration also increased the size of basic pension benefit to obtain the vote of all union legislators (Madrid 1999: 224). In their analyses of the pension reform, Alonso (1998), Brooks (1998), and Madrid (1999) stress that, in contrast to pensioner organizations and opposition political parties, the CGT was the only group effective in changing the government proposal to introduce its demands.

[34] By February 28, 1995, the three largest union-run pension funds were Claridad (215,163 members), Futura (34,152 members), and San José (22,420 members). The largest pension fund, Consolidar, had half a million affiliates (DGI 1995).

[35] Unions administered health and other social services, such as recreation, tourism, complementary pensions, and training. Payroll deductions for union fees and welfare funds contributions (depending on particular laws or collective contracts) fostered the administrative capacity of unions and increased their ranks.

[36] Employers contribute 6% of the salary and employees contribute 3% and 1.5% extra for each family member (law 23,360, art. 16 and 18).

316). Welfare funds provided unions with funding, selective incentives for members, and sanction power over sections while closing this market to private health insurance.

In 1989, the government granted the administration of the compensatory fund to the proreform CGT-San Martín, thus biasing the costs of the financial adjustment in favor of the loyal CGT faction. Two years later decree 2,284 deprived unions of the control of fees by centralizing their collection into the national tax agency. In 1992, the government proposed to let wage earners choose among welfare funds and private sector providers while establishing a universal contribution (Danani 1994: 23). The CGT unified with the explicit aim of rejecting this reform. After the unified CGT organized the only general strike of the period on November 11, 1992, the government compromised by excluding private providers and restricting competition to the existing welfare funds during an undefined transitional period (decrees 9 and 576 of 1993).[37] Because the government also reduced employers' contribution to welfare funds to promote employment (decree 2,609/93), the CGT obtained subsidies and a special schedule for unions paying tax debts (decree 1,829/94). However, the implementation of this reform kept being postponed. In 1995, unions obtained loans for restructuring their welfare funds and the definition of a minimum medical coverage (Fernández 1997: 111–12, welfare fund administrator F. Simonotti, personal interview, 1995).[38]

Labor Flexibility. The Argentine labor market was very rigid. Several laws – originally passed by Perón between 1946 and 1955 – regulated individual and collective work conditions and labor organization by establishing compulsory collective bargaining at the industry/activity level and the indefinite duration of collective and individual contracts (laws 14,250 and 20,744). Although the Menem administration drafted twenty bills to reform work conditions and increase labor market flexibility, only a few of

---

[37] The government also accepted CGT's demand that welfare funds add only a number of people equal to 20% of their enrollment per year (*Ambito Financiero*, April 2, 1993).

[38] These concessions accompanied a smaller reduction in the employer contributions than originally planned although they extended to further activities at the beginning of the second Menem administration (decree 922/95). However, the implementation of competition among welfare funds would continue to be postponed until 1997 when a complex process of choice restricted to a specific time of the year was established (Anses 1997). Even then, Menem did not include private providers. At the end of his second administration, he decreed the return of the collection of funds to an institution controlled by labor unions.

them became law due to union rejection.[39] In 1991, Congress passed the Employment Law (24,013) after two years of changes in the original bill. This law introduced limited external flexibility through temporary hiring contracts for a percentage of workers and derogated article forty-eight of the Law of Economic Emergency that had increased severance payments. To gain the acceptance of the proreform CGT, the law established unemployment insurance and required union agreement for the implementation of the new temporary contracts. The law did not satisfy business. The legal advisor of the Industrial Union of Argentina (UIA) argued that it was useless for job creation (Funes de Rioja, personal interview, 1995). Even a high official in the labor ministry compared the law to trying to accelerate and brake simultaneously (cited in Etchemendi and Palermo 1998: 569). Congress also passed law 24,028 on work safety that put limits on workers' compensation for accidents that year.

Labor Minister Enrique Rodríguez proposed a new labor code in 1993 that would decentralize collective bargaining and increase internal and external flexibility.[40] Despite business' pressures for labor deregulation, the bill never became a law. In 1994, the government signed an agreement with the CGT and the employers' associations to obtain support for the laws on work conditions in small and medium firms, work accidents, and the suspension of collective-bargaining contracts under bankruptcy (Ministry of Labor 1994a). These laws were very moderate and did not fulfill either business or government expectations in terms of labor market flexibility.[41]

---

[39] Congress passed only eight of the twenty bills on labor flexibility sent by the administration in contrast to ten out of eleven bills on privatization (Etchemendi and Palermo 1998).

[40] Internal flexibility refers to the organization of work within the firm whereas external flexibility refers to hiring and firing. The bill included changes in work time, hiring, multifunctional tasks, and annual work schedule as well as a finite duration for contracts (Ministry of Labor 1993).

[41] Echemendi and Palermo (1998) describe the bargaining process for the agreement. Funes de Rioja (1994), Pessino (1997), and Cox Edwards (1997) classified the reform as extremely mild. The laws on work accidents included a compulsory insurance that was criticized by the UIA but supported by unions, small companies, and the insurance lobby (Funes de Rioja, personal interview, 1995). In a personal interview (1995), CGT Secretary-General Antonio Cassia explained his signing of the agreement as "a strategy of negotiation, as the only way to have our concerns listened to. Otherwise, the reforms would have ignored union demands. For instance, the first proposed statute for small and medium sized firms did not include union participation while the final project established the need for agreement through collective bargaining with the union holding the monopoly of representation."

Although neither of the two CGTs wanted labor flexibility, the pro-reform CGT-San Martín negotiated the employment law and obtained the inclusion of provisions on collective-bargaining authorization for temporary contracts and law 24,070 that bailed out union debts (Etchemendi and Palermo 1998: 566–7, Catalano and Novick 1994: 11). The unified CGT rejected the broad reform of the labor code proposed by Minister Rodríguez.[42] The July 1994 agreement established the introduction of the bills mentioned previously together with other bills to provide workers' right to firm information and the extension of employee-owned stock systems to the private sector. It also created a union-business committee to draft a labor flexibility bill (CGT 1994a, Labor Minister A. Caro Figueroa, personal interview, 1994).

Although none of these bills was passed, the government allowed welfare funds to establish insurance firms for work accidents (created by the new law). It also provided institutions for union surveillance in the new regime for small and medium firms and withdrew a bill that reduced severance payments. During the second Menem administration, a new labor reform reinforced the bargaining power of national-level unions and cancelled some of the flexible clauses approved in 1991 and 1994.[43]

The CTA and later the MTA rejected any legal attempt at labor deregulation (Ramírez 1993, CTA 1994, MTA legal advisor H. Recalde, personal interview, 1995). In fact, they demanded the cancellation of the employment law, the establishment of regulations to increase job protection and work safety, the prevalence of work conditions more favorable to workers, a reduction of the work week, and the extension of vacations (CTA n.d., Recalde 1994). The government ignored CTA's proposals.

Reform of Labor Organization Regulation. The regulations on labor organization were at the core of the alliance between union leaders and Perón in the 1940s. They subsidized labor organization and guaranteed monopolies of representation per industry/activity to recognized unions

---

[42] The CGT rejected the proposal and claimed that it reduced the pay of extra time, deteriorated work and hiring conditions, abolished the special conditions for certain trades, reduced severance payments, and menaced the role of nationwide collective bargaining (CGT n.d.).

[43] This reform of 1998 was modified again by a new law proposed by Menem's successor in the presidency, Fernando De le Rua, from the UCR. This last reform reintroduced the flexible provision and the right of unions at any level for collective bargaining.

unless another union had at least 10% more members for a period of six months (Law 23,551, art. 28; decree 467/88, art. 21). These monopolies covered collective-bargaining prerogatives, administration of automatic check-off dues, and tax exceptions on union-related activities, thus reducing union competition. These resources and the regulations on union elections gave an advantage to incumbent union leaders. In 1991, the Menem administration drafted a bill to abolish monopolies of representation and ease competition for union leadership positions (Ministry of Labor 1991).[44] Both CGTs rejected the proposal. The administration drafted a new bill that reduced the threat of leadership competition and maintained monopolies of representation – although a union could claim for a monopoly of representation with a simple majority of union members instead of having to have 10% more members than the current holder. This bill also permitted the decentralization of collective bargaining (Executive Power 1992).

Supporters of reforming the regulations on labor organizing made strange bedfellows. On the one hand, employers wanted freedom of association to increase union competition and supported the decentralization of collective bargaining to lower levels (Funes de Rioja 1992/93).[45] On the other hand, the CTA demanded changes in the conditions for leadership competition within the unions plus some decentralization of collective bargaining that would reduce the resources of incumbent union leaders to control dissidents at the local level.[46] The unified CGT, instead, rejected changes to monopolies of representation (affecting union competition) against the employer demands and to rules on union elections (influencing leadership competition) against CTA demands. It also rejected the decentralization of collective bargaining if it were to replace national unions holding monopolies of representation with local unions or shop stewards as workers' representatives. The government halted the reform as demanded by the CGT.

---

[44] The proposal forbade the incumbent leadership to select the electoral commission to ease the legalization of challenging slates.

[45] Decree 470/93 only facilitated collective bargaining at the company level but required unions holding the monopoly of representation to sign the contracts, thus reducing the real impact of decentralization.

[46] CTA Secretary General V. De Gennaro and CTA advisor H. Maguira denounced the current law for restricting competition for union leadership and denying formal recognition to the CTA (personal interviews, 1995). The first conference of CTA lawyers concluded by calling for the decentralization of collective bargaining, the end of monopolies of representation, and the democratization of union elections (CTA 1997).

Summary

The CGT accepted stabilization, trade liberalization, and privatization after its unification following the positions of the proreform faction but rejected restrictions on wage bargaining. Although it obtained some relaxation of wage restraint, it failed to achieve more gradualism in trade liberalization. The CGT supported privatization in return for compensation for workers and worker and union ownership in privatized companies. The urgency of these reforms for fiscal stability and the fact that they were not a priority in the CGT agenda like social and labor reforms reinforces the importance of these concessions. After its unification, the CGT obtained concessions on the implementation of the pension reform, the design of the social security reform, and important limitations to labor flexibility and the absence of reform on labor organization regulations.

Peronist Identity and Union Cooperation

The interaction between the CGT and Menem provides the last national-level case study for the theory presented in Chapter 2. The theory states that partisan loyalty promotes labor collaboration with allied administrations unless leadership competition creates a replacement threat for allied union leaders that increases their militancy. The effect of labor militancy or restraint, however, depends on whether the union is competing with others for the representation of workers because union competition makes coordination more difficult and weakens every union. In Argentina, despite the impact of Menem's reforms on unions and their constituencies, partisan loyalty explains why he did not suffer nearly as much labor unrest as did his predecessor. Peronist union leaders reduced their militancy and organized only one general strike during this administration, although the CGT had called thirteen general strikes against Alfonsín's policies. General militancy also dropped in relation to the Alfonsín administration (Figure 6.2).[47] The average number of monthly strikes dropped from

---

[47] The source for the strike data is the monthly *Tendencias Económicas y Financieras* published by the Consejo Técnico de Inversiones. I used a data set provided by James McGuire for the total number of strikes until 1993, completed the series until 1995, and used the same publication for the entries of the five individual sectors I studied. Although the monthly collection multiplies the number of strikes when they extend to the following month, McGuire (1996a) justifies the use of this source, shows the high correlation of its measures with less complete ones, and describes the data collection methods.

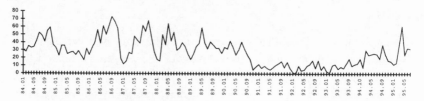

Figure 6.2 Monthly strikes 1984–95.
Sources: McGuire (1996b) and *Tendencias Económicas*.

thirty-eight under Alfonsín (January 1984–June 1989) to eighteen during the first administration of Menem (July 1989–June 1995).[48] In contrast to Venezuela, partisan competition within individual unions dropped since 1990, further reducing incentives for militancy. Between the second semester of 1986 and the second semester of 1990 when militancy was higher (Figure 6.1), the mean of Peronist union victories was 42%. In contrast, between the first semester of 1992 and the last semester of 1994, when militancy declined, the mean of Peronist union victories was 87% (Centro de Estudios para la Nueva Mayoría 1996).[49]

The policy shift of Peronism, though, provoked a division in the CGT between October 1989 and March 1992, thus weakening its bargaining power. The proreform CGT-San Martín supported Menem's policies and the populist CGT-Azopardo rejected market reforms whereas other unions remained independent. Neither of the two CGT factions organized general strikes, but the populist CGT-Azopardo organized a demonstration against market-oriented reforms, and its individual unions were more militant than those in the proreform faction.[50] The government manipulated the competition among factions by shrinking state resources to punish the populist faction and reward the loyal one, thus inducing defection of individual unions from the CGT-Azopardo. As a result, various unions that wanted to avoid the loss of scarce resources abandoned the

[48] Although the most dramatic drop in strikes under Menem coincided with his regulation of strikes in public services by decree 2,448 in October 1990, the monthly peak of strike activity under Menem was surpassed by the number of monthly strikes during more than 40% of Alfonsín's administration.

[49] Peronist union victories dropped in the first semester of 1995 coinciding with an increase in militancy and partisan competition inside the CGT after the MTA informally supported Octavio Bordón, a Peronist dissident, as FREPASO presidential candidate.

[50] Although the populist faction retained 38% of CGT members, its unions accounted for 62% of strikes during the division period (author's calculations).

populist CGT.[51] Subsequently, the leadership of the populist CGT-Azopardo reduced its demands and approached the positions of the pro-reform CGT-San Martín at the end of 1991. Peronist unions were aware that their division permitted the government to manipulate union competition within the same monopolistic party. Union competition cost them control of the contributions to welfare funds, decrees restraining wage bargaining and strike activity in the public services, and the employment law.

The event that triggered unification was the government's attempt to deregulate welfare funds at the beginning of 1992. Aiming to solve co-ordination problems and recover bargaining power, they unified into a single CGT in March 1992.[52] By reducing union and leadership competition with its unification, the CGT-government interaction shifted from subordination (ineffective restraint) to cooperation (effective restraint).

The unified CGT retained its partisan loyalty and organized the only general strike of the first Menem administration against the deregulation of welfare funds in November 1992. However, the CGT had been more militant when calling thirteen general strikes against Alfonsín's policies and had already called a general strike during a Peronist administration in 1974. This general strike was a signal of the value of its restraint, which continued during the rest of this administration. In return for the CGT collaboration, the government provided concessions that included a relaxation of wage bargaining, compensation for workers in privatized firms, subsidies for union ownership, and union participation in the pension reform. In welfare fund deregulation, the CGT obtained the exclusion of private health insurance, subsidies for restructuring welfare funds, and delays in its implementation, as well as a bailing out of union debts. Finally, Peronist unions also halted the reform of regulations on labor organization and collective bargaining and limited modifications of individual labor relations to mild reforms that mostly required union approval. The

---

[51] For instance, in 1990, the important unions of metalworkers, state oil workers, water provision workers, gas provision workers, and postal workers, among others, abandoned the CGT-Azopardo. Food workers and other private sector unions followed them the following year.

[52] The new CGT leadership excluded the unions in the populist faction. It included representatives of five large unions: the railroad workers, the automobile workers, the light and power workers, the construction workers, and the postal workers. Three of these unions had been in the proreform CGT-San Martín, one had been an independent union, and one had abandoned the populist CGT-Azopardo in 1990.

unification of the CGT curtailed union competition and thereby increased labor capacity to obtain concessions. Partisan loyalty continued to restrain CGT militancy because partisan competition was very limited.

Two of the more militant unions in the populist CGT-Azopardo – ATE (state employees) and CTERA (teachers) – and smaller unions and some dissident groups in local unions organized the CTA. ATE and CTERA competed for membership with other Peronist unions in their sectors. Their leaders broke with Peronism and participated in the foundation of FREPASO. Because they were in sectors that experienced both union competition and partisan competition, these unions were more militant and less successful in obtaining concessions than the Peronist unions. Indeed, the incentives for militancy created by partisan opposition and their location in the public sector resulted in education and public admin- istration being the sectors that experienced the highest number of strikes in the period between 1991 and 1995 (Gonda 1995b, McGuire 1996a). Despite their militancy, the leaders of CTERA and ATE claimed that the government refused to bargain with them and ignored their demands (personal interviews with CTERA's M. Maffei and ATE's V. De Gennaro, 1995). The break of partisan loyalties provoked by market reforms explains the more militant position of the CTA and the unwillingness of the gov- ernment to give in. In 1994, truckers' and bus drivers' unions organized the MTA as an internal faction in the CGT. Although they collaborated with the CTA in the organization of a national strike and a major demon- stration in 1994, they joined the CGT ranks when they were granted influence in the selection of its new leadership after the 1995 reelection of Menem.

Sector-level Analysis: Introducing Variation within the Same Country

As in Venezuela and Mexico, the five individual sectors analyzed in Argentina show patterns of union-government interaction different from those of the CGT that cannot be explained by national-level variables. Both interest-based theories and my own theory can explain variation in union behavior within the same country. As in the previous two chapters, this section describes the union-government interactions in oil, auto- mobile, telecommunications, electricity, and education to compare the explanatory power of alternative theories. Oil and automobile were trad- able sectors affected by increasing international exposure (and by privatization in the case of the former).[53] The latter three were services. Whereas telecommunications and electricity were privatized, the education sector was decentralized from the national to the provincial jurisdiction.

Oil. Created in 1922, the state-owned oil company Fiscal Oil Reserves (YPF) carried out 98% of oil production (62.5% under its own management and 35.5% through contracts with private enterprises) and controlled prices and export authorizations (Margarethis 1997: 250). In 1989, the government opened exploration to foreign capital. To increase its ability to compete internationally before privatization, YPF went through a dramatic restructuring. By 1989, YPF had 37,367 employees who enjoyed job stability and numerous indirect benefits, whereas the union had management and hiring prerogatives. In 1990, the government suspended the old collective-bargaining contract (decree 1,757). The new contract included internal flexibility, and reduced work categories and indirect benefits. It also increased working time, curtailed union prerogatives, and excluded managerial employees from collective bargaining. YPF downsized its staff to 1,906 personnel covered by collective bargaining and 3,784 under individual contracts, and nonskilled workers dropped from 56% to 22% (YPF n.d.). YPF also excluded the union from its health fund.[54] Despite its affiliation with the populist CGT until 1990, the SUPE reacted by reducing its militancy after 1990 and accepted the changes (Figure 6.3).

Privatization followed this process. In September 1992, the Congress approved YPF's privatization. By July 1993, YPF had sold more than $2.1 billion in nonessential assets and made a stock offering on the New York Stock Exchange, which raised $3 billion (U.S. billion) (Albarracín 1995, Ministry of the Economy 1993). Privatization threatened the existence of the YPF union, which organized state oil workers (there was another union that affiliated private oil workers). The Ministry of Labor had originally defined these as different "activities" when granting their

---

[53] By 1991, oil accounted for 6.4% of exports and 5.5% of imports, whereas automobiles accounted for 2.7% of exports and 2.5% of imports (Ministry of the Economy 1993: 43, INDEC 1994: 495, 502).

[54] Collective Bargaining Contract (CCT) No. 16 of 1975, and Collective Bargaining Contract (CCT) No. 144 of 1995 between YPF and SUPE, and personal interview with YPF's Labor Relations Manager Roberto Teglia and Chief Economist Federico Sturzenegger, 1995.

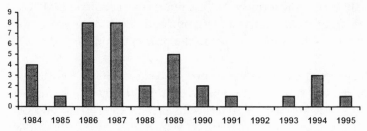

Figure 6.3   SUPE's strikes, 1984–95.

Source: *Tendencias Económicas.*

official recognition, and although the monopoly of representation avoided union competition before privatization, it may have been threatened by it. Despite its previous rejection to the opening of exploration to foreign capitals under Alfonsín, SUPE restrained its militancy to facilitate privatization in 1993 (SUPE's Secretary General A. Cassia, personal interview, 1993).

That union leaders did not confront union or leadership competition and held a monopoly of representation facilitated restraint. In spite of the decentralized constitution of SUPE, Peronist leaders had controlled the union since the eighties.[55] Induced by the Peronist identity of the unions, strikes peaked during the Alfonsín administration (Figure 6.3) in support for wage demands and in protest over the opening of exploration to foreign investment. Although the union had openly rejected privatization as late as 1989, partisan loyalty changed the attitude of the union under the Peronist administration causing it to reduce its militancy in the 1990s (Figure 6.3) in return for concessions (cooperation).

The Peronist government compensated SUPE for its restraint during restructuring and privatization. Job rationalization adopted the form of voluntary retirements with generous benefits and retraining courses. The union organized cooperatives of former workers and obtained subsidies to buy the YPF fleet and a YPF-derived firm of oil equipment. SUPE organized approximately 250 cooperatives and firms, which gathered approximately 8,000 laid-off workers. The union also obtained YPF contracts for the provision of services by these new enterprises for starting up. In addition, the government extended the union monopoly of representation to

---

[55] They won union elections with percentages that surpassed 60% until 1992 when the union election went uncontested (Centro de Estudios Unión para la Nueva Mayoría 1996).

YPF and all the companies emerging from its privatization. Government subsidies also permitted the organization of SUPE's welfare fund to serve the workers of the newly created firms and the pensioners who had been excluded from the health system of YPF.[56] In sum, partisan loyalty reduced SUPE's incentives for militancy when Peronism came to power. Because leadership competition did not grow as a result of this behavior, loyal union leaders maintained the restraint of the union. In return, the union obtained compensations for workers, union and worker ownership of privatized firms in the sector, and subsidies from the state for its welfare fund because their partisan allies did not want other union leaders to take control of the union. The lack of union competition or leadership competition thus brought about cooperation (effective restraint) as the union-government interaction during restructuring and privatization.

Automobiles. In 1959, decree 3,963 restricted imports and imposed limits on the import content of domestically produced cars, thus protecting an industry of high profit and low efficiency that created well-paid jobs. Collective bargaining was decentralized to the firm level although a nationwide union represented workers. Regional integration with Brazil provoked some mild industrial restructuring under Alfonsín. Yet, hyperinflation, the end of credit, economic recession, and trade liberalization provoked a big shock in 1989 and 1990. Sales plummeted, and so did production and employment (Catalano and Novick 1998).[57]

SMATA represented workers in car manufacturing firms and firms supplying parts, selling, and repairing units.[58] Although collective bargaining was decentralized to the level of automobile companies, SMATA was a

---

[56] This information derives from personal interviews with SUPE's Secretary-General A. Cassia (1993 and 1995), YPF's Labor Relations' Manager R. Teglia (1995), SUPE's Health Fund President A. Betancour (1995), Labor Minister E. Rodríguez (1995), SUPE (1992: 40–2, 1993a, 1993b, and 1994: 173), Cassia (1994a), *Clarín* (July 8, 1993), YPF (n.d.), *Página 12-CASH* (August 5, 1994), *La Nación* (August 2, 1993), and *Ambito Financiero* (October 4, 1990).

[57] According to Adefa (1993: 6), the number of employed personnel fell from 21,313 in 1988 to 19,281 in 1989 and 17,430 in 1990.

[58] SMATA was created along with the definition of the mechanical activity. However, the Union of Metal Workers (UOM) disputed this characterization and obtained the monopoly of representation for two plants working during the period studied. Because union competition is drastically reduced by monopolies of representation, it takes place only when new plants are opened. During the period studied, General Motors opened a new plant and played one union against the other to obtain an exceptionally flexible contract signed by SMATA before the establishment of the plant.

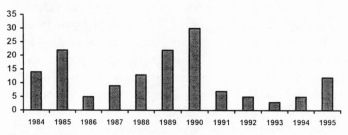

Figure 6.4 Automobile strikes, 1984–95.
Source: *Tendencias Económicas.*

centralized union and its sections had little autonomy. Hence, Peronist national leaders played a key role in bargaining even at the company level.[59] The union experienced leadership competition in 1984 when the winner obtained a close victory by 6% of votes, contested by the loser in the Ministry of Labor (SMATA 1985). Subsequent union elections were uncontested showing the decline in leadership competition (Centro de Estudios Unión para la Nueva Mayoría 1996). Despite partisan loyalty, its affiliation with the proreform CGT-San Martín, and of the futility of fighting job redundancies, labor militancy grew during the recession of 1989 and 1990 (Figure 6.4).

In 1991, Menem established a special trade regime for the automobile sector, which was agreed upon with business and labor, and the liberalization of this industry. The government kept tariffs at 35% while raising the import component of vehicles, reducing tariffs for imported components, restricting the import of models not produced in Argentina, and curtailing taxes on automobile consumption. In return, dealers reduced their commissions, component makers reduced their prices, labor restrained its militancy, and automobile producers maintained prices and employment and had to achieve export targets. Aided by this policy and economic recovery and credit expansion, automobile production increased from 99,639 units in 1990 to 138,958 in 1991 and kept growing to reach 408,777 in 1994 (Catalano and Novick 1998: 43). Employment grew from 18,317 to 23,027 between 1991 and 1993 (Adefa 1993: 6).

---

[59] SMATA is not a federation but a national union, and its constitution granted the national leadership the power to sanction and put its sections into receivership for a large and vague array of reasons (SMATA 1989, art. 79).

In spite of the growth in employment, collective bargaining introduced many forms of internal flexibility and reduced workers' indirect benefits. Real wages did not keep up, although productivity doubled between 1991 and 1993.[60] Facing these challenges, the union reacted by reducing its militancy after the 1991 boom (Figure 6.4), following the logic of partisan loyalty in the absence of leadership competition. In return, management fulfilled its promise to rehire laid-off workers and expand employment benefiting the union from the expansion in its ranks. The government also provided loans for the modernization of SMATA's welfare fund and renewed the automobile regime in 1994. SMATA, in turn, used government subsidies to develop new strategies of social service provision. For instance, it associated with other unions to create a pension fund and reorganized its welfare fund to merge with other unions.[61] The combination of leadership monopoly and union monopoly in this Peronist union led to cooperation (effective restraint) except under the dire economic circumstances of 1989 and 1990 when the union-government interaction was opposition (effective militancy). This militancy in the initial period contradicts the predictions of my theory and the industrial-relations literature. It also contradicts Golden's (1997) view of strikes against job losses that are triggered by the targeting of union activists during redundancies because labor regulations prevented firing shop stewards. The militancy is explained, instead, by the survival of an economic coalition similar to those existing under import substitution industrialization that obtained trade protection despite market reforms.[62]

Telecommunications. The law of state emergency (23,696/89) allowed the privatization of the state-owned telephone company, National

---

[60] Catalano and Novick (1998) analyze the 1991 automotive regime, the evolution of productivity and wages, and the collective contracts. SMATA reports that the average wage increase for automakers was 19.6% for 1991–2 (SMATA 1992: 10), and 19.9% for 1992–3 (SMATA 1993: 8). SMATA's secretary of collective bargaining, Manuel Pardo, explained union demands and the compromise reached under the 1991 regime but complained that wages did not keep up with productivity growth (personal interview, 1995).

[61] Cf. personal interviews with SMATA's Raitano and Pardo (1995), Anses (1997), and Catalano and Novick (1998).

[62] Catalano and Novick (1998) argued that the union followed a strategy of alliance with the employers aimed at influencing policies for the industry. They argue that "in the midst of the deep crisis that affected this economic sector, SMATA pressed the national government to promote and coordinate a collaborative effort on the part of all the sector's representatives. This gave rise to the Automotive Reactivation Agreement, signed on 25 March 1991 . . ." (p. 53).

Company of Telecommunications (ENTEL).[63] ENTEL was split into two companies with seven-year exclusive licenses to provide basic telecommunications services in their different areas of coverage. The first 60% of the shares in these companies were sold by competitive international bidding with management rights. Twenty-five percent of the remaining shares were sold in public auction, 10% were sold to ENTEL employees, and 5% to cooperatives (decrees 59 to 62/1990). Private consortia led by Telefónica of Spain and STET-France Telecom paid $214 million (U.S. million) in cash and $5 billion (U.S. billion) in debt bonds at their nominal value for the 60% share whereas the government took over ENTEL's pending debts (Ministry of the Economy 1993: 48).

Privatization had a large effect on the stability and work conditions of ENTEL's 47,000 employees. ENTEL downsized its staff by 6,000 employees before privatization and an additional 16,000 employees followed suit in the first year after privatization. Approximately half of the job losses were covered with new hiring, and labor productivity increased dramatically after the two companies extended telephone lines, introduced digitalization, new technologies, and training programs. As in YPF, the new collective-bargaining contract curtailed union management prerogatives and union shop arrangements for hiring, while decreasing indirect benefits for workers, abolishing seniority, reducing the number of work categories, and increasing the work week by five hours.[64]

FOETRA had no union competition, and its leaders were Peronist. However, as a decentralized federation it provided more opportunities for leadership competition within its sections, and its elections were generally

---

[63] On September 3, 1946, Perón had nationalized the Telephonic Union (UT), arguing that "telephone and telegraph services are essential for the economy and the defense of the country" (Petrazzini 1996: 111). Although the company involved public-private ownership, Perón made it entirely public in March 1948 and kept buying privately owned telecommunications companies in the interior of the country. By the early 1970s, ENTEL controlled 92% of the market. This privatization was used to signal Menem's commitment to market reforms and reduce the fiscal crisis, thereby prioritizing speed to the point of leaving the regulatory framework undefined until the time of the bidding (decree 1,185/90) according to Gerchunoff and Torre (1996) and former Minister of Public Works R. Dromi (personal interview, 1998). Hill and Abdala (1996), Petrazzini (1996), and Molano (1997) analyze the privatization of ENTEL.

[64] This information comes from a comparison of collective-bargaining contracts of 1975 and 1992 (CCT 165/75 and FOETRA 1992a), a report of the Ministry of Labor on the innovations of the 1992 contract (MTSS, n.d.), personal interviews with labor relations' managers R. Giordanengo of Telefónica and J. Giar of Telecom, and union leader Salazar (1995), and Walter and Senén González (1998: 50–55).

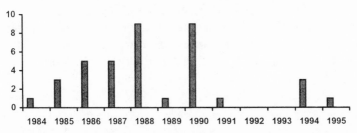

Figure 6.5 FOETRA's strikes 1984–95.

Source: *Tendencias Económicas.*

competitive (FOETRA 1989). FOETRA had been militant under Alfonsín and denounced his privatization efforts until late 1988, when the national leadership accepted that foreign investment was necessary to overcome the bankruptcy of the company. In 1989, Menem appointed union leader Julio Guillán as undersecretary of communications. Guillán's support for privatization fed the growth of an antiprivatization populist faction led by Héctor Esquivel, who challenged his leadership in the union of Capital Federal. Although Guillán moderated his support by proposing only partial privatization, Esquivel won the election in November 1989 with 54% of votes to Guillán's 32%.[65] This was the largest union of the federation, and the populist victory signaled the growth of leadership competition for the proreform Peronist national leaders. Despite their affiliation with the proreform CGT-San Martín, the fear of replacement made them more militant in 1990 (Figure 6.5).[66] Yet, whereas the union of Capital Federal called strikes, demonstrations, and boycotts to explicitly reject privatization, the demands of the national leadership were not political but work related.

Because the government did not want loyal leaders in a monopolistic union to be replaced, the government granted concessions to the national leadership of FOETRA but remained inflexible with the union in Capital

---

[65] Esquivel campaigned against privatization and for the defense of "a state-owned, monopolistic, and efficient" telephone company. Guillán argued that foreign investment was necessary to overcome the crisis of the sector although it did not imply full privatization (*Nuevo Sur*, November 11, 1989).

[66] Esquivel participated in the populist CGT-Azopardo, and later in the CTA. He was supported by dissident Peronists and an array of center-left parties, but he failed to gain enough support to split the union of Capital Federal from the federation to affiliate it to the CTA in 1992.

Federal. [67] That is, in the context of increasing leadership competition and no union competition, the government wanted labor restraint to facilitate the success of the privatization and preferred to avoid the growth of the populist faction. Concessions included the distribution of 10% of capital to employees through a shared-ownership program, a wage increase of 42%, the promise of no firings, and handsome early and voluntary retirements for all job redundancies. Union leaders were put in charge of the trust fund for employee-owned stocks, and the union gained complete control of the welfare fund (previously shared with the company). These concessions help to reduce leadership competition to the point that Guillán won the 1993 union elections for the union in Capital Federal. After leadership competition dropped, militancy also went down (Figure 6.5), but the monopolistic union continued to receive concessions from the private management. It obtained contracts for provision of services to Telecom by union-organized cooperatives of former workers, contributions to the union and the welfare fund from nonunionized workers, and participation in the training program of Telecom.[68] It also received subsidies for the modernization of its welfare fund.[69] In short, the combination of leadership competition and union monopoly brought about opposition (effective militancy) as the union-government interaction during the privatization. However, after the decline of leadership competition, militancy declined and the interaction shifted to cooperation (effective restraint).

Electricity. By 1989, three large state-owned enterprises – Electricity Services of the Great Buenos Aires (SEGBA) for Buenos Aires and its suburbs, Hidronor for the Northern Patagonia rivers, and Agua y Energía for the rest of the country – concentrated most of the electricity industry

[67] The union of the Capital Federal lost a one-month antiprivatization strike, which ended with more than three hundred dismissals after the government declared it illegal. McGuire (1996a) argues that this loss discouraged further strike activity in the country. However, FOETRA called four national strikes in 1990 and two in 1991 and obtained both the rehiring of those dismissed in Capital Federal and wage hikes.

[68] Personal interviews with FOETRA annual reports from 1990 to 1994, FOETRA (1992), and Giar and Giordanengo (1995).

[69] Moreover, the Telephone Workers' Welfare Fund (OSTEL) associated with the health funds of the unions in water provision, shoe production, plastic production, and garage attendance to increase both its clientele and efficiency. By 1995, it was also attempting to organize an insurance fund for job accidents (personal interviews with Salazar and Simonotti, 1995).

from generation to distribution.[70] The distortion in electricity prices created by taxes and subsidies across provinces, and the politicization of management resulted in financial deficits and a deterioration of services (Bastos and Abdala 1995: 75–95).[71] In 1991, the secretary of energy announced the privatization of electricity after dividing the existing companies into several units and defining a regulatory framework, which was passed by Congress a year later as law 24,065. This law divided existing monopolies into power generation, transmission, and distribution companies, thus creating limits for the ownership or control of companies in the different segments. It also allowed the privatization of eighteen distribution companies, six transmission companies, and twenty-eight power generation companies (ENRE 1998: 16–24).[72]

As in the previous two cases, privatization affected job stability and work conditions. The division and privatization of the state-owned enterprises decentralized collective bargaining. New collective contracts introduced internal flexibility; reduced workers' indirect benefits; extended vacations; and curtailed special funds for training, housing, and tourism as well as union shop privileges.[73] Despite its partisan loyalty, FATLyF increased its militancy during the years of privatization (1992–4) (Figure 6.6).

---

[70] Perón created the predecessor of Agua y Energía in 1947 to produce, buy, and sell energy. SEGBA emerged from the nationalization of two private companies in 1958 (Argentine Company of Electricity – CADE) and in 1979 (Italian-Argentine Company of Electricity – CIAE). Hidronor was born as a public corporation in 1967 (Bastos and Abdala 1995: 7–13). Some provinces, such as Buenos Aires and Córdoba, also had their own distribution companies.

[71] In 1989, the treasury subsidized Agua y Energía by $9.1 million, SEGBA by $127 million, and Hidronor by $78 million (all U.S. million) (Bastos and Abdala 1995: 94).

[72] The law created a regulatory agency and a Wholesale Electricity Market (MEM). Power-generating companies compete among themselves to sell to a power pool. Company for the Administration of the Wholesale Electricity Market (CAMMESA) – a nonprofit company, whose shares were equally divided among the national government, generating companies, transmission companies, distributors, and large users – supervised the power poll and regulated the spot price based on marginal costs and seasonal demand (decree 1,192/92).

[73] See the reports of the Ministry of Labor on the collective bargaining contracts of FATLyF with Edenor, Edesur, and Edelap (Expte. # 939,030/93) and Collective Bargaining Contract (CCT 225 of 1993), with Central Térmica San Nicolás S.A. (Expte. # 952,524/93 and CCT 36 of 1975), with Central Puerto S.A. (Expte. # 934,393/92 and CCT 88 of 1993), with Central Pedro de Mendoza S.A. (Expte. # 948,830/93 and 949,542/93 and CCT 78 of 1975), and with Central Térmica Guemes S.A. (Expte. # 945,639/93 and CCT 97 of 1994) and personal interview with union leader J. Taccone and Under-Secretary of Energy A. Mirkin (1995).

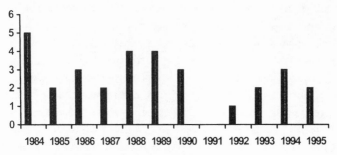

Figure 6.6 FATLyF strikes, 1984–95.

Source: *Tendencias Económicas.*

FATLyF held a monopoly of representation over the sector, and the Peronists controlled its national leadership. Because it was a decentralized union, there were more opportunities for leadership competition in the sections, and populist leaders controlled the unions in Mar del Plata and Córdoba (FATLyF 1988). During the Alfonsín administration, FATLyF was not only more militant but had also rejected privatization, although its secretary-general, Carlos Alderete, briefly served as labor minister in 1987. However, by the end of 1990, FATLyF – which had remained independent during the division of the CGT – has come to accept privatization and reduced its militancy (C. Alderete, personal interview, 1993).[74] As in ENTEL, this support for privatization fed the expansion of populist faction that rejected privatization within the federation. In the national conference of December 1991, the Mar del Plata union of the federation denounced the national leadership as sold out. The following year, this local union joined the CTA, thus breaking ties with the Peronist CGT. The growth in leadership competition for the loyal Peronist leaders of the national federation increased their incentives for militancy to show more responsiveness to the rank-and-file (Figure 6.6). Besides the increase in the number of strikes in 1993 and 1994, the loyal union in the Capital Federal and the national federation organized protest demonstrations in 1994.

To achieve restraint and avoid the growth of union leaders allied with the opposition, the government gave considerable concessions to the loyal

---

[74] At the end of 1990, the secretary-general of the union in Capital Federal, Oscar Lescano, said that it was necessary and unavoidable to open SEGBA to private capital to avoid its bankruptcy (*Clarín*, November 24, 1990).

leadership of the federation despite its militancy (opposition). In addition to the employee-owned stocks programs, electricity workers obtained handsome voluntary and early retirements to reduce the workforce before privatization. They also received contracts to provide services for the new companies guaranteed by the government for union-organized cooperatives of former employees.[75] FATLyF also bought five of the privatized units, including three utility groups (Patagonia, Litoral, and Northwest) and two transportation companies (Transnea and Transnoa). It also obtained special conditions for the concession of the state-owned coal-mining zone (Yacimientos Carboníferos Fiscales) providing input for electricity utilities. This strategy allowed the union to reduce job losses and participate in energy production in less profitable areas.[76] FATLyF also received loans to modernize and privatize some services in its welfare fund. In addition, the union created a life insurance company, opened a pension fund in its headquarters, bought a bank and a series of pharmacies, and developed new training facilities.[77]

In 1995, FATLyF expelled the union in Mar del Plata and the union in Córdoba put down its criticism of the national leadership for its "entrepreneurial" strategy (personal interviews with union leaders J. Rigane and N. Calegaris, 1995). The subsequent reduction of leadership competition within the federation induced the restraint of the loyal national leaders who did not call any protests during that year. The union in Mar del Plata called all the strikes in the sector during 1995 to protest the privatization of a provincial electricity company in Buenos Aires. In sum, Peronist union leaders could obtain important concessions to restrain the militancy

---

[75] These companies included Electricity Transmission, Inc. (TRANELSA), Resource Evaluation, Inc. (EVARSA), Company of Environmental Issues, Inc. (EMASA), Engineering Projects, Inc. (PROHINSA), Sistemas Cuyo, Canal Federal, and Taller Mecánico Regional Mendoza providing services to diverse stages in the production, transmission, and distribution of electric energy (Bastos and Abdala 1995:145).

[76] Carlos Alderete (secretary-general) and Néstor Callegaris (secretary of energy policies) argued that taking part in the privatization of energy generators was a way of accomplishing workers' participation in management, influencing national energy policies, reducing the social costs of privatization, and obstructing the decline of organizational resources (personal interviews, 1993).

[77] Information derived from FATLyF's Annual Reports from 1992 to 1995, FATLyF (1992), personal interviews with union leaders Callegaris, Raitano, and Rigane and Under-Secretary of Energy Mirkin in 1995, from Ieraci (1995), Ministry of Economy (1995), and Murillo (1997a: 87). In its twenty-fourth congress, the union separated itself from a newly created corporation, which was to seek market opportunities in electricity and social services to generate resources for the organization and its affiliates (FATLyF 1992: 1).

generated by populist competitors, making this interaction a case of opposition until the expulsion of dissidents turned it into cooperation.

Education. The Argentine education system established in 1881 by law 1,420 had involved a large role for the central government, which controlled 42.7% of primary schools, 74.8% of secondary schools, and 82.5% of vocational schools by 1952. The decentralization policies of the last military regime focused on elementary education. As a result, only 1.9% of primary schools – as compared with 44.7% of secondary schools and 26.8% of vocational schools – were under national jurisdiction by 1987 (Paglianitti 1991). However, education personnel still accounted for 41% of the public administration by 1989 (Indec 1994: 452). As a part of the reform of the state provoked by fiscal austerity, Menem introduced a bill in 1991 to decentralize the schools and teachers remaining in the national jurisdiction to the provinces. It became law 24,049 at the end of that year.

CTERA was founded in 1973 by 147 provincial unions that were trying to reduce the high fragmentation of the sector. Eighteen years later, successive mergers led to a union per province and a union of teachers under national jurisdiction (CTERA 1992b). CTERA had a tradition of partisan pluralism and a Radical leader during democratic transition. In the mid-1980s, Mary Sánchez, a Peronist union leader, won the national union elections and affiliated CTERA to the CGT while increasing its militancy during the rest of the Radical administration (Figure 6.7). In 1989, CTERA became part of the populist CGT-Azopardo. Two years later, it broke with the Peronist CGT and was one of the founding unions of the CTA. Mary Sánchez also participated in the organization of FREPASO and later became a legislator. Her successor, Marta Maffei, was also affiliated with a center-left party in FREPASO.

There were other teachers' unions unaffiliated to CTERA, which sometimes reached loose coordinating agreements of short duration. Two of the main CTERA competitors were unions of teachers under national jurisdiction, Union of Argentine Teachers (UDA) and Association of Vocational Teachers (AMET), which were hit harder than CTERA's provincial unions by decentralization despite their loyalty to the government. UDA and AMET usually led the coalitions of teachers' unions competing with CTERA, along with the FEB (Federation of Buenos Aires' Teachers), which was the largest provincial union.

All teachers' unions rejected decentralization. Their main concerns were the lack of provision for adequate financing for provinces and the

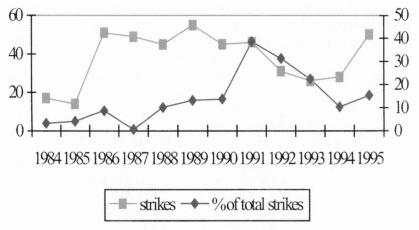

Figure 6.7 Teachers' strikes.
Source: *Tendencias Económicas.*

effect of decentralization on their declining real wages and provincial wage dispersion, once the national government relinquished its financial responsibilities.[78] Teachers backed their demands with strikes and public demonstrations. As a result, when the reform was announced in 1991, militancy was high, and teachers organized more than one-third of the total strikes (Figure 6.7). Teachers' unions kept protesting with fewer but longer strikes during the implementation of the law in 1992.[79] In particular, partisan opposition enhanced the militancy of CTERA while the government did not want to appear to give in to a union associated with the electoral opposition.[80] Yet, non-CTERA unions could not control the sector because CTERA was larger and grew at their expense during this period (personal interview with former education official, T. Sozio, 1995).

The competition between CTERA and non-CTERA unions for teachers' membership weakened them all. Government officials had few

[78] Although teachers' real salaries declined relative to real national GNP per capita throughout the country, the variance across provinces in mean teacher salary per year and its evolution was large (Vegas, Pritchett, and Experton 1999: 5).
[79] McGuire's (1996b) data set shows an increase in the duration of strikes by counting the number of days lost during this period (education and health strikes accounted for 80% of lost days between 1991 and 1993).
[80] The political motivation of CTERA's militancy during this administration is shown by the attempt of its secretary-general to make strikes coincide with the CTA strike schedule and by the exit of two provincial Peronist unions of CTERA.

165

incentives to give in to CTERA because they were aware of the difficulties for competing unions to coordinate their actions while overcoming the temptation of union competition. Moreover, CTERA's leaders were associated with the electoral opposition. CTERA routinely complained about government manipulation of union competition as it rejected wage agreements reached by non-CTERA unions and defined different strike schedules.[81] As a result, despite being the most militant sector, even by combining strikes with public demonstrations and marches, teachers were unable to influence the government (Gonda 1995a). In its 1992 annual report, CTERA complained that "despite all the actions we organized to deter the sanctioning of the law without adequate funding, we did not achieve much" (CTERA 1992b: 8). CTERA's Secretary-General Marta Maffei said that they opposed law 24,049 because of the lack of adequate resources at the provincial level, but they could not achieve concessions despite multiple strikes and mobilizations (personal interview, 1995). Even unions competing with CTERA received few concessions because they could not guarantee labor restraint in the sector. In short, the overlapping between union competition and partisan competition increased the incentives of teachers for militancy and reduced their capacity to obtain concessions from the government, thus bringing about resistance (ineffective militancy) as the interaction between them.

Summary

The unions of oilworkers (SUPE) and autoworkers (SMATA) collaborated with the Peronist government by restraining their militancy. In return, workers and the unions were compensated for the cost of oil privatization and the automobile workers were protected from trade competition. The combination of partisan loyalty and the lack of union competition or leadership competition induced the restraint of these unions and gave incentives for the government to grant them concessions to avoid the

---

[81] CTERA complained of the government manipulating union competition by granting registration to competing organizations (annual reports 1991: 9 and 1994: 1), favoring other unions as bargaining partners, and trying to grant them the control of the teachers' welfare fund (personal interviews with union leaders G. Araoz and M. Maffei, 1995). An example of disjointed coordination of militancy that failed to achieve wage demands is the CTERA March 1990 three-day strike, followed by a five-day strike by Federation of Workers of the National Education (FETEN) (UDA, AMET and others), another two-day strike by CTERA, and a final three-day strike called by FETEN.

replacement of loyal leaders (cooperation). However, in the case of SMATA, militancy was higher than expected until the government conceded a shelter from liberalization to this sector showing the persistence of a protectionist coalition between employers and employees similar to those forged during the populist period.

The unions of telephone workers (FOETRA) and electricity workers (FATLyF) reacted differently from SUPE to the privatization of their state-owned companies. In both cases, the support of the loyal leadership for privatization left void a space that was occupied by the antiprivatization or populist faction. The hike in leadership competition created by the increasing influence of the populist faction raised the incentives of loyal leaders for militancy to show that they had not sold out. Because there was no union competition in these sectors, the government wanted to grant concessions to loyal leaders to avoid their replacement by populist ones. In both cases, workers and unions received compensation for privatization and ownership in the privatized sectors. That is, their militancy was effective in bringing them concessions (opposition). As a result, when loyal leaders recovered control of both unions, thus reducing leadership competition, their incentives for militancy receded and their interaction shifted from opposition to cooperation.

Finally, the overlapping of union competition and partisan competition in the education sector, as in Venezuela, increased the incentives for militancy for hostile unions and caused loyal unions to follow them for fear of losing members to their more bellicose rivals. Despite teachers' militancy, union competition prevented coordination among multiple unions and weakened their bargaining power vis-à-vis the government, thus hindering their ability to exercise any policy input regarding the decentralization of education (resistance).

Conclusion

Labor unions had been the backbone of Peronism before democratization and they have organized key constituencies for electoral and policy support since then. Indeed, the partisan loyalty of labor unions to Peronism facilitated the implementation of market reforms because it restrained their militancy, which had debilitated the previous Radical administration in the absence of partisan ties. Despite the effect of Peronist loyalty on labor militancy, Menem's conversion from populism to neoliberalism provoked a division in the Peronist-controlled CGT that increased union competition. The government manipulated union competition, thus reducing labor bargaining power until 1992. The costs of union competition became too high when the Peronist unions risked losing their main source of organizational resources – their welfare funds – prompting their reunification into a single CGT. The unified CGT had a near monopoly over organized labor and was able to obtain multiple concessions in return for keeping labor peace after a general strike showed the value of such restraint. The lack of union competition increased their ability to obtain concessions and shifted their interaction with the Peronist government from subordination (ineffective restraint) to cooperation (effective restraint). However, although partisan loyalty reduced the incentives for militancy in the Peronist unions, it would increase the incentives for a few unions that broke ranks with Peronism to join the CTA and later, the FREPASO.

The policy shift of Peronism not only put the CGT under stress, but also threatened the five individual unions studied. Privatization in oil, telecommunications, and electricity; trade liberalization in the automobile sector; and decentralization in education challenged organized labor. However, the respective unions interacted differently with the Peronist government. Cooperation characterized the union-government interaction during the privatization and restructuring of the oil industry where the Peronist SUPE faced no union competition and no leadership competition. That is, partisan loyalty created incentives for restraint, and the government granted concessions to this monopolistic union to back the loyal leadership. In the case of telecommunications and electricity, leadership competition from populist factions that denounced the loyalty of the national leaders to the Peronist government increased incentives for labor militancy for union leaders who wanted to show they had not sold out. Because these unions held monopolies of representation and the government wanted to keep loyal leaders in control, the unions received concessions that compensated workers for the costs of reforms (opposition). However, after leadership competition receded, the incentives for militancy declined for loyal union leaders, and these unions shifted toward cooperation. In the automobile sector, the combination of union monopoly and no leadership competition brought cooperation only after the government granted restrictions to trade liberalization to a joint coalition of discontented employers and militant workers protesting the consequences of a sharp recession and import competition. Finally, the overlapping of union competition and partisan competition in the education sector

Table 6.2. *Summary of Union-Government Interactions*

Union	Union Competition	Partisan Competition	Interaction
CGT t-1	yes	no	Subordination
CGT t-2	no	no	Cooperation
SUPE t-1	no	no	Cooperation
SUPE t-2	no	no	Cooperation
SMATA t-1	no	no	Opposition
SMATA t-2	no	no	Cooperation
FOETRA t-1	no	yes	Opposition
FOETRA t-2	no	no	Cooperation
FATLyF t-1	no	yes	Opposition
FATLyF t-2	no	no	Cooperation
CTERA t-1	yes	yes	Resistance
CTERA t-2	yes	yes	Resistance

increased teachers' militancy, but decreased the government's willingness to give in to political opponents or weak allies, thus bringing about resistance (unsuccessful militancy) as the union-government interaction (Table 6.2).

It is worth noting that the behavior of individual unions was not very constrained by the CGT, in contrast to what happened in Mexico and Venezuela where the confederations were more centralized. Indeed, although SMATA and FOETRA had joined the proreform CGT, they increased their militancy during the period of the division based on their internal dynamics. The decentralized authority of the CGT permitted the largest unions to control the confederation and allowed the coexistence of diverse strategies even among loyal unions.[82] Although some adapted to

---

[82] The process of trade liberalization weakened the traditional predominance of the metalworkers' union and established a balance between the largest service unions reinforced by the formal rules mentioned in Chapter 3 and an array of informal practices. For instance, in 1995, I attended a CGT congress and witnessed how the majority of delegates waited in the convention center for the outcome of closed-door bargaining among a group of a dozen leaders of the largest unions who were drafting the slate of candidates in a separate building. This decentralized authority also explains that the large unions that controlled the confederation openly supported the competition among welfare funds because they thought they would win affiliates at the expense of smaller unions. These unions also obtained subsidies to foster mergers and modernize their welfare funds. Two unions, commerce employees and bank employees, received loans for $57 million and $40 million (U.S. million) respectively. The electricity workers' union explicitly supported union competition for health provision: "the Union's present health service association will not only

state retrenchment by buying companies or providing social security services, others continued to seek traditional concessions, such as political appointments. Among the Peronist unions that used concessions to adapt to the new environment were FATLyF, FOETRA, SUPE, and SMATA. They devised new endeavors to protect their ranks from unemployment and provide them with social services that compensated for the uncertainty of political resources (Murillo 1997a). They remained Peronist but prepared for a future of dwindling political resources although partisan loyalties continued to influence the union-government interactions. Indeed, Menem passed a labor reform that reinforced the power of national union leaders to reduce replacement threats based on local unions during his second administration (law 25,013/98).

A minority of unions adopted a different strategy to confront the new environment: they moved to a new labor confederation (CTA) and broke their Peronist loyalty. Allied with Peronist dissidents and center-left groups, they helped to construct a new political party, the FREPASO, but at the same time they retained their autonomy.[83] Similar to the "new unionism" in Venezuela and the independents in Mexico, they refused to build functional ties with their partisan allies because they wanted to challenge corporatist subsidies to Peronist control of unions justified by such a relationship.

The cross-national comparison among the national confederations in all three countries shows that, after its unification, the CGT had a larger policy influence than the Mexican CTM although both restrained their militancy to support an allied government. Because the CGT did not suffer the union competition that weakened the multiple confederations affiliated to the PRI, it could obtain more concessions in return for its collaboration (cooperation). However, the restraint of the Argentine CGT was sustained because most unions remained Peronist and there was little partisan competition in contrast to the Venezuelan experience of AD union leaders that resulted in opposition.

provide medical care to the present beneficiaries of Luz y Fuerza but will also set out to capture a vast sector of this large market" (FATLyF 1995: 4).

[83] The FREPASO was more successful in attracting votes in national elections than in extending its influence among unions. Its growth since 1993 has brought it to an alliance with the Radical Party that won the 1999 presidential election, bringing its main leader, Carlos Alvárez, a former Peronist, to the vice presidency although he resigned eleven months after his inauguration.

From Pickets to Prices: Labor Unions and Market Reforms in Argentina

The collaboration of Peronist unions with Menem facilitated the quick implementation of market reforms in Argentina. Peronist labor unions joined Menem's proreform coalition, which also included traditional provincial bosses and new allies in the business sector (Gibson 1997, Corrales 1997). The contending view based on leadership charisma and imposition explains labor restraint by repression and cooptation of union leaders (Acuña 1995, Palomino 1995), but this chapter shows a great deal of compromise in the interaction between Peronist labor leaders and government officials. This chapter does not dismiss the role played by formal institutions in the reform process but qualifies the "delegative" character of Argentine democracy based on Menem's abundant use of decrees. It shows that some decrees – such as the decrees on wage bargaining and welfare fund deregulation – involved direct negotiations with labor unions rather than imposition, although they did exclude the legislature and therefore the electoral opposition.

Labor loyalty follows the expectations of neocorporatist theories on the importance of the partisan identity of the government. The authority of national leaders to control their followers is a key component of the exchanges with the government (Offe and Wiesenthal 1985). In Argentina, the high unemployment that resulted from the fast implementation of market reforms reinforced their authority. In this context, strikes are less effective and negotiations became a more viable strategy than militancy, further shifting the internal balance of power in favor of union leaders – in charge of bargaining – at the expense of the rank-and-file-essential for mobilization. However, neocorporatism can not explain the institutional change from union competition to union monopoly in the case of the CGT, nor can it account for the changes in leadership competition within the telephone and electricity workers' federations. Although militancy declined when unemployment went up as predicted by industrial-relations theories, the success of the CGT in obtaining concessions increased at the same time that unemployment kept growing.

Finally, economic pluralists can explain that unions in the tradable sector rejected unrestricted trade liberalization after so many years of protectionism as automobile workers did, although it does not explain that they took longer to restrain their militancy than oil workers. In addition, economic interests also account for the fact that almost 35% of all the conflicts against job redundancies occurred in the exposed manufacture sector and 35% of the conflicts based on salary demands occurred in the public services – where state retrenchment and job stability constrained salaries (Gómez 1997: 668, 675). However, economic interests do not explain the resistance of the CTA, composed mainly of public sector unions, to trade liberalization. Nor do they explain the variation in the capacity of the CGT to obtain concessions before and after its unification, or the fact that among service unions, FOETRA (telecommunications) and FATLyF (electricity) were able to extract concessions with their militancy whereas the government ignored teachers' unrest.

Institutions cannot account for changes in the internal dynamics of unions, and interests cannot explain differences in bargaining power. My theory explains the changes in union dynamics by looking to the patterns of leadership competition and their effect on incentives for militancy and to the perceptions of union leaders of the effect of union competition on their interaction with government officials – in the case of the CGT unification. Simultaneously, union competition explains labor bargaining power. The absence of union competition strengthened SMATA, SUPE, FOETRA, and FATLyF in the same way it strengthened the CGT after its unification in 1992 despite their different reactions in terms of militancy and restraint. In contrast, union competition weakened both the divided CGT and the teachers' unions, although their patterns of militancy were different. In sum, this chapter does not deny the importance of macroeconomic conditions, economic interests, or national institutions to influence union-government interactions. Instead, it shows that partisan loyalty and leadership or partisan competition account for labor reaction in terms of militancy or restraint. Simultaneously, union competition explains the strength of the union and its capacity to obtain concessions. Furthermore, these variables apply to the CGT considering a variety of market reforms, and explain better than alternative theories the differences across the studied individual unions in different economic sectors.

7

Multilevel Comparison

He had learned, without effort, English, French, Portuguese, Latin. I suspect, however, that he was not very capable of thinking. To think is to forget differences, to generalize, to abstract. In the over stocked world of Funes there was nothing but details, almost immediate details. **Jorge Luis Burges (1944).**

The theory of union-government interaction presented in Chapter 2 focuses on the effect of partisan loyalties, leadership competition, and union competition on the relationships among governments, union leaders, and labor constituencies. Partisan loyalty influences the relationship between union leaders and government officials. Leadership competition, however, can interact with partisan loyalty by making leaders more aware of their constituencies to avoid replacement by rival union leaders. Union competition, in turn, affects the strategies of union leaders by shaping their relationship with other labor organizations when competing for constituencies and subsequently their bargaining power vis-à-vis governments. Chapter 3 shows the original influence of these variables at the onset of the alliance between labor unions and populist labor parties. Chapters 4 to 6 test their explanatory power in three different countries, five different economic sectors, and two different types of labor organizations (multisectoral confederations and industry-specific unions). This chapter brings together all the pieces of the puzzle in a cross-national comparison of all the case studies in Argentina, Mexico, and Venezuela. At the same time, it makes an explicit comparison of the explanatory power of different theories to account for the variation observed in the case studies.

The Comparability of the Case Studies

The case studies in Argentina, Mexico, and Venezuela are comparable because in all three countries the relationship between governing parties, labor unions, and their constituencies was shaped by similar historical legacies and faced a similar policy stimulus.[1] That is, they provide a "most similar" context regarding the variables that could affect the interaction studied. This similitude makes possible the cross-national comparisons.

In all three countries, an exogenous shock or economic crisis – which could be traced to the failures of import substitution industrialization and state-led development with closed economies – was behind the decision of populist labor-based parties to embrace the promises of market reforms. Peronism, the PRI, and AD had all previously supported protectionism and state intervention and gained the label of workers' representatives. Their conversion was a question of political survival and economic necessity. Each of the three presidents made it clear that he was not truly neoliberal. Their conversions were forced by the economic circumstances and the national interest. They understood the need to add a social aspect to the market, reaffirming that they were the true heirs of the great original mythology of their respective parties. For that very reason, their market reforms had to be drastic to persuade skeptical business actors about their commitment. Symbolism was important. In Venezuela, Pérez announced a "Great Turnaround." In Mexico, Salinas's began his administration by imprisoning Joaquín Hernández Galicia, a powerful union leader who had supported the populist Cuauhtémoc Cárdenas. In Argentina, Menem surrendered monetary policy to a currency board.

All three presidents followed the "Washington Consensus." The three countries instituted stabilization packages that included trade liberalization, privatization, and deregulation. That is, prices were turned into market signals, economies were opened to foreign competition, and private sector development received a boost. Also common to the three countries were social security reforms sought to increase savings rates and reduce payroll taxes and the inclusion of labor cost and flexibility into the policy agenda due to the pressures of international competition.

---

[1] These countries also share a common cultural heritage as former Spanish colonies. They all gained independence in the early nineteenth century and instituted presidential systems.

In the three countries, the policy turn also generated drastic changes in the formerly protected industries and nationalized sectors. The automobile industry, a symbol of import substitution industrialization, was opened to international competition and forced to restructure for exporting. The nationalized oil sector, which had been a source of patronage, was either streamlined or privatized. Increasing capital mobility caused infrastructure to become a key factor in the competition for investment and highlighted the importance of the telecommunications and electricity sectors. Fiscal deficits had prevented state-owned enterprises from joining the telecommunications revolution and hurt the efficiency of the electricity sector. Privatization promised revenue, investment to the fast-growing telecommunications sector, and dramatic improvements to the electricity sector. Finally, in competitive international markets the value of an educated workforce became salient. However, this coincided with the decline in the quality of education (IADB 1996: 277). The organization of education, and particularly centralization, was signaled as a main culprit of this malaise, and administrative reform or decentralization were pursued in all three countries.

The policy convergence in all three countries created challenges to labor unions that had grown influential under the previous economic conditions and were still tied by old vows to the governing parties. Stabilization programs constrained wage bargaining. Trade liberalization and privatization provoked job losses, hindered labor bargaining power by increasing exposure, and triggered drastic changes in the organization of labor. The reforms of pensions in Argentina and Mexico and severance payments in Venezuela were aimed at increasing individual savings, thus hindering solidarity among union constituencies. The reform of union-administered health funds in Argentina, union-administered housing funds in Mexico, and the Venezuelan Institute of Social Security also attempted to reduce the mechanisms for union patronage. The labor reform challenged the subsidies for labor organization obtained as institutional guarantees of the original alliance. Industry-specific reforms curtailed employment and dramatically changed work conditions while challenging the viability of the old patterns of labor relations. It is in this common context – where economic interest would predict a negative labor reaction across-the-board – that variation in union-government interaction became interesting and brought the importance of political variables to the fore.

Comparing National Confederations

Despite the common context in all three countries, the main national confederations reacted differently. Effective militancy (opposition) characterized the interaction between the Venezuelan CTV and President Pérez. Ineffective restraint (subordination) featured the CTM-Salinas relationship. The interaction between the CGT and President Menem shifted from ineffective restraint (subordination) to effective restraint (cooperation) when the Peronist unions reunited in a single CGT.

Industrial-relation theories cannot explain this variation. The empirical association of labor restraint with recession and unemployment is explained by the increasing cost of militancy when the reserve army of unemployed workers is growing, while labor bargaining power declines due to the effect of economic constraints on the probability of employers giving in to labor demands (Ashenfelter and Johnson 1969). However, unemployment and recession do not explain the patterns of militancy or its effectiveness in the three countries during the period studied. In Venezuela, the general rise in militancy in the period between 1989 and 1991 coincides with a sharp recession in the first year and economic growth in the other two years, but high unemployment persisted during the whole period (from 8.7% to 10.4%). In contrast, Mexican unions exercised restraint despite growth and low unemployment (below 4.4%). In Argentina, the first drop in militancy corresponds with poor economic performance and high unemployment (above 8%) in 1989 and 1990. Beginning in October 1990, there is a further plunge in general militancy, although economic prosperity returned only the next year, and unemployment remained high.

Because all three countries suffered high inflation, it is likely that the illusion of wage gains brought about by nominal hikes did not hide the real losses for workers. Labor militancy, thus, could be related to the defense of purchasing power regardless of the real conditions of the economy.[2] In Venezuela, militancy increased at the same time that inflation grew in 1989, apparently giving some credence to this hypothesis. However, when inflation was halved the following year, militancy continued growing until 1992. In Mexico, inflation dropped dramatically

[2] Zapata (1986: 166) found an empirical correlation between inflation and labor militancy in Chile, Mexico, and Venezuela for the 1960s and early 1970s. He related this correlation with the political influence of labor unions in setting national policies.

during Salinas's first year in office and remained low or decreased for the rest of his administration in tandem with labor restraint. On the other hand, in Argentina the militancy of individual unions showed a slow decline following Menem's inauguration despite the hyperinflation. Additionally, beginning in October 1990, there was a sharp drop in labor militancy despite the high inflationary context. Restraint, however, continued even when inflation dropped to double digits in 1992 and to single digits two years later.

Corporatist theories rely on the organizational characteristics of the labor movements to explain their restraint. In some cases, union density is used to explain labor strength and behavior. For instance, Shalev (1992) argues that the decline in union density was correlated with drops in labor militancy in OECD countries during the 1980s. Others emphasize the need for coordination to achieve wage restraint and emphasize the importance of characteristics that make labor movements more "encompassing." These features include, besides union density, the centralization of wage bargaining at the peak level, the statutory authority of peak confederations over union members, and the concentration of the labor movement in a few large organizations.[3] The expectation is that labor movements that are more concentrated, centralized, and able to control their affiliates are more likely to exercise restraint. A variation of these arguments focuses on the combination of partisanship with these organizational variables, such as party in government and the level of wage bargaining.[4] In this case, labor

[3] Most of these studies analyzed cross-national variation of economic performance in the OECD, assuming the effect of labor militancy. Cameron (1984) analyzes both strike activity and economic performance during the 1960s and 1970s in the OECD. In his description of corporatist labor movements, he assesses their unity or fragmentation, the power of confederations in collective bargaining, and the level of collective bargaining. Golden (1993) argues that centralization may be less important than concentration, where concentration refers to the extent to which union members are concentrated in a few large unions, as opposed to being divided into a large number of smaller organizations. Because coordination is easier among fewer unions (and free-riding less likely), it facilitates wage restraint. Calmfors and Driffill (1988) find that wage militancy is lower when wage bargaining is centralized at the peak level or decentralized at the company level and higher in the cases of industry-level bargaining. Golden and Wallerstein (1994), Western (1997), and Wallerstein and Western (1999) analyze the evolution of these variables for the OECD in the 1980s and 1990s.

[4] Cameron (1984) and Lange (1984) analyze the influence of labor or left parties on union behavior. Garrett and Lange (1985) and Alvarez, Garrett, and Lange (1991) combine partisanship with Calmfors and Driffill's (1988) finding about wage-bargaining levels. They argue that restraint and good economic performance are associated with left-wing parties and peak-level wage bargaining or right-wing parties and company-level bargaining.

Table 7.1. *Organizational Characteristics of Labor in Argentina, Mexico, and Venezuela*

	Argentina	Mexico	Venezuela
Unionization/Wage earners	57.2% (1986) 67.4% (1995)	42.6% (1974) 59.6% (1995)	34.6% (1980) 28.9% (1995)
Fragmentation (number of unions)	low	high	medium
Number of Peak Organizations	single predominant	multiple	single predominant
Centralization of Authority by Peak Organizations	low	very high	high
Predominant Wage-bargaining Level	industry	company	company/state

Sources: Union density in McGuire (1997: 264) and ILO (1997: 237), fragmentation in Ministry of Labor and Social Security (1997: 20, 40), Zazueta and De La Peña (1981: 761, 775), Leal (1986: 12), and Diaz (n.d.: 27), peak organization and the predominant wage-bargaining level in Feldman (1991), Zazueta and De La Peña (1981), and Díaz (n.d.).

restraint is associated with wage bargaining centralized at the peak level – with a labor movement concentrated in few unions and labor confederations with strong authority over members – if a labor party is in power.

Although both partisanship and organizational variables are key to understanding the observed variation, this stylized picture does not account for the differences between the Mexican CTM, Venezuelan CTV, and Argentine CGT in their interaction with labor-based administrations. A labor-based party was in power in all three countries. In contrast to Shalev's findings, union density (as a proportion of wage earners) was lower and declining more rapidly in Venezuela than in Argentina and Mexico (Table 7.1). However, militancy was increasing in Venezuela and decreasing in the latter countries.

Other characteristics of corporatist labor movements are also insufficient to explain the variation in the interaction studied. In Venezuela, company-level wage bargaining was predominant, and there was a single labor confederation with centralized authority over members. In Mexico, wage bargaining also was predominantly company level, although it was occasionally centralized by the government in social pacts that imposed wage ceilings. However, the labor movement was very fragmented, and although confederations have strong authority over members, there were many of them. In Argentina, union fragmentation was low, most union-ized workers were concentrated in a few large unions, and there was a single labor confederation recognized by law. Nevertheless, the authority of this confederation over members was very weak and industry-level wage bargaining was predominant. Nor was there any informal kind of wage coordination. In sum, in none of the three countries was the labor move-ment really encompassing – concentrated and centralized by an authori-tative confederation – to justify the labor restraint considering that a labor-based party was in government. Indeed, both the Mexican and Argentine labor movements exercise restraint despite their different organizational features.

The Latin American version of corporatism had paid more attention to characteristics of the state vis-à-vis labor than the organizational dimen-sions of the union movement. The previous three chapters analyze the impact of labor institutions on union-government interactions for each country. In a comparative study, Collier and Collier (1979: 974–5) measure state-labor relationships through the levels of "inducements" and "con-straints" for labor organization introduced in labor codes. Because labor legislation has remained unchanged, these measures should still be valid. According to this data, both Argentina and Mexico have higher levels of "inducements" than Venezuela in their labor legislation. That is, they have regulations that provide more subsidies for labor organization and thus strengthen unions more than those of Venezuela. If "inducements" made labor stronger in Argentina and Mexico, we should expect labor restraint, because strong unions do not need to exercise their muscle to obtain con-cessions. In contrast, the Venezuelan workers had to go to the streets to be effective. However, labor restraint did not yield concessions in Mexico or in Argentina from 1989 to 1992. In fact, these formal measures of labor codes cannot explain that without any changes on the regulations of labor organization, the Argentine CGT became more effective in exercising policy input beginning in 1992.[5]

The literature on political institutions focuses on the capacity of governments to control labor militancy and their permeability to labor demands. Part of this literature looks at the character of the regime and distinguishes between authoritarian governments and democracies, which can explain some of the facets of the Mexican case studies as discussed in

---

[5] In 1990, a decree curtailed strike activity in the public services. This legal change, though, should have had the opposite effect.

the following text.[6] Other versions of this literature focus on government institutions. In particular, due to the predominance of presidentialism in Latin America, the power of the president has been described as an essential variable to explain success or failure of market reforms. Using formal measurements of presidential power, Shuggart and Carey (1992: 155) originally placed all three countries in the same category. However, empirical analysis of the functioning of institutions categorized the Mexican presidency as stronger (Weldon 1997) and the Venezuelan presidency as weaker (Crisp 1997) than the Argentine one (Jones 1997). Like the studies on regime type, the strength of the Mexican presidency can explain Salinas's control over labor militancy and impermeability to labor demands in contrast to the Venezuelan President Carlos A. Pérez. This type of analysis, however, has limitations. It fails to explain that the restraint of the Argentine CGT was ineffective in getting the president's attention until 1992, even though the Argentina political institutions did not change at that time. It does not explain that the Mexican CTM was effective in halting the reform of the labor code even when it failed to achieve other policy demands under the same political institutions. More importantly, political institutions, just as the previous national-level variables, cannot be applied to account for the subnational variation in the union-government interaction observed in each of the three countries.

Partisan Loyalties, Leadership Competition, and Union Competition

The theory presented in Chapter 2 incorporates partisanship and institutional context while accounting for the fact that economic interest created labor preferences against policies that hurt the bulk of their constituencies in the protected and public sectors. It states that the labor unions' interactions with governments are affected by partisan loyalties, organizational characteristics of labor, and internal union dynamics, holding constant the institutional and macroeconomic variables. The benefit of this theory is that partisan loyalties, leadership competition, and union competition are variables that travel across countries, sectors, and levels of organization. These variables also explain the variation in the interaction between labor confederations and populist labor-based parties converting to the market creed.

[6] See, for instances, Nelson (1990, 1992, 1994), Remmer (1991), Przeworski (1991, 1995), and Haggard and Kaufman (1992, 1995).

The effect of leadership competition and union competition on union-government interactions varies according to the identity of the party in government. When those implementing market reforms are labor-based parties tied to labor unions, labor leaders affiliated with these parties are likely to trust their partisan allies in government and restrain labor militancy to collaborate with them. However, market reforms make leadership competition more likely by providing rival union leaders with a populist cause – the rejection of market reforms. Leadership competition increases the militancy of union leaders allied with the governing party, because they want to avoid being replaced by populist rivals. Thus, we should expect militancy to increase after leadership competition grows – either immediately after the policy shift or during the process – regardless of the effect of such militancy, because it is related to the internal dynamics of the union. Instead, if there is no leadership competition, we should expect partisan loyalty to cause union leaders to restrain labor militancy.

Union competition, in turn, explains the effect of either militancy or restraint to achieve labor demands. It weakens each of the competing unions because none can control the militancy or restraint of the whole sector but just a portion of it. Moreover, union competition causes coordination problems among rival unions and creates incentives to undermine joint strategies, because unions attempt to differentiate themselves in their bid for members. Hence, union competition reduces the effectiveness of either the labor restraint or militancy due to an interunion dynamic that affects labor unions' relationship with the government. Union monopoly, instead, makes the union stronger because it controls the whole sector, and the government does not want to lose its loyalty. Thus, if there is union competition, we should see few or no concessions, whereas union monopoly should increase the effectiveness of the union to achieve its demands.

In Venezuela, the CTV broke a long tradition of restraining labor militancy under AD administrations when Pérez announced his "Great Turnaround." Although AD controlled the CTV, other parties had competed for the leadership and displaced AD briefly in the 1960s, making partisan competition a regular form of leadership competition. The pluralism of the CTV was also reinforced by a proportional representation electoral system that resulted in the inclusion of minority parties in its executive committee. In 1989, urban riots followed Pérez's announcement of market reforms. AD union leaders became afraid that popular discontent would spread to their constituencies and jeopardize their control over the CTV in the face of opposition parties that were protesting against the reforms. They took the urban riots as a signal of increasing partisan competition. Torn between partisan loyalty and the threat of replacement, they increased their militancy by calling the first economic general strike in Venezuelan history. Labor militancy was effective because the CTV was a monopolistic confederation, and Pérez's concessions included emergency wage hikes, suspension of layoffs, and retaining price controls for basic staples. Partisan competition continued to grow when the anti-neoliberal Causa R defeated AD in union elections. AD union leaders further increased their militancy, and the CTV called additional protests despite Perez's decision to halt the reform of the severance payment system and social security and accept union demands for the resignation of his labor minister. Because CTV had a near monopoly over Venezuelan workers, and the AD administration did not want their allied labor leaders replaced by more hostile ones, Pérez gave in to many CTV demands, thus making labor militancy effective in achieving concessions (opposition).

In Argentina, the interaction between Menem and the CGT shifted from ineffective restraint (subordination) to effective restraint (cooperation). The Peronists faced no competition from other political parties for the control of unions. Because, in contrast to Venezuela, there was no partisan competition, labor restraint prevailed. Although the CGT had had a union monopoly, Menem's announcement of market policies divided the CGT into three factions – all of which retained their partisan loyalty to Peronism. Unlike the union monopoly of the CTV, the division of the CGT allowed Menem to manipulate union competition among the three factions, thus making their restraint ineffective in achieving concessions (subordination). Peronist labor unions were unable to block a new law introducing temporary hiring and decrees establishing wage restraint and depriving them of the collection and administration of welfare fund fees. The weakening provoked by union competition resulted in a reunification of the CGT in early 1992. Lacking partisan competition, Peronist union leaders continued to restrain labor militancy after calling a single general strike a few months after reunification to signal their capacity to mobilize. Once the CGT recovered its union monopoly, its restraint was effective in obtaining concessions (cooperation). These included changes in the reforms of pensions, social security, subsidies for their welfare funds, and the maintenance of legislation on collective bargaining and labor organization.

In Mexico, ineffective restraint (subordination) characterized the inter-action between the CTM and Salinas. As in Argentina, partisan loyalty without partisan competition resulted in labor restraint, particularly after the PRI almost lost the 1988 elections. As in Argentina until 1992, union competition among the CTM and other PRI-affiliated confederations made the CTM policy demands ineffective in achieving concessions except in regard to the labor code. To bring them under its control, the govern-ment manipulated union competition for scarce resources. The only exception to this pattern was the unanimous rejection by the CTM and all other PRI-confederations of the reform of the labor code that reduced union competition and increased their bargaining power. Hence, the lack of partisan competition induced labor restraint, whereas union competi-tion made that restraint ineffective in achieving concessions.

In short, partisan loyalties, leadership competition, and union compe-tition explain the cross-national variation of national confederations in the context of partisan loyalty to the governing party. Increasing partisan competition explains the militancy of the Venezuelan CTV, whereas the absence of partisan competition explains the predominance of partisan loyalty and the restraint of the Mexican CTM and the Argentine CGT. In turn, union monopoly explains why the CTV and the CGT after its re-unification in 1992 were effective in achieving concessions – albeit with different reactions – whereas union competition weakened the CTM and the divided CGT before 1992. For labor unions tied to the government by partisan loyalty, partisan competition provoked militancy, and union monopoly increased their capacity to obtain concessions – regardless of militancy.

Comparing Sector-specific Unions

The comparison of unions in the same sector across countries provides further testing of the theory by introducing two control dimensions. Firstly, it determines whether the theory works in different economic contexts (telecommunications, electricity, oil, automobile, and education). Secondly, it tests the theory's viability for diverse types of organization because the labor confederations analyzed in the previous section gathered unions of different sectors, whereas these unions were specific to a single industry.

Economic pluralists expect economic interest to drive the policy demand of unions and other economic actors. In a closed economy, the interest of workers and employers could be reconciled with higher wages and profits at the expense of consumers, which explains the emergence of populist coalitions in Latin America. However, in open economies higher prices are not a possibility for tradable goods that could be imported. The divide between the tradable and the nontradable sectors widens. Whereas in the tradable sector workers are likely to lose their jobs if the costs of the goods they produce are not competitive, in the nontradable sectors domestic workers have more leverage because production was not exposed to international competition. This explains the higher militancy of workers in the public sector in the OECD countries during the 1980s (Shalev 1992, Garrett and Way 1995). In the case of *opening* economies, labor unions in the tradable sectors should have a negative reaction against losing the protection that had made them nearly nontradable for many years. These sectors are going to be harder hit than the public sector until they become competitive when the usual incentives for restraint in open economies should apply. As a result we expect a pattern of declining militancy in these sectors.

Regarding the public sector, the transition to the market brought privatization and state retrenchment that created challenges for employment and work conditions. Even if public services cannot be imported, fiscal deficits provide sharp incentives to cut costs. The bulk of the adjustment is likely to occur at the beginning when fiscal urgency is at its height. Thus, the pattern should be the opposite of the case of tradable goods with increasing militancy once the threat of job loss starts to decline. Finally, fiscal deficits hurt teachers in the public administration by cutting their salaries, which dropped in the whole region during the 1980s (ILO 1996), and by compromising their work conditions. Teachers were also protected from dismissal by public sector regulations. The logic of nontradable sectors in open economies also applies to this sector, where militancy should be high. The following section compares these expectations with those derived from the theory presented in Chapter 2.

Telecommunications

In all three countries, the large fiscal deficit deprived the monopolistic state-owned telephone companies of the investment necessary to join the telecommunications revolution. Privatization promised to improve infrastructure – which was crucial for global business – and bring revenue to the state coffers, especially because exclusive licenses for a predetermined number of years made investment more attractive in the three countries. Looking at the end of the exclusive licenses, all privatized companies restructured their working conditions and labor technologies, thus challenging the privileged collective contracts of state-owned enterprises.

In Argentina, the militancy of the union during the privatization process was effective in achieving worker-owned stocks, wage increases, subsidies for the union, and handsome voluntary retirements rather than layoffs (opposition). After privatization, militancy went down, but restraint was effective in achieving union participation in training programs, contracts for union-organized companies, and subsidies for union-provided health services (cooperation). In Venezuela, the union effectively restrained its militancy during privatization in return for worker-owned stock, job stability, and no changes in the collective contract (cooperation). In contrast to Argentina, militancy grew after privatization although the Venezuelan union retained its bargaining power (opposition). In Mexico, there were no changes in union behavior or bargaining power. The Mexican union restrained its militancy during privatization in return for worker-owned shares, wage hikes, job stability, the expansion of employment, and subsidies for union-provided social services (cooperation). After privatization, the union continued to exercise restraint when bargaining over restructuring and it continued to receive concessions. These included union participation in programs for quality, productivity, and training as well as generous benefits for workers (cooperation).

The expansive characteristic of the industry is probably related to the fact that either labor militancy or restraint was effective for achieving concessions related to privatization and restructuring. This commonality makes it even more intriguing that there were variation in union reaction and even changes in the same union from restraint to militancy. The transformation of union strategies in Argentina and Venezuela followed different directions with labor militancy dropping in the former and increasing in the latter. Although the increasing militancy of the Venezuelan union could be associated with the delay in industrial restructuring, no change in behavior was observed in the Mexican union, and most of the restructuring in Argentina also took place after privatization. The conditions of the industry, are therefore insufficient to explain these patterns of variation.

In these case studies, leadership competition is a key variable in explaining the differences across countries and the changes within a single union.

Leadership competition increased the militancy of the Argentine union during privatization and the Venezuelan union after privatization. In both cases, the loyal union leaders lost control of the largest local union in the telephone workers' federation to an antiprivatization group. Afraid of replacement, the national leadership of the federation followed their internal contenders in increasing labor militancy to show their responsiveness to the rank-and-file. In contrast, the lack of leadership competition explains the restraint of the Mexican union before and after privatization and of the Venezuelan union before privatization. Even the Argentine union restrained when leadership competition receded after privatization and the loyal union leaders won the election of the previously lost local union. In these cases, partisan loyalty prevailed because there was no threat of replacement. In the three cases, union monopoly made the unions effective in achieving concessions through either militancy or restraint. Partisan allies in the government valued the loyalty of strong unions that could control the militancy of all workers in the sector.

Electricity

Electricity was controlled by the state in all three countries. Fiscal deficits provoked a drop in investment that eroded the provision of services in all three countries and drove all three governments toward reform. However, only the Peronist government in Argentina went as far as privatizing the industry – from generation to distribution. In Argentina, there were three national electricity companies: SEGBA, Agua y Energía, and Hidronor. They were divided before their privatization. In Mexico, although business demanded the privatization of the deficit-ridden Compañía de Luz y Fuerza del Centro, the government backed away from its attempt to liquidate the company and implemented only some labor restructuring. In Venezuela, the government decentralized CADAFE and unsuccessfully attempted to restructure labor relations but dropped plans to privatize this company.

During the privatization process, the Argentine union increased its militancy and effectively achieved important concessions that included worker-owned stocks, handsome voluntary retirements, contracts for union-organized companies of former employees, and subsidized conditions for union purchasing of public utilities (opposition). Despite its effectiveness, the national federation of electricity workers restrained its militancy after privatization at the end of Menem's administration (cooperation). As in the previous case, the Venezuelan union exhibited the opposite pattern. The union restrained its militancy and supported the decentralization of CADAFE in return for concessions (cooperation), but then increased its militancy and halted industrial restructuring and privatization afterward (opposition). Finally, the Mexican union restrained its previous militancy and ensured the survival of the company by compelling the government to abandon plans for its privatization or bankruptcy (cooperation). However, militancy increased at the end of Salinas's administration, effectively reducing productivity targets previously included in a new collective contract (opposition).

The effectiveness of either labor militancy or restraint in electricity, as in telecommunications, may be related to the characteristics of the industry. However, it is intriguing that all three unions changed their behavior during the short period studied here, making the patterns of militancy less clear. Whereas privatization took place only in Argentina and perhaps justified the initial militancy of the union, the increases in militancy by the Venezuelan and Mexican unions cannot be explained by a privatization that never took off. In fact, militancy grew in Mexico after privatization had already been prevented.

In electricity, as in telecommunications, leadership competition was an essential variable to explain labor choices for militancy or restraint. Leadership competition justifies the militancy of the Argentine union during privatization, the Venezuelan union after decentralization, and the Mexican union after restructuring and the survival of the company. Leadership competition took the form of an antiprivatization coalition that denounced the loyal Argentine union leaders and led to Causa R's capture of the largest section of the Venezuelan federation. In Mexico, a sudden increase in leadership competition resulted in the loyal union leader losing reelection and bringing about a break in partisan loyalty. Union monopolies explain the effectiveness of the three unions to obtain concessions – through either militancy or restraint.

Oil

In all three countries state-owned oil companies were a source of government revenue, although to a much larger extent in Mexico and Venezuela than in Argentina. Salinas, Pérez, and Menem tried to open the sector to foreign investment and improve the efficiency of the companies to raise fiscal revenue. Thus, these companies underwent labor restructuring and work force reductions to improve labor productivity. Moreover, the Mexican government divided and decentralized PEMEX, the state-owned company, and the Argentine government privatized YPF, its Argentine counterpart.

In Argentina, a dramatic restructuring – including job losses and new work conditions – was followed by privatization. The union restrained but was effective in obtaining concessions that included retraining courses, voluntary retirement, and subsidies for the union to buy the YPF fleet and organize firms with former workers (cooperation). In Venezuela, restructuring included a new payment scheme, the reduction of union prerogatives, and subsidies for workers. Whereas effective restraint (cooperation) was the reaction of the union to the first round of collective bargaining, it shifted to effective militancy (opposition) in the second round. Finally, in Mexico, the union restraint became ineffective because it obtained no compensations for a restructuring process that included many job losses and dramatic changes in the collective contract (subordination).

The conditions of the industry are not sufficient to explain such a variety of militancy and its effectiveness. There was no obvious pattern of decreasing militancy – due to larger exposure – or increasing militancy – due to immediate fiscal needs that affected public enterprises. The Venezuelan case study even changed from cooperation to opposition during the period studied. Although oil was a main source of exports in both Venezuela and Mexico but not in Argentina, there was not any clear pattern linking the oil sector unions in the former two countries.

Instead, the internal dynamics of the unions and their relationship with government help explain this variation. Partisan loyalty without partisan competition explains the restraint of the Argentine union and the Venezuelan union during the first round of collective bargaining. Without the replacement threat, union leaders collaborated with their allies in government. The emergence of partisan competition in the Venezuelan union explains the hike in militancy during the second round of collective bargaining. That is, the emergence of a replacement threat made them more militant to avoid being perceived as having sold out and losing control of the union. Strengthened by the absence of union competition, the Argentine and Venezuelan unions were able to obtain concessions. Their restraint and militancy were effective to achieve labor demands because the government valued the restraint of the sector and gave in to these monopolistic unions. In Mexico, the monopolistic PRI union had effectively restrained during De La Madrid's administration in return for concessions. However, Salinas and the CTM forced this union into ineffective restraint (subordination). Political dynamics rather than the economic interest of the union explain this exception. The undemocratic nature of the Mexican regime explains the repression of a union that supported Cárdenas in the 1988 election.

Automobiles

The automobile industry was drastically restructured due to the effect of the economic opening and its swift integration into the transnational production of large multinational corporations in all three countries. Moreover, in the aftermath of economic recessions, automobiles suffered a drop in domestic demand due to the shortage of credit and the fall in real incomes. The main effects of industrial restructuring were the elimination of workforce redundancies and the introduction of new work technologies aimed at increasing labor productivity.

In Venezuela, the Ford Motor Company restructured its single plant after trade liberalization and the 1989 recession provoked large layoffs. The union restrained and effectively obtained participation in the restructuring and rehiring of workers (cooperation). In Argentina, trade liberalization and recession affected automobile sales and provoked job shedding. The militancy of the union and business pressures achieved a more protected regime in this sector (opposition). In the context of economic prosperity, industrial restructuring did not provoke militancy but restraint, which was effective in obtaining the rehiring of workers, subsidies for the union, and continuation of the trade regime (cooperation). In Mexico, the local section of the Ford Motors' union in Cuautitlán was the last "brownfield" plant of the company. As such, the company put it in line with work conditions in the more modern plants of northern Mexico. Workers resisted militantly initially and then exercised restraint during both rounds of collective bargaining. However, they were unable to achieve any change in the employers' proposal thus shifting from resistance to subordination.

Economic theories should have a stronger explanatory power in the automobile sector because it is the only private sector example in the set. The variation in the studied interactions within this single industry across the three countries suggests that additional variables affected the economic demands of workers who wanted to retain the good conditions received during the period of import substitution industrialization. These economic demands explain the initial militancy of both Argentine and Mexican workers, but not the success of the former and the failure of the latter to obtain concessions. The Venezuelan case study does not fit the pattern because labor restraint was maintained despite the changes in work conditions and even layoffs, which had provoked the militancy of Argentine automobile workers.

The focus on the partisan loyalties of union leaders provides crucial information for understanding the different labor reactions and their effectiveness. The lack of partisan competition in union leaders affiliated with the governing party explains the restraint of the Venezuelan union and the Argentine union since 1991. Partisan loyalty prevailed, and they chose not to increase unrest that could damage an allied administration. In turn, their restraint was effective in achieving concessions because they lacked union competition (cooperation). In Argentina, however, the Peronist union was militant during the 1989–90 recession, because it could build an alliance with employers to persuade the government to provide trade protection to the sector. In Mexico, the local section of the SITRAFORD voted a new leadership associated with the electoral opposition to the PRI while trying to leave the CTM for the COR. Although the change in partisan loyalty provoked the expected effect of increased militancy, the CTM took over the section and forced it into subordination to management's demands.

Because this was a private industry from the beginning, the role of private employers is more salient than in the other case studies. In Argentina, employers allied with the unions to demand trade protection from the government, returning to the kind of coalitions usual during a period of import substitution industrialization. In Mexico, employers allied with the government and the CTM to impose changes in the collective contract that made their plant more competitive in an open and integrated economy. The violent methods used by the CTM to achieve this goal are related to the undemocratic nature of the Mexican regime and its competition for union affiliates with other confederations. The theory does not fit this case as well as others, because it is more prepared to deal with the union-government interaction. However, its main insight of looking at the political dynamics on unions remained unchallenged even for these exceptions.

Education

In all three countries, the national government committed to decentralizing public education and improving its quality. In fact, decentralization was supposed to promote efficiency in the use of resources and improve quality by removing layers of bureaucracy between providers and users and by promoting competition across jurisdictions (Savedoff, Haussmann, and Piras 1996, Savedoff 1996). Argentina and Mexico decentralized education, transferring all national teachers to the provinces in Argentina and to the state in Mexico. In Venezuela, states themselves needed to demand the transfer of teachers according to the decentralization law. Thus, decentralization was slower because few states demanded the transfer, and the minister of education was not very convinced of their capacity to administer education. Instead, he implemented an administrative reform and directed subsidies to private education to increase competition for promoting efficiency in the public sector.

In Argentina and Venezuela, teachers' unions militantly rejected the reforms but were not effective in making the government incorporate their policy input or grant them concessions (resistance). Instead, the Mexican teachers' union reacted militantly, but it was effective in achieving concessions that changed the proposal of reform and compensated teachers for the impact of decentralization (opposition). That is, only in Mexico did the government substantially modify the original reform to include union demands in its design.

As expected from public sector employees, teachers' militancy was high in all three cases, despite regulations on strike activity for the public administration in Mexico. However, the conditions of education as part of the public sector are not sufficient to account for the cross-national variation in the effectiveness of teachers' militancy. Nor is it the fact that the reform implies large decentralization only in Argentina and Mexico because unions in both countries had different capacity to make themselves heard by the government.

Partisan competition explains the militancy of the education sector, whereas differences in union competition account for the effectiveness of teachers in obtaining concessions. In the three countries there was partisan competition in this sector. Partisan competition increased militancy in the Mexican union and even induced the loyal teachers' unions in Argentina and Venezuela to follow the militancy of the unions associated

191

with the electoral opposition. However, because the Mexican SNTE was a monopolistic union, its militancy was effective in achieving policy input. In contrast, in Argentina and Venezuela, there were various education unions competing for the membership of teachers. Teachers unions had different political affiliations, including some allied with the governing parties and some with other parties in the electoral opposition. Partisan competition made unions allied with the opposition parties and those loyal to the government militant. Union competition made it more difficult for all of them to coordinate their collective action and made each one weaker because neither could control the whole sector. Consequently, governments paid little attention to their demands, and their militancy was ineffective.

In sum, partisan loyalties, leadership competition, and union competition are useful to illustrate the cross-national variation within particular sectors in the context provided by populist labor-based governments converting to neoliberalism. By focusing on the effect of political variables, even for individual unions, this theory complements economic interest in explaining patterns of union-government interaction. For individual unions, as for labor confederations, partisan identity and leadership competition affect the preferences of union leaders for militancy or restraint, whereas union competition affects the willingness of government officials to spend on union concessions.

National Patterns

The importance of political factors at the level of sector-specific individual unions highlights the legacies of state corporatism in the three countries. In particular, institutional legacies made union competition more resilient to change than leadership competition during the period studied here. However, leadership competition was more prevalent in Venezuela than in the other two countries. Partisan loyalties emerging from the populist alliances changed in a few case studies. That is, leadership and partisan competition grew but allied union leaders retained control of the unions studied in most cases. In those case studies where allied union leaders were replaced, the partisan change produced the expected effect of increasing the militancy of the unions won by nonallied union leaders who had no incentives to exercise restraint if market reforms hurt their constituencies. In fact, they have incentives to be militant not only because of electoral alliances, but also because they replaced union leaders who had sold out to governmental allies. However, partisan loyalties also remained relatively stable in the case studies although they experienced the most dramatic changes in Mexico. Two unions abandoned their partisan loyalty to the PRI and were repressed into subordination by a regime that was not totally democratic (Ford Motors' at Cuautitlán and oil workers). The SME also abandoned its partisan loyalty, but the government tolerated this because this union had kept a more independent tradition. On the other hand, the SNTE did not openly break the partisan loyalty although it ended the official affiliation with the PRI, because its leader was active in the party. It is remarkable that most breaks to partisan loyalty took place in the country where partisan competition was repressed the most.

The Mexican cases highlight the importance of embedding the explanatory variables within the constraints created by the political regime on the means of expressing militancy and the costs of partisan competition. Yet, at the same time, even in the most constrained environment (Mexico), where the regime was not completely democratic and the president was powerful, there was variation in the interaction between unions and the government. This variation cannot be explained by traditional theories based only on the features of the Mexican regime. Without denying the importance of political institutions, it is important to recognize the diversity in the same national context as a result of the different effects of institutions on organizational and partisan variables. Hence, by focusing on both the national and subnational level, the relevance of political variables in shaping economic trends becomes manifest.

Comparing Multilevel Case Studies

The multilevel comparison shows the explanatory power of the theory presented in Chapter 2 for the analyzed case studies across different countries, economic sectors, and types of labor organization. Building upon the summary tables at the end of the previous three chapters, Table 7.2 presents all case studies. It includes two observations for each case to account for changes within the same union to show the correspondence between the explanatory conditions in the theory and the cases with the expected outcome.

These case studies highlight the importance of the interactions among union leaders, union members, and government officials in the explanation of union-government interactions after the policy shift of labor-based parties. Partisan loyalties retained from the original alliance still tied labor

Table 7.2. *Explanatory Conditions and Union-Government Interaction in Argentina, Mexico, and Venezuela*

Explanatory Conditions Assuming Partisan Loyalty (independent variables)		Expected Outcome	Number of Observations with Explanatory Conditions	Number of Observations with Expected Outcome
Partisan Competition	Union Competition			
no	no	COOPERATION effective restraint	13	13
no	yes	SUBORDINATION ineffective restraint	6	3
yes	no	OPPOSITION effective militancy	12	11
yes	yes	RESISTANCE ineffective militancy	5	5
			36	32

leaders and politicians. Partisan loyalties promoted labor restraint and collaboration with partisan allies in power, whereas nonallied union leaders were usually more militant in their demands against market reforms. Partisan loyalties, however, interacted with leadership competition and union competition. On the one hand, leadership competition explains labor choices for militancy or restraint based on union leaders' fear of being replaced if they did not protest against market reforms. On the other hand, union competition influenced the effectiveness of either strategy for obtaining concessions by weakening rival unions that were unlikely to coordinate their collective action due to the bid for members. In fact, the case studies that do not correspond to the conditions predicted in the theory are not explained by general economic theories but by particular political conditions.

Finally, this study suggests that further research should focus on the interaction between different levels of analysis. This implies moving beyond the national-level bias to include units of analysis defined at the level of sectors, subnational units, and even organizations in the study of comparative politics. The multilevel research design of this study combined comparisons across and within countries to facilitate the testing of alternative explanations within a relative small number of cases. In turn, a small number of cases made possible the collection of the data necessary to test causal mechanisms based on organizational dynamics. The theoretical benefit of this research design is the possibility to maintain national institutions and macroeconomic conditions constant in the comparisons within countries and sector-level variables constant in the comparison within sectors. Its empirical advantage is to provide a better picture of the complex reality of the studied countries and the organizational dynamics of each case while advancing comparative analysis.

8

Labor Competition and Partisan Coalitions

The mark of the immature man is that he wants to die for a noble cause, while the mark of the mature man is that he wants to live humbly for one. **J.D. Salinger (1991)**

This book provides a new framework for understanding the interactions between labor unions and their allied parties on the road to market reforms based on labor competition and partisan coalitions. It incorporates multiple stories about the path of transition for several labor unions in Argentina, Mexico, and Venezuela. Yet, it also sheds light on a much larger story. The book's theory addresses one of the political challenges created when increasing capital mobility and trade integration make state intervention more difficult in nations across the world. The explanation for union-government interactions presented in this book includes economic interests, macroeconomic conditions, and political institutions. The comparisons within each country enabled me to hold macroeconomic conditions and political institutions constant at the country level and assess their impact on the patterns of interaction. The comparison within sectors enabled me to hold economic interests constant and evaluate their influence on union-government interactions. Within these different contexts, the evidence demonstrates that partisan coalitions and labor competition were crucial to understand the interactions between labor unions and labor-based governments that had been converted to the market creed. In particular, partisan loyalties and leadership competition shaped the unions' reactions to market reforms, whereas union competition influenced the response of the governments to labor demands.

196

Partisan Loyalties. Emerging from an original alliance that benefited workers and facilitated labor organization, partisan loyalties influenced union leaders' attitudes vis-à-vis the government. Unions were more likely to restrain their militancy when partisan allies were in the government even after the latter had converted to neoliberalism.

Leadership Competition. Leadership competition for the control of unions resulted from the challenges created by alternative leaders who protested against market reforms and accused loyal union leaders of having sold out to partisan allies. If leadership competition created a replacement threat for them, even loyal union leaders were likely to follow their contenders becoming more militant in order to show their responsiveness to the rank-and-file.

Union Competition. Union competition for membership made each union less valuable for the government. The competition created incentives for labor unions to break coordination efforts in their bid for affiliates, thus weakening their strategies – whether militancy or restraint. Hence, union competition reduced government's incentives to yield to labor demands.

The interaction of these three variables explains the origin of the relationship between unions and labor-based parties in Argentina, Mexico, and Venezuela. In these three countries, the desire for political survival had united the populist politicians who were searching for political constituencies and the labor leaders who were trying to avoid replacement in alliances that generated partisan loyalties for organized labor. Politicians wanted political power, whereas labor leaders wanted concessions for their followers and limits for their rivals. The industrial weakness of workers in these late industrializing countries made the alliance with political parties more valuable. After labor support had helped populist labor-based parties gain power, these parties' policies changed labor market conditions by closing the economy and expanding state ownership, and they transformed collective bargaining through labor regulations. Labor regulations increased the collective bargaining power of workers and reduced the opportunities to challenge incumbent labor leaders.

Partisan loyalties were also crucial when these labor-based parties implemented market reforms in the 1990s. Because uncertainty was very high, and interests were harder to define due to the reshaping of eco-

197

nomic and political institutions, partisan ties provided a cue for labor behavior. Labor leaders could trust their allies who claimed that these policies were necessary, even though workers and unions were paying the costs of the transition. Partisan loyalties thus created incentives for labor restraint, because they facilitated bargaining by providing union leaders with longer time horizons for their relationships with partisan allies.

Partisan loyalties did not guarantee labor quiescence, however. Because some workers resented the costs of the transition or bore a larger share of it – most likely due to productivity differentials – alternative union leaders could increase their appeal by protesting market reforms. Incumbent union leaders wanted to remain in office and were torn between their partisan loyalty and the replacement threat that was created by the effects that market reforms implemented by their partisan allies had on their constituencies. The emergence of leadership or partisan competition made incumbent union leaders more militant to show that they had not sold out to their partisan allies, as rivals contended.

In turn, militancy did not necessarily lead to significant policy influence. Union monopoly made either militancy or restraint effective for achieving concessions because allied governments valued having loyal union leaders in organizations that controlled all workers in a sector. Instead, union competition weakened each of the competing unions that represented only a fraction of workers. Competition caused coordination problems by creating incentives to undermine other unions' strategies in their bids for members.

Therefore, when labor-based parties implemented market reforms, partisan loyalty induced the collaboration of allied union leaders. Assuming partisan loyalty, hence, the absence of leadership competition or union competition rendered labor's effective restraint (cooperation); that is, loyal unions collaborated in return for concessions. The emergence of leadership or partisan competition in a monopolistic union increased its militancy but did not affect its capacity to extract concessions from the allied government. It thus resulted in effective militancy (opposition). In contrast, union competition reduced the incentives of the government to make concessions. If combined with partisan monopoly, partisan loyalty facilitated labor restraint, but this collaboration was poorly paid by allies in government. The likely outcome was ineffective restraint (subordination) that rendered few or no concessions to labor unions. Finally, if the unions that were dealing with the government were competing for members and each one was affiliated with different political parties, they were combining union competition and partisan competition. In that case, their partisan competition increased their militancy, but this strategy was ineffectual for achieving their demands. In this case, the militancy of competing unions was ineffective (resistance).

The Role of Labor on the Bumpy Road to the Market

This book illuminates the Latin American transition to open economies and polities. Both transitions are part of larger global trends, but their simultaneity makes the region of particular importance for the comparative study of transitions. The findings of this study show that although economic constraints explain the policy shift of labor-based parties, state-centered arguments based on the skill of a handful of policy makers or "technopols" are not sufficient to explain the conflicts behind policy making during market reforms.[1] In a context of increasingly competitive polities, economic liberalization involves strategic interactions between the government and different social actors with a variety of ties with policy makers. As a result, the analysis of partisan coalitions and labor competition exemplifies the importance of building coalitions with social actors for the success of market reforms implemented in a competitive political environment. This analysis shows that coalition building exceeds the aggregation of economic interests and is profoundly influenced by institutional constraints and political dynamics.[2]

This book examines one of these interactions based on the influence of partisan ties and political dynamics on government and labor strategies. The literature that focuses on the insulation of policy makers disregards

---

[1] Williamson, ed. (1994), Geddes (1994), and Dominguez, ed. (1997) stress the importance of skillful policy makers and the concentration of authority in the executive for success of reforms.

[2] Contrary to the arguments of economic pluralists, this book demonstrates that economic interests were redefined politically in the interactions between unions and labor-based parties following a path opened by the new institutionalist literature – either rational choice (Bates 1989) or historic (Hall 1986) – on how political forces transform economic interests. Hence, along with a growing literature on the politics of economic transitions, these findings stress the political character of coalition building (Gibson 1997, Kessler 1998, Stark and Bruszt 1998, and Hagopian 1999) instead of deriving it from the aggregation of economic interest (Treissman 1998, Schamis 1999).

the role that concessions can play on the road to the market. It also assumes that labor had no influence in the process, following Geddes's (1995: 67) dictum that "working class opposition to adjustment has resulted in neither systematic defeats for incumbent politicians nor the wholesale abandonment of reform policies." However, this study describes the policy consequences of union-government interactions in a variety of instances and demonstrates that labor unions had policy input in the process of market reforms to different degrees. Even if labor unions did not derail the reform process, they contributed to its obstruction or success, and pace or shape in the three countries studied.[3] The quiescence of Argentine and Mexican unions facilitated the tasks of Menem and Salinas respectively, although unions were more successful in exercising policy input in the former country than in the latter. In Venezuela, labor unrest not only derailed Pérez's social and labor policies, but it also contributed to the demise of his reforms. These findings add nuance to an understanding of the scope and types of labor influence in the process of market reforms and highlight the importance of politics on the road to the market.

The institutionalist literature in political science has recognized the importance of politics in economic policy making. However, the units of analysis have been mainly constrained within geographical boundaries, either national or subnational. This book goes beyond emphasizing the political conflicts behind market reforms in three Latin American countries to provide a mechanism for assessing the different political dynamics at the national and sectoral level and even short-term changes within each unit of analysis. Moreover, the applicability of the theory presented here to different contexts within the three countries studied enhances its comparative implications for countries and economic sectors beyond those examined here. By facilitating theory testing for a small number of cases and the study of subnational units of analysis, its multilevel research design provides an alternative tool for theory building in comparative politics beyond union-government interactions. In particular, it can be used to develop theories that illuminate the impact that relationships between

---

[3] From an institutional perspective, O'Donnell's (1994) "delegative democracy" depicts the conditions that facilitate the emergence of plebiscitarian leaders who implement neoliberal reform in democratic contexts. These leaders are only episodically accountable to the electorate but lack accountability to other democratic institutions (O'Donnell 1994) or linkages to organized groups (Weyland 2000). The findings of this book show that market reforms have also been achieved with bargaining and inclusion of policy input by organized groups.

governments and other social actors have on policy making in other regions and contexts.

Labor-party Alliances Beyond Market Reforms

The uncertainty of economic interests during the time of reform reinforced the effect of partisan loyalties, leadership competition, and union competition on union-government interactions. Labor unions' political strategies had proved useful in the process of labor incorporation by populist parties. The expansion of state ownership and regulation in closed economies further reinforced the effectiveness of the unions' political strategies.

Political strategies still served unions at the critical juncture of institutional design when they could demand concessions in return for labor support for market reforms. In this context, partisan loyalties also served labor-based governments that retained labor support despite their drastic policy shift. Drastic policies served to show skeptical business actors the commitment of recent converts to the market creed. Hence, labor-based parties needed to retain the loyalty of their labor allies to implement reforms as smoothly and quickly as possible. Even if business demanded labor market deregulation, changes in labor organization regulations could have modified the opportunities for leadership competition and even reshaped the patterns of union competition. It was an opportunity for labor unions to recover their autonomy but at the expense of lost state subsidies when dealing with employers and increasing the exposure of incumbent union leaders to the threat of replacement. Governing labor-based parties refrained from reforming these regulations for two reasons. First, these parties wanted to limit the opportunities for the emergence of labor rivals associated with the electoral opposition by keeping their allies in control of unions. Second, these parties needed to signal to their labor allies that economic circumstances rather than ideological change had forced their conversion to neoliberalism. Keeping these regulations intact was necessary (but insufficient) to retain labor loyalty during the process of market reforms. Indeed, the reform of regulations on labor organization would have amounted to filing for "divorce," and hence reduced the comparative advantage provided by partisan loyalty in tempering labors' reaction to market reforms.

Partisan loyalties were valuable for both unions and partisan allies in government during the period of dramatic institutional change. However, for labor unions, the value of political resources and partisan loyalties was doomed to decline in open economies with restricted state intervention. Increasing capital mobility limited the ability of states to regulate labor markets and boost demand. Trade liberalization prevented employers from transferring higher labor costs to domestic consumers, making them more aware of the effect of such cost on competitiveness. State retrenchment curtailed public sector employment, and private managers paid more attention to profit than to partisan loyalties and electoral coalitions.[4] In addition, the growth of the informal sector to approximately half of nonagricultural employment also eroded the value of labor unions' political strategies. First, it curtailed the power of labor regulations, which applied only in the formal economy, thus prompting unions to generate alternative strategies based on the accumulation of organizational or industrial resources. Second, it reduced the electoral influence of formal workers in the government coalition, thereby inducing labor leaders toward new political alliances with groups in the informal sector and different political parties.

Hence, after economic liberalization, labor unions found it difficult to continue exchanging their autonomy for concessions. In some cases, they sought alternative strategies to reduce the dependency on the state that emerged from their original alliances. This book presents examples of unions that pursued new organizational and industrial strategies in Argentina and Mexico. In Argentina, the predominant strategy of large unions was to emphasize their role as service organizations rather than their industrial or political representation. In the process of privatization, they became private entrepreneurs who owned railroads, public utilities, cargo fleets, and mines. The unions expanded their social and professional service provision beyond their traditional membership in market competition among themselves.[5] In Mexico, large non-CTM unions also expanded their provision of social services, even if these services were still restricted to members. These unions were more aggressive, however, in adopting new forms of participation with management in industrial

---

[4] Between 1990 and 1997, public sector employment dropped 34% in Argentina, 13.2% in Mexico, and 14.8% in Venezuela (ILO 1998).
[5] Streek and Visser (1998) note a process of union regrouping in Germany and Netherlands provoked not by political strategies or interest representation, but by an evolutionary dynamic of unions as service organizations responding to the general principles of adaptive-economic rationality. Although labor reaction was different, the logic of adaptation was similar to my findings in Argentina.

restructuring. Although these new strategies did not imply the construction of new political alliances, in all three countries some union leaders helped to build opposition parties and attempted to extend their appeal to social movements in the informal sector. This strategy was followed by the Venezuelan "new unionism" allied with Causa R, the Argentine CTA loosely linked to the FREPASO and the Mexican independents often associated with the PRD.

The later strategy reverberated in the political arena. The new parties' electoral success with the citizenry further enhanced partisan competition in the unions. Electoral competition and partisan competition grew most dramatically in Venezuela after Pérez combined economic reforms with political decentralization, thus opening governorships and majorships to electoral competition. Causa R politicians and union leaders expanded their labor and electoral influence with those of MAS during the Pérez administration. Two factors made partisan competition in the labor movement easier in Venezuela than in Argentina and Mexico. Venezuela had a long tradition of partisan plurality in the union movement and included minorities in union executive committees through a proportional representation electoral system. In contrast, the Mexican "exclusion clause" and the Argentine electoral system with no minority representation in union leadership restricted leadership competition in those two countries.

The effect of partisan competition on the union movement was crucial for the policy and electoral achievements of labor-based parties that implemented market reform. Limited partisan competition prevented labor opposition to these parties and explains that Argentine and Mexican unions exercised restraint whereas Venezuelan unions militantly protested against reforms. The absence of labor unrest contributed to the success of Peronism and the PRI in implementing market reforms while winning elections during most of the 1990s. In contrast, labor unrest contributed to the demise of Pérez's market reforms and AD's electoral erosion.

The importance for labor-based parties of partisan competition in the unions lies in the dispute for their core constituencies. The erosion of labor support allowed the growth of electoral competition on the left, challenging the "popular" or "labor" character of labor-based parties. Electoral victories could persuade the most populist sectors of the party that the majority of the population supported the policy shift, while these sectors continued to have access to elective positions. In contrast, increasing electoral competition fostered internal tension within labor-based parties, which centered on the costs of the policy shift. The loss of votes to parties that challenged economic policies called into question the policy shift and contributed to the slowdown of reforms. Policy indecision further hindered the electoral appeal of these parties. Whereas AD suffered electoral decay, and market reforms lagged in Venezuela, both Peronism and the PRI sustained electoral support until 1997 and successfully implemented market reforms. In Chile, as well, a labor-based coalition including Socialist and Christian Democratic Parties gained power and implemented promarket policies.[6] The absence of labor opposition and the weakness of the Communist Party restricted electoral competition to the left of this coalition and facilitated its success in keeping these policies and electoral power during the 1990s. The importance of labor appeal for labor-based parties is crucial in terms of policy implementation and its symbolic value for electoral competition. It thus contributes to the failure or success of labor-based parties on the road to the market.

I began this book by discussing the simultaneous implementation of market reforms by labor-based governments and the challenges faced by labor unions. I concluded by pointing to the implications of union-government interactions for labor-based parties after their conversion to the market creed. At a moment of high uncertainty created by institutional change, political interactions were crucial in shaping the path of political and economic transitions. However, mere words cannot convey what I learned from various personal accounts of workers, union leaders, politicians, and individual citizens in the three countries. The distance imposed by geography and scholarly analysis has helped me to understand the complexity of this political phenomenon by simplifying it. Only the close experience of living in the three countries has enabled me to understand the importance of politics as a collective enterprise.

[6] General Pinochet adopted promarket policies in Chile. However, the new center-left coalition continued with similar macroeconomic policies, privatization, and trade liberalization, albeit with a larger social component (Weyland 1999).

Bibliography

Acedo Agulo, Blanca Margarita. 1990. "En la construcción y consolidación del estado cardenista. 1936–1940." In *Historia de la CTM, 1936–1990*, vol 1. Mexico City: UNAM.

Acuña, Carlos. 1994. "Politics and Economics in the Argentina of the Nineties (Or, Why the Future No Longer Is What It Used to Be)." In *Democracy, Markets and Structural Reform in Latin America*. William Smith, Carlos Acuña, and Eduardo Gamarra, eds. New Brunswick, NJ: Transaction Publishers.

———. 1995. "Política y economía en la Argentina de los 90 (o porque el futuro no es lo que solía ser)." In *La nueva matriz política argentina*. Carlos Acuña, ed. Buenos Aires: Nueva Visión.

ADEFA (Association of Automotive Industries). 1993. *Industria Automotriz Argentina 1993*. Buenos Aires: ADEFA.

Agosín, Manuel R., and Ricardo Ffrench-Davis. 1995. "Trade Liberalization and Growth: Recent Experiences in Latin America." *Journal of Interamerican Studies and World Affairs*, 37, no. 3: 9–58.

Aguilar García, Javier, and Lorenzo Arrieta. 1990. "En la fase más aguda de la crisis y en el inicio de la reeestructuración o modernización." In *Historia de la CTM: 1936–1990*, vol. II. Javier Aguilar García, ed. Mexico City: Instituto de Investigaciones Sociales, UNAM.

Albarracín, Santiago. 1995. "Privatisation of the Argentine State-owned Oil Company." *Journal of Energy and Natural Resources Law* 13 (May): 108–19.

Aldana, Francisco. 1988. "La renta petrolera y el ascenso del quinismo." In *Cuatro sindicatos nationales de industria*. Javier Aguilar García, ed. Sinaloa, Mexico: Universidad Autónoma de Sinaloa.

Alonso, Guillermo V. 1998. "Democracia y reformas: las tensiones entre decretismo y deliberación. El caso de la reforma previsional argentina." *Desarrollo Económica* 38, no. 150 (July–September): 595–626.

Alvarado, Arturo. 1990. "La fundación del PNR." In *El partido en el poder*. Mexico City: IEPES.

Bibliography

Alvarez, Michael, Geoffrey Garrett, and Peter Lange. 1991. "Government Partisanship, Labor Organization, and Macroeconomic Performance." *American Political Science Review* 85, no. 2 (June): 539–57.

Ambrus, Steven. 1992. "Causa R: The Power of Persuasion that Draws and Repels Business." *Veneconomy Monthly* (Caracas), December: 5–6.

Anses (National Administration of Social Security) Argentina. 1997. "Decreto 1590/96. Libre elección de activos. Variación neta de titutales que ejercieron la opción. Período enero-abril de 1997." Administración Nacional de Seguridad Social, Buenos Aires.

Arismendi, León, and Francisco Iturraspe. 1990. "Sistemas electorales sindicales." In *Mandatao Político, Evolución Electoral, Comunicación y Sociedad*. Manuel Vicente Magallanes, ed. Caracas, Venezuela: Publicaciones del Consejo Supremo Electoral.

Arnaud, Alberto. 1992a. "La decentralización educativa y el Sindicato Nacional de Trabajadores de la Educación, 1978–1988." CIDE, Mexico City. Unpublished working paper.

1992b. "La evolución de los grupos hegemónicos e el SNTE." Working paper, no. 3, *Estudios Políticos*. CIDE, Mexico City.

1993. "Historia de una profesión: maestros de educación primaria en México: 1887–1993." Centro de Estudios Internacionales, El Colegio de México. Unpublished master's thesis.

1994. "La federalización de la educación básica y normal (1978–1994)." *Política y Gobierno* (Mexico City) 1, no. 2.

Arteaga, Arnulfo. 1990. "Ford: un largo y sinuoso camino." In *Negociación colectiva y conflicto laboral en México*. Graciela Bensusán and Samuel León, eds. Mexico City: Fundación Ebert and Flacso.

1992. "La reestructuración de la industria automotriz en México y sus repercusiones en el viejo núcleo fabril." In *Proceso de trabajo y relaciones laborales en la industria automotriz en México*. Arnulfo Arteaga, ed. Mexico City: Fundación Ebert and UAM-Iztapalapa.

Ashenfelter, Orley, and George E. Johnson. 1969. "Bargaining Theory, Trade Unions and Industrial Strike Activity." *American Economic Review* 59, no. 40: 35–49.

Aspe, Pedro. 1993. *El camino mexicano de la transformación económica*. Mexico City: Fondo de Cultura Económica.

Avila Carrizo, Enrique, and Humberto Martínez Brizuela. 1990. *Historia del movimiento magisterial 1910–1989*. Mexico City: Ediciones Quinto Sol.

Aziz Nassif, Alberto. 1989. *El estado mexicano y la CTM*. Mexico City: Editorial La Casa Chata.

Azpiazu, Daniel, Eduardo Basualdo, and Miguel Khavisse. 1987. *El nuevo poder económico en la Argentina*. Buenos Aires: Nueva América.

Baizán, Mario. 1993. *Conversaciónes con Carlos Menem*. Buenos Aires: Editorial Fraterna.

Banamex. 1993. *Mexico Social*. Mexico City: Grupo Financiero Banamex-Accival.

Barbosa, Fabio. 1992. "La reestructuración de Pemex." In *El Cotidiano* (Mexico City) 46, March–April: 45–8.

1993. "Los retos del sindicalismo petrolero." In *El Cotidiano* (Mexico City) 56, July: 24–6.

1995. "Los trabajadores petroleros hoy." In *Trabajo y democracia hoy* (Mexico City) 23: 12–13.

Bastos, Carlos, and Manuel Abdala. 1995. *La transformación del sector eléctrico argentino*. Santiago, Chile: Editorial Antártica.

Basualdo, Eduardo. 1987. *Deuda Externa y Poder Económico en la Argentina*. Buenos Aires: Editorial Nueva América.

Basurto, Jorge. 1999. "Populism in Mexico: From Cárdenas to Cuauhtémoc." In *Populism in Latin America*. Michael L. Conniff, ed. Tuscaloosa: University of Alabama Press.

Bates, Robert. 1989. *Beyond the Miracle of the Market: The Political Economy of Agrarian Development in Kenia*. Cambridge: Cambridge University Press.

Bates, Robert and Anne Kruger. 1993. "Generalizations Arising from the Country Studies." In *Political and Economic Interaction in Economic Policy Reform*. Robert Bates and Anne Kruger, eds. Cambridge, MA: Blackwell.

Bensusán, Graciela. 1990. "Políticas de Modernización y Relaciones Laborales en las empresas paraestatales." In *Relaciones laborales en empresas paraestatales*. Graciela Bensusán and Carlos García, eds. Mexico City: Fundación Ebert.

1992. "Institucionalización laboral en México. Los años de la definición (1917–1931)." Facultad de Ciencias Políticas y Sociales, Universidad Nacional Autónoma de México, Mexico City. Unpublished doctoral dissertation.

1994a. "Los determinantes institucionales de la flexibilización laboral." *Revista Mexicana de Sociología* (Mexico City) 1: 45–78.

1994b. "Entre candados y dientes. La agenda laboral del TLCAN." *Perfiles Latinoamericanos*, 3d year, no. 4 (June): 109–41.

1997. "Estrategias sindicales y relaciones laborales frente al TLC: el caso de México." Paper presented at the meeting of the Latin American Studies Association, April 17–19.

Bensusán, Graciela and Carlos García. 1993. *Opiniones sindicales sobre la reforma laboral*. Mexico City: Fundación Ebert.

Bertranou, Julián F. 1995. "La política de la reforma a la seguridad social en México. Análisis de la formulación del Sistema de Ahorro para el Retiro." *Estudios Sociológicos* 37 (January–April).

Betancourt, Keila, Samuel Freije, and Gustavo Marquez. 1995. *Mercado laboral. Instituciones y regulaciones*. Caracas, Venezuela: IESA.

Bizberg, Ilán. 1990. *Estado y sindicalismo en México*. Mexico City: El Colegio de México.

Bocco, Arnoldo and Repetto Gaston. 1932. "Elarte Narrativo y La Magia," Diswsión. In *Obras Completes*. Buenos Aires: Emecé Editores, 1974.

1944. "Funes el Memovioso," Ficciones. In *Obras Completes*. Buenos Aires: Emecé Editores, 1974.

1991. "Empresas públicas, crisis fiscal y restructuración financiera del Estado." In *Privatizaciones. Restructuración del Estado y la Sociedad*. Arnoldo Bocco and Naum Misnburg, eds. Buenos Aires: Ediciones Letra Buena.

Borges, Jorge Luis. 1964. "Buenos Aires, El Otro, El Nismo." In *Obras Completes*. Buenos Aires: Emecé Editores, 1974.

Bottome, Robert. 1989. "The Economic Program: A Progress Report." *Veneconomy Monthly* (Caracas), March: 2–5.

———. 1992. "IVSS Restructuring Plan: Radical, Ambitious and Maybe Even Workable." *Veneconomy Monthly* (Caracas), September: 10–12.

———. 1993. "The Privatization Effort: Back on Track." *Veneconomy Monthly* (Caracas), February.

Bottome, Robert and John Sweeney. 1989. "Trade Policy: The Doors Open at Last." *Veneconomy Monthly* (Caracas), May: 3–5.

Bouzas, Roberto. 1993. "La economia argentina a comienzos de los 90." *Desarrollo Económico* (Buenos Aires) 33, no. 129.

Brooks, Sarah. 1998. "Political Dynamics of Pension Reform in Argentina." Paper presented at the 1998 meeting of the Latin American Studies Association, Chicago, September 24–6.

Britos, Oraldo, ed. 1984. *Mensajes del Coronel*. Buenos Aires: Pequén Ediciones.

Burgess, Katrina. 1995. "Un divorcio a medias: reforma económica y políticas laborales en España." *Política y gobierno* (Mexico City), vol. II, no. 2: 207–42.

———. 1996. "Thresholds of Institutional Change: Economic Reform and Party-Labor Relations in Mexico." Paper prepared for the conference "Economic Reform and Civil Society in Latin America." David Rockefeller Center for Latin American Studies, Harvard University, April 12.

———. 1998a. "Alliances Under Stress: Economic Reform and Party-Union Relations in Mexico, Spain, and Venezuela." Department of Politics, Princeton University. Unpublished doctoral dissertation.

———. 1998b. "Is the Party Over? Economic Reforms and Party-Union Relations in Venezuela." Paper presented at the 1998 meeting of the Latin American Studies Association, Chicago, September 24–6.

Calmfors, Lars and John Driffill. 1988. "Centralization and Wage Barganing." *Economic Policy* 3, no. 1 (April): 13–61.

Calvo, Ernesto. 1999. "Promoting Power: From Import Protection to Export Promotion in Latin America." Paper presented at the Annual Meeting of the American Political Science Association, Atlanta, September 2–5.

Camacho, Manuel. 1980. *El futuro inmediato*. Mexico City: Editorial Siglo XXI.

Cameron, David. 1984. "Social Democracy, Corporatism, Labor Quiescence, and the Representation of Economic Interest in Advance Capitalist Society." In *Order and Conflict in Contemporary Capitalism*. John H. Goldthorpe, ed. New York, NY: Oxford University Press.

Campuzano Montoya, Irma. 1990. "El impacto de la crisis en la CTM." *Revista Mexicana de Sociología* (Mexico City) 52, no. 3: 161–90.

Canitrot, Adolfo. 1980. "Discipline as the Central Objective of Economic Policy: An Essay on the Economy Programme of the Argentine Government since 1976." *World Development* 8: 918.

———. 1981. "Teoría y práctica del liberalismo: Política antiinflacionaria y apertura económica en la Argentina, 1976–1981." *Desarrollo Económico* 21, no. 82 (July–September): 131–89.

1994. "Crisis and Transformation of the Argentine State (1978–1992)." In *Democracy, Markets, and Structural Reform in Latin America. Argentina, Bolivia, Brazil, Chile, and Mexico.* William Smith, Carlos Acuña, and Eduardo Gamarra, eds. New Brunswick, NJ: North-South Center and Transaction Publishers.

CANTV. 1991. "Contrato Colectivo 1991–92." CANTV, Caracas.

1993. "Contrato Colectivo 1993–94." CANTV, Caracas.

1995. "Contrato Colectivo 1995–96." CANTV, Caracas.

1996a. "Pliegos presentados desde 1991." Internal document of the Industrial Relations Department, Caracas.

1996b. "Evolución del salario promedio vs. salario mínimo nacional (Personal amparado por el Contrato Colectivo)." Internal document of the Industrial Relations Department, Caracas.

Cardoso, Fernando Henrique and Enzo Faletto. 1971. *Dependencia y desarrollo en America Latina.* Mexico City: Siglo Veintiuno.

Carr, Barry. 1976. *El movimiento obrero y la política en Mexico, 1910–1929.* Two volumes. Mexico City: SepSetentas.

Carrillo, Jorge. 1993. "La Ford en México: restructuración industrial y cambio en las relaciones sociales." El Colegio de México, Centro de Estudios Sociológicos, Mexico City. Unpublished doctoral dissertation.

Cassia, Antonio. 1994a. "No soy un dirigente empresario." Interview by Luis Vásquez. *Revista Gremial*, year 3, no. 29 (March).

1994b. "Mensaje del secretario general de la CGT ante la asamblea de la OIT." Buenos Aires: CGT.

Catalano, Ana María, and Marta S. Novick. 1994. "Reconversión productiva y estrategias sindicales en la Argentina: renovación o ajuste táctico?" Buenos Aires. Unpublished manuscript.

1998. "The Argentine Automotive Industry: Redefining Production Strategies, Markets, and Labor Relations." In *Transforming the Latin American Automobile Industry.* John P. Tuman and John T. Morris, eds. Armonk, NY: M.E. Sharpe.

Cavarozzi, Marcelo. 1984. *Sindicatos y política en Argentina.* Buenos Aires: Estudios Cedes.

1987. *Autoritarismo y democracia (1955–1983).* Buenos Aires: Centro Editor de América Latina.

CENM (Center for Studies of the New Majority). *Informes sobre elecciones gremiales,* various issues. Buenos Aires: Centro de Estudios para la Nueva Mayoría.

Centeno, Miguel Angel. 1994. *Democracy Within Reason: Technocratic Revolution in Mexico.* University Park: Pennsylvania State University Press.

Central Bank of Venezuela. 1990. "Estadísticas Socio-Laborales de Venezuela. Series Históricas, 1936–1990." Hector Valecillos, ed. Sections I and II. Caracas: Banco Central de Venezuela.

CGT (General Confederation of Labor). 1992. "Proyecto del sindicalismo ante la reestructuracion de las relaciones laborales." Buenos Aires. Internal document.

1993. "Las cuentas fiscales cierran; las cuentas sociales no." Declaration of the Central Confederal Committee of the CGT. Buenos Aires, May 19.

1994a. "Posición sobre reforma laboral en la conferencia Ciosl-Orit: desarrollo económico y derechos laborales." Buenos Aires. Internal document.
1994b. "Declaración del Comité Central Confederal." Buenos Aires, September 2.
1994c. "Constitution." Buenos Aires.
1995. "Exclusión laboral, políticas gubernamentales y del sindicalismo en la Argentina." Lima, Peru: Instituto Jaureche. Paper presented at ILO Regional Forum on Social Exclusion, Lima, January 17–19.
n.d. "Empleo y Flexibilidad Laboral." Internal document.
Chalmers, Douglas A., Carlos M. Vilas, Kathrine Hite, Scott B. Martin, Kerianne Piester, and Monique Segarra. 1997. *The New Politics of Inequality in Latin America: Rethinking Participation and Representation.* Oxford, UK: Oxford University Press.
Clark, Marjorie Ruth. 1934. *Organized Labor in Mexico.* Chapel Hill: University of North Carolina Press.
Clifton, Judith. 1995. "The Restructuring of State-Labour Relations in Mexico during the Salinas de Gortari Presidency: The Case of the Sindicato de Telefonistas de la República Mexicana." St. Anthony's College, Oxford University, March. Unpublished manuscript.
Collier, David. 1995. "Trajectory of a Concept: 'Corporatism' in the Study of Latin American Politics." In *Latin America in Comparative Perspective: New Approaches to Method and Analysis.* Peter Smith, ed. Boulder, CO: Westview Press.
Collier, Ruth Berins. 1992. *The Contradictory Alliance: State-Labor Relations and Regime Change in Mexico.* Berkeley, CA: Institute for International and Area Studies, University of California.
Collier, Ruth Berins, and David Collier. 1991. *Shaping the Political Arena.* Princeton, NJ: Princeton University Press.
1979. "Inducement versus Constraints: Disaggregating 'Corporatism.'" *American Political Science Review* 73: 967–86.
Collier, Ruth Berins, and James Samstad. 1995. "Mexican Labor and Structural Reform: New Unionism or Old Stalemate?" In *The Challenge of Institutional Reform in Mexico.* Riordan Roett, ed. Boulder, CO: Lynne Rienner.
Commission for the Restructuring of the IVSS. 1989. "Informe al Presidente Carlos Andrés Pérez." Presidential report from representatives: Ivan Lansberg Henríquez for the Presidency, Angel Zerpa Mirabal for the CTV, and Luis Jose Silva Luongo for Fedecámaras. Caracas.
1992. "Informe de Agosto de 1992." Caracas.
Conaghan, Catherine, and James Malloy. 1994. *Unsettling Statecraft: Democracy and Neoliberalism in the Central Andes.* Pittsburgh, PA: Pittsburgh University Press.
Congress of the Republic of Venezuela. 1990. "Proyecto de Ley Orgánica de Prestaciones Sociales de los Trabajadores." Caracas.
Conniff, Michael L. 1999. "Introduction." In *Populism in Latin America.* Michael L. Conniff, ed. Tuscaloosa: University of Alabama Press.
Cook, Maria Lorena. 1996. *Organizing Dissent.* University Park: Pennsylvania State University Press.

1995. "State-Labor Relations in Mexico: Old Tendencies and New Trends." In *Mexico Faces the 21ˢᵗ Century*. Donald E. Schulz and Edward J. Williams, eds. Greenwich, CT: Greenwood Press.

Coppedge, Michael. 1993. "Parties and Society in Mexico and Venezuela." *Comparative Politics* 23, no. 3 (April): 253–72.

1994. *Strong Parties and Lame Ducks*. Stanford, CA: Stanford University Press.

Cordera, Rolando, and Ricardo Rocha. 1994. *Mexico: Los años del cambio. Una conversación con Carlos Salinas de Gortari*. Mexico City: Editorial Diana, Mexico.

CORDIPLAN. 1990. *El gran viraje: lineamientos generales del VIII Plan de la Nación*. Caracas: CORDIPLAN.

Cornelious, Wayne A. 1973. "Nation Building, Participation and Distribution: The Politics of Social Reform Under Cárdenas." In *Crisis, Choice and Change: Historical Studies in Political Development*. Gabriel A. Almond, Scott C. Flanagan, and Robert J. Mundt, eds. Boston, MA: Little, Brown.

CORPOVEN (Division of Petroleum of Venezuela). 1991. "Contrato Colectivo de Trabajo 1990." Caracas: Cromotip C.A.

1993. "Contrato Colectivo de Trabajo 1992." Caracas: Cromotip C.A.

Corrales, Javier. 1996. "From Market-Creators to Market-Correctors: Executive-Ruling Party Relations in the Economic Reforms of Argentina and Venezuela, 1989–93." Harvard University, Cambridge, MA. Unpublished doctoral dissertation.

1998a. "Do Economic Crises Contribute to Economic Reform? Argentina and Venezuela in the 1990s." *Political Science Quarterly* 112, no. 4 (Winter): 617–44.

1998b. "Coalitions and Corporate Choices in Argentina, 1976–1994: The Recent Private Sector Support for Privatizations." *Studies in Comparative International Development* 32, no. 4 (Winter): 24–51.

Forthcoming. "Co-opting Bolivar: Chavez plays 'Simon Says.'" Hopscotch.

Corrales, Javier and Imelda Cisneros. 1999. "Corporatism, Trade Liberalization, and Sectoral Responses: The Case of Venezuela, 1989–1999." *World Development* 27, no. 12: 2090–122.

Cortés, Fernando. 1999. "Acerca de la reforma y la desigualdad económica." Paper presented at the conference on Democracy and Distribution, Yale University, New Haven, CT, November 11–12.

Cox Edwards, Alejandra. 1997. "Labor Market Regulation in Latin America: An Overview." In *Labor Markets in Latin America*. Sebastian Edwards and Nora Lustig, eds. Washington, DC: Brookings Institution.

Craig, Anne L., and Wayne A. Cornelious. 1995. "Houses Divided: Parties and Political Reform in Mexico." In *Building Democratic Institutions: Party Systems in Latin America*. Scott Mainwaring and Timothy R. Scully, eds. Stanford, CA: Stanford University Press.

Crisp, Brian. 1997. "Presidential Behavior in a System with Strong Parties: Venezuela, 1958–1995." In *Presidentialism and Democracy in Latin America*. Scott Mainwaring and Matthew Soberg Shuggart, eds. Cambridge: Cambridge University Press.

1998. "Lessons from Economic Reform in the Venezuelan Democracy." *Latin American Research Review* 33, no. 1: 7–41.

Crouch, Colin. 1982. *Trade Unions: The Logic of Collective Action*. Cambridge, UK: Fontana Paperback.

Cruz Bencomo, Miguel Angel. 1989. "El quinismo, una historia del charrismo petrolero." *El Cotidiano* (Mexico City) 28, March–April: 19–21.

CTA (Argentine Workers Central). 1994. "CTA y CGT frente al proyecto oficial de reforma laboral." Buenos Aires.

1997. "Conclusiones del 1er Congreso Nacional de Abogados." Buenos Aires: CTA (October 10–11).

n.d. "Documento del Congreso de los Trabajadores Argentinos sobre el proyecto de Reformas a la Legislación Laboral." Buenos Aires.

CTERA (Argentine Federation of Teachers). 1991. *Memoria 1990/91*. Annual report. Buenos Aires.

1992a. *Estatuto*. Constitution. Buenos Aires.

1992b. *Memoria 1991/92*. Annual report. Buenos Aires.

1993. *Memoria 1992/93*. Annual report. Buenos Aires.

1994. *Memoria 1993/94*. Annual report. Buenos Aires.

CTM (Confederation of Mexican Workers). 1990. "Memorias de la CXI Asamblea Ordinaria de la CTM." Annual report. Mexico City.

1991. "Memorias de la CXII Asamblea Ordinaria de la CTM." Annual report. Mexico City.

1992. "Memorias de la CXIII Asamblea Ordinaria de la CTM." Annual report. Mexico City.

1993a. "Memorias de la CXV Asamblea Ordinaria de la CTM." Annual report. Mexico City.

1993b. "La CTM y la economía de los trabajadores." Internal document. Mexico City.

1994a. "Memorias de la CXVI Asamblea Ordinaria de la CTM." Annual report. Mexico City.

1994b. "Congreso Nacional de Empresas y Organismos del Sector Social." In *CTM: Cincuenta años de lucha obrera*. Mexico City: Instituto de Capacitación Política, PRI.

CTV (Venezuelan Confederation of Workers). 1987. *Antecedentes y Testimonios de los Congresos de la CTV*, vol. IV. Caracas: INAESIN/ILDIS.

1990a. "Informe del Comité Ejecutivo." Report of the Executive Committee of the Confederación de Trabajadores de Venezuela, Caracas.

1990b. "Privatización y reestructuración. Lineamientos de la CTV." Commission on Privatization, X Congress of the Venezuelan Workers Confederation, Caracas, March 16–17.

1991a. "Estatutos." Constitution. Caracas.

1991b. "Posición de la CTV frente a la propuesta de Cambio del Régimen de Prestaciones Sociales." Internal document. Caracas (April).

n.d. "La seguridad social, crisis y alternativas para un nuevo modelo." Comisión de Seguridad Social del XI Congreso de la Confederación de Trabajadores de Venezuela, Caracas.

Cukierman, Alex, and Mariano Tommasi. 1998. "When Does it Take a Nixon to Go to China?" *American Economic Review* 88, no. 1 (March): 180–97.

Bibliography

Danani, Claudia. 1994. "El proyecto de libre afiliación a las obras sociales: análisis y perspectivas." Buenos Aires. Unpublished manuscript.

De La Garza, Enrique. 1989. "Quién ganó en Telmex?" *El Cotidiano* (Mexico City) 32, November–December: 27–30.

——— 1993. *Reestructuración productiva y respuesta sindical en México.* Mexico City: Instituto de Investigaciones Económicas (UNAM), División Ciencias Sociales y Humanidades (UAM-I).

——— 1994. "Sindicato y restructuración productiva en México." *Revista Mexicana de Sociologia* (Mexico City), no. 1: 3–28.

De La Garza, Enrique, et al. 1994. *Historia de la Industria Eléctrica en México*, vol. I. Mexico City: Universidad Autónoma Metropolitana.

De La Garza, Enrique, and Javier Melgoza. 1998. "Restructuración y cambio en las relaciones laborales en la telefonía mexicana." In *La privatización de las telecomunicaciones en América Latina.* Jorge Walter and Cecilia Senén González, eds. Buenos Aires: Eudeba.

De Lara Rangel, Maria Eugenia. 1990. "De la dispersión a la unificación del movimiento obrero." In *Historia de la CTM: 1936–1990*, vol. 1. Javier Aguilar García, ed. Mexico City: Instituto de Investigaciones Sociales, UNAM.

DGI (General Tax Agency). 1995. "Número de afiliados por AFJyP y tipo de afiliado al 28 de febrero de 1995." Buenos Aires: Dirección General Impositiva.

Díaz, Rodolfo. 1997. "Engaging Labor and Labor Unions to Strenghen Democratic Politics in a Market Economy." Paper presented at the X NOMOS seminar of the Center for International Affairs in Harvard University, American Academy of Science, Cambridge, MA, May 1–3.

Díaz, Rolando. n.d. "El movimiento sindical ante la crisis." Caracas: Instituto Latinoamericano de Investigaciones Sociales, Fundación Friederich Ebert.

Díaz-Alejandro, Carlos. 1984. "Latin America in the 1930s." In *Latin America in the 1930s.* Rosemary Thorp, ed. Oxford, UK: Macmillan.

Di Tella, Guido. 1983. *Argentina under Perón, 1973–76.* London: Macmillan.

Di Tella, Torcuato. 1965. "Populism and Reform in Latin America." In *Obstales to Change in Latin America.* Claudio Veliz, ed. London: Oxford University Press.

——— 1981. "Working-class Organization and Politics in Argentina." *Latin American Research Review* 16, no. 2: 61–95.

Domínguez, Jorge I., ed. 1997. *Technopols: Freeing Politics and Markets in Latin America in the 1990s.* University Park, PA: Pennsylvania State University Press.

Domínguez, Jorge I., and James McCann. 1992. "Whither the PRI? Explaining Voter Defection in the 1988 Mexican Presidential Elections." *Electoral Studies* 11, no. 3 (September): 207–22.

Doyon, Louise. 1988. "El crecimiento sindical bajo el peronismo." In *La formación del sindicalismo peronista.* J.C. Torre, ed. Buenos Aires: Legasa.

Drake, Paul. 1991. "Comments to The Political Economy of Latin American Populism." In *The Macroeconomic of Populism.* Rudiger Dornbush and Sebastian Edwards, eds. Chicago: Chicago University Press.

ECLAC (United Nations Economic Commission on Latin America and the Caribbean). 1983. *Statistical Yearbook for Latin America*. Santiago, Chile: United Nations.

1984. *Precios, Salarios y Empleo en la Argentina*. Santiago, Chile: United Nations.

1985. *Statistical Yearbook for Latin America*. Santiago, Chile: United Nations.

1993. *Economic Survey of Latin America and the Caribbean 1991*, vol. II. Santiago, Chile: United Nations.

1995. *Economic Survey of Latin America and the Caribbean 1994*, vol. II. Santiago, Chile: United Nations.

Edwards, Sebastian. 1995. *Crisis and Reform in Latin America*. New York: Oxford University Press.

Elizondo, Carlos, and Blanca Heredia. 1999. "La instrumentación política de la reforma económica en México, 1985–1999." CIDE, Mexico. Unpublished manuscript.

Ellner, Steve. 1980. *Los partidos políticos y su disputa por el control del movimiento sindical en Venezuela, 1936–1948*. Caracas: Universidad Católica Andrés Bello.

1989. "Organized Labor's Political Influence and Party Ties in Venezuela: *Acción Democrática* and its Labor Leadership." *Journal of Interamerican Studies and World Affairs* 31, no. 4 (Winter): 91–120.

1993. *Organized Labor in Venezuela, 1958–1991*. Wilmington, DE: Scholarly Resources Inc.

1999. "The Impact of Privatization on Labor in Venezuela: Radical Reorganization or Moderate Adjustment?" *Political Power and Social Theory* 13: 109–45.

ENRE (National Regulator of Electricity). 1998. "El informe eléctrico: Cinco años de regulación y control. 1993-abril-1998." Buenos Aires: ENRE.

Etchemendy, Sebastian, and Vicente Palermo. 1998. "Conflicto y concertación. Gobierno, Congreso y organizaciones de interés en la reforma laboral del primer gobierno de Menem (1989–1995)." *Desarrollo Económico* 37, no. 148 (January–March): 559–90.

Executive Power of Argentina. 1992. "Projecto de reforma a la ley de asociaciones sindicales no. 23,551." Project of law presented to the National Congress, Buenos Aires.

Farber, Henry. 1986. "The Analysis of Union Behavior." In *Handbook of Labor Economics*. Orley C. Ashenfelter and Richard Layard, eds. Amsterdam: North-Holland.

FATLyF (Federation of Light and Power Workers). 1988. "Estatutos." Buenos Aires: FATLyF.

1992. "XXXIV Congreso Ordinario de la Federación Argentina de Trabajadores de Luz y Fuerza." Proceedings of the annual congress, Mar del Plata, Argentina.

1993. *Memoria y Balance 1992*. Annual report. Buenos Aires.

1994a. "Luz y Fuerza Garantia de Excelencia." Buenos Aires: FATLyF.

1994b. *Memoria y Balance 1993*. Annual report. Buenos Aires.

1995. *Memoria y Balance 1994*. Annual report. Buenos Aires.

1996. *Memoria y Balance 1995*. Annual report. Buenos Aires.

Feldman, Silvio. 1991. "Tendencias a la sindicalización en Argentina." *Estudios del Trabajo* (Buenos Aires), no. 2: 79–109.

Fernández, Arturo. 1997. *Flexibilización laboral y crisis del sindicalismo.* Buenos Aires: Espacio Editorial.

Fernández, Raquel and Dani Rodrik. 1991. "Resistance to Reform: Status Quo Bias in the Presence of Individual-Specific Uncertainty." *American Economic Review* 81, no. 5 (December): 1146–55.

Fernández, Roque. 1991. "What Have Populists Learned from Hyperinflation?" In *The Macroeconomics of Populism in Latin America.* Rudisher Dornbush and Sebastian Edwards, eds. Chicago: University of Chicago Press.

Ferreira Rubio, Delia, and Mateo Goretti. 1996. "Cuando el presidente gobierna solo: Menem y los decretos de necesidad y urgencia hasta la reforma constitucional (Julio 1989–Agosto 1994)." *Desarrollo Economómico* 36: 443–74.

FETRATEL (Federation of Telephone Workers). 1981. "Estatutos." Constitution, Caracas.

——— 1989. "Fetratel ante la Privatización." VII Conference of Fetratel Workers, Barquisimeto, Venezuela, September 26–9.

——— 1993. "Reglamento Electoral para los Directores Accionarios Tipo 'C' de la Junta Directiva de CANTV." Regulations for the election of the directors in representation of workers' share holders. Caracas.

FIV (Investment Fund of Venezuela). 1991. "Agreement between Gerber Torres, President of the FIV in representation of the Republic, Carlos Lander and Cesar Olarte in representation of the CTV and Salomón Coronel in representation of Fetratel." Caracas, November 15.

FOETRA (Federation of Telephone Workers of the Republic of Argentina). 1989. *Estatuto de Foetra.* Constitution. FOETRA, Secretariado Nacional, Buenos Aires.

——— 1991. *Memoria y Balance 1990.* Annual report. Buenos Aires.

——— 1992a. "Nuevo Convenio Colectivo de Trabajo No. 201/92." Collective bargaining agreement, *Unidad Telefónica.* Buenos Aires: FOETRA.

——— 1992b. *Memoria y Balance 1991.* Annual report. Buenos Aires.

——— 1993. *Memoria y Balance 1992.* Annual report. Buenos Aires.

——— 1994. *Memoria y Balance 1993.* Annual report. Buenos Aires.

——— 1995. *Memoria y Balance 1994.* Annual report. Buenos Aires.

Foewaker, Joe. 1993. *Popular Mobilization in Mexico: The Teachers' Movement, 1977–87.* Cambridge: Cambridge University Press.

Ford Motor Company. 1989. "Contrato Colectivo de Trabajo, 1989–92." Valencia, Carabobo, Venezuela.

——— 1989–91. "Contrato Colectivo de Trabajo que celebran por una parte Ford Motor Company, S.A. de C.V. y por la otra parte el Sindicato nacional de Trabajdoares de Ford Motor Company-CTM." Mexico City.

——— 1991–3. "Contrato Colectivo de Trabajo que celebran por una parte Ford Motor Company, S.A. de C.V. y por la otra parte el Sindicato nacional de Trabajdoares de Ford Motor Company-CTM." Mexico City.

——— n.d. "Programas de Mejora de Calidad y Productividad del Sector." Industry pamphlet.

n.d. "Impact of Pay for Knowledge System." Industry pamphlet.

Francés, Antonio, Felipe Aguerreve, Raquel Benbunam, and María Eugenia Boza. 1993. *Aló Venezuela! Apertura y privatización de las telecomunicaciones*. Caracas: Ediciones IESA.

Franzosi, Roberto. 1995. *The Puzzle of Strikes: Class and State Strategies in Postwar Italy*. Cambridge: Cambridge University Press.

Frieden, Jeffry. 1991. "Invested Interests: The Politics of National Economic Policies in a World of Global Finance." *International Organization* 45, no. 4 (Autumn): 425–51.

1992. *Debt, Development and Democracy*. Princeton, NJ: Princeton University Press.

1995. "Labor and Politics of Exchange Rates: The Case of the European System." In *The Workers of Nations: Industrial Relations in a Global Economy*. Sanford Jacoby, ed. New York: Oxford University Press.

Friedmann, Santiago, Nora Lustig, and Arianna Legovini. 1995. "Mexico: Social Spending and Food Subsidies during Adjustment in the 1980s." In *Coping With Austerity*. Nora Lustig, ed. Washington, DC: The Brookings Institution.

Funaro, Rita. 1990. "Severance Benefits Law: Promises, Promises." *Veneconomy Monthly* (Caracas), November: 2–4.

Funes de Rioja, Daniel. 1992–3. "Necesidad de adecuación del régimen laboral y de la seguridad social: sus condicionantes e implicancias." Consejo Empresario Argentino, Buenos Aires.

1994. "El impacto de la globalización sobre las normas laborales en el contexto latinoamericano." Unión Industrial Argentina, Buenos Aires. Unpublished manuscript.

Gamboa, Teresa. 1993. "La privatización y sus efectos laborales." Proceedings of the III Venezuelan Congress of Labor Relations, Universidad del Zulia. Maracaibo: Editorial Astro Data SA.

Garip-Bertuol, Patricia. 1993. "Oil and the Labor Race." *Veneconomy Monthly* (Caracas), March: 5–6.

Garrett, Geoffrey, and Peter Lange. 1985. "The Politics of Growth: Strategic Interaction and Economic Performance in the Advanced Industrial Democracies: 1974–80." *Journal of Politics* 47: 792–827.

1989. "Government Partisanship and Economic Performance." *Journal of Politics* 51, no. 3 (August).

1995. "Internationalization, Institutions, and Political Change." *International Organization* 49, no. 5 (Autumn): 627–55.

Garrett, Geoffrey, and Christopher Way. 1995. "The Rise of Public Sector Unions, Corporatism and Macroeconomic Performance, 1970–1990." In *The Political Economy of European Integration*. Barry Eichengreen and Jeffrey Frieden, eds. New York: Springer-Verlag.

Garrido, Luis Javier. 1982. *El partido de la revolución institucionalizada: la formación del nuevo estado en México, 1928–1945*. Mexico City: Siglo Veintiuno Editores.

Gaudio, Ricardo, and Jorge Pilone. 1988a. "El desarrollo de la negociación colectiva durante la etapa de modernización industrial en la Argentina, 1935–1943."

Bibliography

In *La formación del sindicalismo peronista*. Juan Carlos Torre, ed. Buenos Aires: Legasa.

1988b. "Estado y relaciones laborales en el período previo al surgimiento del peronismo, 1935–43." In *La formación del sindicalismo peronista*. Juan Carlos Torre, ed. Buenos Aires: Legasa.

Gaudio, Ricardo, and Andrés Thompsom. 1990. *Sindicalismo peronista/gobierno radical. Los años de Alfonsín*. Buenos Aires: Fundación Frederich Ebert and Folio Ediciones.

Geddes, Barbara. 1994. *Politician's Dilemma: Building State Capacity in Latin America*. Berkeley: University of California Press.

1995. "Challenging the Conventional Wisdom." In *Economic Reform and Democracy*. Larry Diamond and Marc F. Plattner, eds. Baltimore, MD: Johns Hopkins University Press.

Gerchunoff, Pablo, and Guillermo Cánovas. 1996. "Privatization: The Argentine Experience." In *Bigger Economies, Smaller Governments: Privatization in Latin America*. William Glade, ed. Boulder, CO: Westview Press.

Gerchunoff, Pablo, and Lucas Llach. 1998. *El ciclo de la ilusión y el desencanto*. Buenos Aires: Ariel Sociedad Económica.

Gerchunoff, Pablo, and Juan Carlos Torre. 1996. "Argentina: la política de liberalización económica bajo un gobierno de base popular." *Desarrollo Económico*, no. 36 (October–December): 733–68.

Germani, Gino. 1973. "El surgimiento del peronismo: el rol de los obreros y de los migrantes internos." *Desarrollo Económico* 13, no. 51 (October–December).

Gibson, Edward L. 1996. *Class and Conservative Parties: Argentina in Comparative Perspective*. Baltimore, MD: Johns Hopkins University Press.

1997. "The Populist Road to Market Reform: Policy and Electoral Coalitions in Mexico and Argentina." *World Politics* 49 (April): 339–70.

Gil Yepes, José Antonio. 1987. "Instituto Venezolano de Seguros Sociales: La Ilusión del Rescate Gerencial." Case study prepared for the meeting of the Santa Lucia Group of November, Curação.

1989. "The CTV at a Crossroads." *Veneconomy Monthly* (Caracas), April: 3–4.

Giordano, Osvaldo, and Alejandra Torres. 1994. "Reflexiones en torno a la reforma de la legislación laboral." *Estudios*, Ministerio de Trabajo y Seguridad Social, (January–March): 3–23.

Golden, Myriam. 1993. "The Dynamics of Trade Unionism and National Economic Performance." *American Political Science Review* 87, no. 2 (June): 439–55.

1997. *Heroic Defeats: The Politics of Job Loss*. New York: Cambridge University Press.

Golden, Myriam and Jonas Pontusson, eds. 1992. *Bargaining for Change: Union Politics in North America and Europe*. Ithaca, NY: Cornell University Press.

Golden, Myriam and Michael Wallerstein. 1994. "Trade Union Organization and Industrial Relations in the Postwar Era in 16 Nations." Paper Prepared for the 1994 Annual Meeting of the American Political Science Association, New York, September 1–4.

Gómez, Marcelo. 1997. "Conflictividad laboral durante el Plan de Convertibilidad en Argentina (1991–1995). Las prácticas de lucha sindical en una etapa de reconstrucción económica y desregulación del mercado de trabajo." *Estudios Sociológicos* XV, no. 45: 639–89.

Gonda, Alejandro. 1994. "Reporte de la Consultora de Investigación Sindical Independiente." Consultora de Investigación Sindical Independiente, Buenos Aires.

——— 1995a. "Cantidad de Medidas de Fuerza realizadas en las principales organizaciones sindicales." Consultora de Investigación Sindical Independiente, Buenos Aires. Unpublished manuscript.

——— 1995b. "El plan dejó afuera a 396 trabajadores por día." Consultora de Investigación Sindical Independiente, Buenos Aires. Unpublished manuscript.

Góngora, Janette, and Horacio Vazquez. 1991. "El sindicalismo mexicano ante el Tratado de Libre Comercio." *Trabajo* (Mexico City) 5–6: 3–4.

González Silva, Pedro. 1990. "Ahorro de 25% tendrá el empresariado en Ley de Prestaciones del Gobierno." *Economía Hoy* (Caracas), November 7.

Gordillo, Elba Esther. 1992. "Modernización y sindicalismo en los tiempos del mercado." Paper presented to the first European and Latin American Conference on Political and Economic Integration, Granada, Spain, November 8–13.

Grupo Santa Lucía. 1990. "El movimiento sindical venezolano y el reajuste estructural de la economía. Retos y desafíos." XIV Meeting of the Santa Lucía Group, Caracas, October.

Gurr, Ted Robert. 1969. "A Comparative Study of Civil Strike." In *Violence in America: Historical and Comparative Perspectives*. Hugh Davis Graham and Ted Robert Gurr, eds. New York: Praeger.

Haggard, Stephan, and Robert Kaufman, eds. 1992. *The Politics of Economic Adjustment*. Princeton, NJ: Princeton University Press.

——— 1995. *The Political Economy of Democratic Transitions*. Princeton, NJ: Princeton University Press.

Hagopian, Frances. 1998. "Negotiating Economic Transitions in Liberalizing Polities." Paper prepared for the annual meeting of the American Political Science Association, Working Paper no. 5/1998, Weatherhead Center for International Affairs, Harvard University, Cambridge, MA.

Hall, Peter. 1986. *Governing the Economy: The Politics of State Intervention in Britain and France*. Oxford: Oxford University Press.

Hart, John Mason. 1987. *Revolutionary Mexico: The Coming and Process of the Mexican Revolution*. Berkeley: University of California Press.

Hayes, Beth. 1984. "Mirrors and Strikes of Assymetric Information." *Journal of Labor Economics* 2: 57–83.

Hellman, Joel S. 1998. "Winners Take All: The Politics of Partial Reform in Post-Communist Transitions." *World Politics* 50, no. 2 (January): 203–34.

Heredia, Blanca. 1994. "Making Economic Reform Politically Viable: The Mexican Experience." In *Democracy, Markets and Structural Reform in Latin America*. William Smith, Carlos Acuña, and Eduardo Gamarra, eds. New Brunswick, NJ: North-South Center and Transaction Publishers.

Bibliography

Hernández, Cruz. 1994. "Estado Actual de las Telecomunicaciones en Venezuela." Paper prepared for the II Continental Conference of Telecommunication Unions, São Paulo, Brazil, November.

Herrera Lima, Fernando. 1992. "Reestructuración de la industria automotriz en México y respuesta sindical." *El Cotidiano* (Mexico City) 46, March–April: 35–7.

Hierro, Jorge, and Allen Sanginés. 1991. "Public Sector Behavior in Mexico." In *The Public Sector and the Latin American Crisis*. Felipe Larraín and Marcelo Selowsky, eds. International Center for Economic Growth, San Francisco.

Hill, Alice and Manuel Angel Abdala. 1996. "Argentina: The Sequencing of Privatization and Regulation." In *Regulations, Institutions, and Commitment: Comparative Studies of Telecommunications*. Brian Levy and Pablo T. Spiller, eds. Cambridge: Cambridge University Press.

Hirshman, Albert. 1968. "The Political Economy of Import Substitution Industrialization in Latin America." *The Quarterly Journal of Economics* 82, no. 1 (February): 1–32.

1970. *Exit, Voice and Loyalty.* Cambridge, MA: Harvard University Press.

Horowitz, Joel. 1990. *Argentine Unions, the State, & the Rise of Peron, 1930–1945.* Berkeley, CA: Institute of International Studies, University of California.

Ieraci, Julio. 1995. "Tenemos una conducción equilibrada." Interview in *Noticias Gremiales* (Buenos Aires), no. 315 (July).

INDEC (National Institute of Statistics and Census). 1992a. "Sintesís: Situación y Evolución Social." Volume 1. Buenos Aires: INDEC.

1992b. Data provided to the Ministry of Labor and Social Security, Buenos Aires: INDEC.

1993a. *Estadística Mensual* 3, no. 4. Buenos Aires: INDEC.

1993b. "Encuesta Permanente de Hogares, Información de Prensa." Buenos Aires: INDEC (May).

1994. *Anuario Estadístico de la República Argentina: 1994.* Buenos Aires: INDEC.

1995a. *Estadística Mensual* 5, no. 6. Buenos Aires: INDEC.

1995b. "Encuesta Permanente de Hogares, Información de Prensa." Buenos Aires: INDEC (May).

1996. *Anuario Estadístico de la República Argentina: 1996.* Buenos Aires: INDEC.

Inter-American Development Bank (IADB). 1996. *Economic and Social Progress in Latin America.* Washington, DC: Johns Hopkins University Press.

International Labour Organization (ILO). 1991. "Informe de la misión de la Organización Internacional del Trabajo sobre el diagnóstico de las relaciones laborales en Venezuela." International Labour Organization. Unpublished manuscript.

1996. "Evolución reciente del sector de la educación." Programa de Actividades Sectoriales, Geneve: International Labour Organization.

1997. *World Labour Report.* Geneva: International Labour Organization.

1998. "OIT Informa. Panorama Laboral." Lima: International Labour Organization.

International Monetary Fund. 1996. *International Financial Statistics, 1996*. Washington, DC: IMF.

1997. *International Financial Statistics, 1997*. Washington, DC: IMF.

1998. *International Financial Statistics, 1998*. Washington, DC: IMF.

Iranzo, Consuelo. 1994. "Respuestas del movimiento sindical venezolano del sector público frente a la reestructuración económica." Paper presented at the first Latin American Meeting of Labor Studies, San Juan, May 15–22.

Iranzo, Consuelo, and Rodrigo Penso. 1996. "El movimiento sindical venezolano frente a los procesos de reestructuración estatal." Caracas: CENDES. Unpublished manuscript.

Iranzo, Consuelo, and Jacqueline Richter. 1998. "Privatización y relaciones laborales en la telefonía venezolana." In *La privatización de las telecomunicaciones en América Latina*. Jorge Walter and Cecilia Senén González, eds. Buenos Aires: EUDEBA.

Iranzo, Consuelo, Luisa Bethencourt, Hector Lucena, and Fausto Sandoval Bauza. 1996. "Competitividad, calificación y trabajo: sector automotriz venezolano." Coordinated by Consuelo Iranzo. Caracas: CENDES. Unpublished manuscript.

Isuani, Ernesto Aldo, and Jorge San Martino. 1993. *La reforma previsional argentina*. Buenos Aires: Miño y Dávila Editores.

Iverson, Torben and Anne Wren. 1998. "Equality, Employment, and Budgetary Restraint: The Trilemma of the Service Economy." *World Politics* 50, no. 4 (July): 507–46.

IVSS (Venezuelan Institute of Social Security). 1993. *Statistical Records*. Caracas: IVSS.

James, Daniel. 1988. *Resistance and Integration: Peronism and the Argentine Working Class, 1946–1976*. Cambridge: Cambridge University Press.

Jones, Mark. 1997. "Evaluating Argentina's Presidential Democracy: 1983–1995." In *Presidentialism and Democracy in Latin America*. Scott Mainwaring and Matthew Soberg Shugart, eds. Cambridge: Cambridge University Press.

Karl, Terry Lynn. 1986. "Petroleum and Political Pacts: The Transition to Democracy in Venezuela." In *Transitions from Authoritarian Rule: Latin America*. Guillermo O'Donnell, Phillipe Schmitter, and Laurence Whitehead, eds. Baltimore, MD: Johns Hopkins University Press.

1997. *The Paradox of Plenty, Oil Booms and Petro-States*. Berkeley: University of California Press.

Kaufman, Robert. 1988. *The Politics of Debt in Argentina, Brazil, and Mexico: Economic Stabilization in the 1980s*. Berkeley: Institute of International Studies, University of California.

Kennan, John. 1986. "The Economics of Strikes." In *Handbook of Labor Economics*, vol. 2. Orley C. Ashenfelter and Richard Layard, eds. Amsterdam: North-Holland.

Kessler, Timothy P. 1998. "Political Capital: Mexican Financial Policy Under Salinas." *World Politics* 51, no.1 (October): 36–66.

Bibliography

King, Gary, Robert Keohane, and Sidney Verba. 1994. *Designing Social Inquiry. Scientific Inference in Qualitative Research*. Princeton, NJ: Princeton University Press.

Knight, Alan. 1986. *The Mexican Revolution*, vol. 1 and 2. Cambridge: Cambridge University Press.

——— 1998. "Populism and Neo-Populism in Latin America, Especially in Mexico." *Journal of Latin American Studies* 30, part 2 (May): 233–46.

Kornblith, Miriam. 1998. *Venezuela en los noventa: las crisis de la democracia*. Caracas: Universidad Central de Venezuela, Facultad de Ciencias Juridicas y Politicas.

Kornblith, Miriam, and Daniel Levine. 1995. "Venezuela. The Life and Times of the Party System." In *Building Democratic Institutions: Party Systems in Latin America*. Scott Mainwaring and Timothy Scully, eds. Stanford, CA: Stanford University Press.

Korpi, Walter. 1978. *The Working Class in Welfare Capitalism*. London: Routledge & Kegan Paul.

——— 1985. "Developments in the Theory of Power and Exchange." *Sociological Theory* 3, no. 2: 46–62.

Korpi, Walter, and Michael Shalev. 1980. "Strikes, Power, and Politics in the Western Nations, 1900–1976." *Political Power and Social Theory* (Greenwich, CT), vol. 1.

La Botz, Dan. 1992. *Mask of Democracy: Labor Suppression in Mexico Today*. Boston: South End Press.

LAGOVEN. 1991. "Contrato colectivo de trabajo." Caracas.

——— 1993. "Contrato colectivo de trabajo." Caracas.

Lamadrid, Alejandro. n.d. "La evolución de la estructura sindical en los años 80." Buenos Aires: Ministerio de Trabajo y Previsión Social. Unpublished manuscript.

Lange, Peter. 1984. "Unions, Workers, and Wage Regulation: The Rational Bases of Consent." In *Order and Conflict in Contemporary Capitalism*. John H. Goldthorpe, ed. Oxford: Clarendon Press.

Lara Rangel, María Eugenia. 1990. "De la dispersión a la unificación del movimiento obrero. La fundación de la CTM. 1933–1936." In *La historia de la CTM 1936–1990*, vol. 1. Javier Aguilar García, ed. Mexico City: UNAM.

Lárez, Fermín. 1992. *El movimento sindical y la lucha política en Venezuela (1936–1959)*. Caracas: Monte Avila Editores, Instituto Nacional de Altos Estudios Sindicales.

Leal, Felipe. 1985. *Agrupaciones y burocracias sindicales en México, 1906–1938*. Mexico City: Ed. Terranova.

——— 1986. "Las estructuras sindicales." In *Organización y Sindicalismo*. Pablo Gonzalez Casanova, ed. Mexico City: Ed. Siglo XXI and Instituto de Investigaciones Sociales de la UNAM.

León, Samuel. 1990. "Del partido de partido al partido de sectores." In *El partido en el poder*. Mexico City: Iepes.

León, Samuel, and Ignacio Marván. 1985. *En el cardenismo, 1934–40*, vol. 10. In *La clase obrera en la historia de México*. Pablo González Casanovas, ed. Mexico City: Siglo Veintiuno Editores.

Levine, Daniel. 1973. *Conflict and Political Change in Venezuela*. Princeton, NJ: Princeton University Press.

Levitsky, Steven R. 1999. "From Laborism to Liberalism: Institutionalization and Labor-Based Party Adaptation in Argentina (1983–1997)." Department of Political Science, University of California, Berkeley, CA: Unpublished doctoral dissertation.

Ley de Seguro Social (Social Security Law). 1991. *Gaceta Oficial*, 3 October.

Ley 14,250 de Convenciones Colectivas. 1991. Buenos Aires.

Ley 23,551 de Asociaciones Sindicales. 1990. Buenos Aires.

Ley 23,660 del Seguro de Salud. 1992. Buenos Aires.

Ley Federal del Trabajo. 1993. Mexico City: Colección Jurídica Esfinge.

Ley Orgánica del Trabajo. 1994. Caracas.

Little, Walter. 1988. "La organización obrera y el estado peronista, 1943–55." In *La formación del sindicalismo peronista*. Juan Carlos Torre, ed. Buenos Aires: Legasa.

Little, Walter and Herrera, Antonio. 1995. "Populism and Reform in Contemporary Venezuela." London: Institute for Latin American Studies, University of London.

Llach, Juan. 1997. *Otro siglo, otra Argentina*. Buenos Aires: Ariel Sociedad Económica.

Llanos, Mariana. 1997. "El poder ejecutivo, el congreso y la política de pirvatizaciones en Argentina (1989–97)." Paper presented to the III National Congress of Political Science "Democracy, Economic Reform, and the Social Question." Argentine Society of Political Analysis, Mar del Plata, November 5–8.

Locke, Richard M. 1995. *Remaking the Italian Economy*. Ithaca, NY: Cornell University Press.

López Cárdenas, Próspero. 1989. "Legislación especial y sindicalismo de trabajadores al servicio del estado." In *Los sindicatos nacionales: educación, telefonistas, y bancarios*. Javier Aguilar, ed. Mexico City: García Valdéz Editores.

López Maya, Margarita. 1992. *El Banco de los Trabajadores de Venezuela: algo más que un banco?* Caracas: Universidad Central de Venezuela.

1997. "El ascenso en Venezuela de la Causa R." In *The New Politics of Inequality in Latin America: Rethinking Participation and Representation*. Douglas Chalmers et al., eds. New York: Oxford University Press.

Loyola, Rafael. 1990a. "1938: El despliegue del corporatismo partidario." In *El partido en el poder*. Mexico City: IEPES.

1990b. "Las implicaciones laborales del neoliberalismo en Petróleos Mexicanos." In *Relaciones laborales en las empresas paraestatales*. Graciela Bensusán and Carlos García, eds. Mexico City: Fundación Ebert.

Loyola, Rafael, and Liliana Martínez. 1994. "Petróleos Mexicanos: la búsqueda de un nuevo modelo empresarial." *Estudios Sociológicos* XII, México City.

Lucena, Hector. 1982. *Las relaciones laborales en Venezuela: el movimiento obrero petrolero: proceso de formación y desarrollo*. Caracas: Ediciones Centauro.

1998. "Recent Development in the Venezuela Automotive Industry: Implications for Labor Relations." In *Transforming the Latin America Automobile Industry*. John P. Tuman and John T. Morris, eds. Armonk, NY: M.E. Sharpe.

Bibliography

Lustig, Nora. 1992. "Equity and Growth in Mexico." In Simon Teitel, ed. *Towards a New Development Strategy for Latin America: Pathways from Hirshman's Thought*. Washington, DC: Inter-American Development Bank.

———. 1995. "The Mexican Peso Crisis: The Foreseeable and the Surprise." Brookings Discussion Papers in International Economics, Washington, DC.

———. 1998. *Mexico, the Remaking of an Economy*. Washington, DC: Brookings Institution Press.

Lustig, Nora, and Darryl, McLeod. 1997. "Minimum Wages and Poverty in Developing Countries: Some Empirical Evidence." In *Labor Markets in Latin America*. Nora Lustig and Sebastian Edwards, eds. Washington, DC: Brookings Institution Press.

Lynch, Menenendez, Nivel y Asociados. Various Years. Encuestas de opinion publica, Capital Federal and Gran Buenos Aires. Buenos Aires (mimeo).

Mackinnon, Maria Moira. 1998. "Unity and Fragmentation: The Conflictive Relationship between Trade Unionists and Politicians in the Early Years of the Peronist Party (1946–50)." Paper prepared for the 1998 meeting of the Latin American Studies Association, Chicago, Illinois, September 24–6.

Madrid, Raul. 1999. "The New Logic of Social Security Reform: Politics and Pension Privatization in Latin America. "Stanford University, Stanford, CA. Unpublished doctoral dissertation.

MARAVEN. 1989. "Taller de negociación de contratos colectivos." Caracas.

———. 1991. "Contrato colectivo de trabajo." Caracas.

Marbrán, Ignacio. 1990. "La dificultad del cambio (1968–1990)." In *El partido en el poder*. Mexico City: IEPES.

Margheritis, Ana. 1997. "Implementing Structural Adjustment in Argentina. The Politics of Privatization." University of Toronto, Ontario, Canada. Unpublished doctoral dissertation.

Marquez, Gustavo, ed. 1994. *Regulación del Mercado de Trabajo en América Latina*. Caracas: Ediciones IESA.

Matsushita, Hiroshi. 1983. *Movimiento Obrero Argentino 1930/1945. Sus proyecciones en los orígenes del Peronismo*. Buenos Aires: Siglo Veinte.

———. 1999. "Un análisis de las reformas obreras en la primera presidencia de Menem: la perspectiva de opción estratégica." In *El sindicalismo en tiempos de Menem*. Santiago Senén González and Fabián Bosoer, eds. Buenos Aires: Ediciones Corregidor.

Maxfield, Sylvia. 1990. *Governing Capital*. Ithaca, NY: Cornell University Press.

McCoy, Jennifer. 1989. "Labor and the State in a Party-Mediated Democracy: Institutional Change in Venezuela." *Latin American Research Review* 24, no. 2 (Spring): 35–68.

McCoy, Jennifer, and William Smith. 1995. "Democratic Disequilibrium in Venezuela." *Journal of Interamerican Studies and World Affairs* 37, no. 2 (Summer): 113–79.

McGuire, James W. 1996a. "Strikes in Argentina: Data Sources and Recent Trends." *Latin American Research Review* 31, no. 3 (Fall): 127–51.

1996b. Dataset on union strikes in Argentina between 1984–1992, based on the reports of *Tendencia Económica* (Buenos Aires), Wesleyan Univerversity, Middleton, CT.

1997. *Peronism Without Perón: Unions, Parties, and Democracy in Argentina.* Stanford, CA: Stanford University Press.

Medina, Luis. 1979. *Civilismo y modernización del autoritarismo.* In *Historia de la revolución mexicana*, vol. 20. Mexico City: El Colegio de Mexico.

Melcher, Dorthea. 1992. *Estado y movimento obrero en Venezuela.* Caracas: Academia Nacional de Historia.

Melgoza, Javier. 1992. "Avances e incertidumbres en la modernización del sector eléctrico." *El Cotidiano* (Mexico City) 46, March–April: 45–7.

1994. "El SME y la productividad: los saldos de la negociación." *Polis* 93 (Universidad Autónoma de México, Unidad Iztapala, Mexico City).

Mendez Berrueta, Luis, and José Quiroz Trejo. 1994. *Modernización estatal y respuesta obrera: historia de una derrota.* Mexico City: Universidad Autónoma Metropolitana.

Meza González, Liliana. 1999. "Cambios en la estructural salarial de México en el período 1988–1993 y el aumento del rendimiento de la educación superior." *Trimestre Económico* 66, no. 262 (April–June): 189–226.

Michels, Robert. 1966. *Political Parties.* New York: Free Press.

Middlebrook, Kevin. 1986. "Political Liberalization in an Authoritarian Regime: The Case of Mexico." In *Transitions from Authoritarian Rule: Latin America.* Guillermo O'Donnell, Phillipe Schmitter, and Laurence Whitehead, eds. Baltimore, MD: Johns Hopkins University Press.

1991. "State-Labor Relations in Mexico: The Changing Economic and Political Context." In *Unions, Workers and the State.* Kevin Middlebrook, ed. La Jolla, CA: Center for U.S.-Mexican Studies, University of California, San Diego.

1995. *The Paradox of Revolution.* Baltimore, MD: Johns Hopkins University Press.

Ministry of Economy of Argentina. 1993. "Argentina: A Growing Nation." Buenos Aires: Ministerio de Economía.

1995. "Privatizaciones en el sector eléctrico argentino." Internal document, Ministerio de Economía, Buenos Aires (July).

Ministry of Education of Venezuela. 1989. *Memoria y cuenta.* Annual report, Ministerio de Educación, Caracas.

1994. *Memoria y cuenta.* Annual report, Ministerio de Educación, Caracas.

Ministry of Labor of Argentina. 1975a. CCT (Collective Contract on Work) 16/75. "Convención colectiva de Trabajo no. 16 de 1975 entre Yacimientos Petrolíferos Fiscales (YPF) y Federación de Sindicatos Unidos Petroleros del Estado (SUPE)." Buenos Aires. Collective bargaining agreement.

1975b. CCT (Collective Contract on Work) 165/75. 1975. "Convenio Colectivo no. 165 de 1975 entre la Federación de Obreros y Empleados Telefónicos de la República Argentina y Unión del Personal Jerárquico de Entel, con Empresa Nacional de Telecomunicaciones, Compañías Argentinas y Entrerrianas de Teléfonos y Federación de Cooperativas Telefónicas." Buenos Aires. Collective bargaining agreement, August 14.

Bibliography

1987. *Estructura sindical en la Argentina*. Buenos Aires: Dirección Nacional de Recursos Humanos y Empleo.

1988. *Sindicatos: Elecciones 1984–1986*. Buenos Aires: Dirección Nacional de Recursos Humanos y Empleo.

1992. "Ley de asociaciones sindicales. Propuesta de modificación." Project of law, Buenos Aires.

1993a. "Proyecto de Ley de Reforma al Régimen de Contrato de Trabajo." Buenos Aires, August 19.

1993b. "La dinámica de la negociación colectiva en el marco de la reforma laboral y algunas aplicaciones de la ley de empleo." Comisión Técnica Asesora de Productividad y Salarios, Buenos Aires.

1994a. "Acuerdo Marco para el empleo, la productividad, y la equidad social." Buenos Aires: Ministry of Labor and Social Security.

1994b. "Estadísticas Laborales." Ministerio de Trabajo y Seguridad Social, Departmento de Estadísticas Laborales, Buenos Aires.

1995. CCT (Collective Contract on Work) 144/95. "Convenio Colectivo de Trabajo no. 144 de 1995 entre YPF S.A. y S.U.P.E." Buenos Aires. Collective bargaining agreement, YPF S.A.

n.d. "Informe sobre el acuerdo salarial entre la Federación Argentina de Luz y Fuerza; Sindicato Salta y Delegados de la Central Térmica Guemes SA y la empresa Central Térmica Guemes SA." Expte 945, 369/93, Buenos Aires.

n.d. "Informe sobre el acuerdo salarial entre la Federación Argentina de Luz y Fuerza y Central Pedro de Mendoza S.A." Expte 924,830/93 and 9494, 542/93, Buenos Aires.

n.d. "Informe sobre el acuerdo salarial entre la Federación Argentina de Luz y Fuerza Capital Federal, y la empresa Central Puerto S.A." Expte 934, 393/92, Buenos Aires.

n.d. "Informe sobre el acuerdo salarial entre la Federación Argentina de Luz y Fuerza y las empresas Edenor S.A., Edesur S.A., y Edelap S.A." Expte 939, 030/93, Buenos Aires.

n.d. "Informe sobre el acuerdo salarial entre la Federación Argentina de Luz y Fuerza, el Sindicato de Luz y Fuerza de San Nicolás, y la Central Térmica San Nicolás S.A." Expte 952, 524/93, Buenos Aires.

n.d. "Informe sobre el acuerdo salarial entre la Federación de Obreros y Empleados Telefónicos de la República Argentina, y las empresas Telecom-Argentina-Stet France Telecom S.A.-Telefónica de Argentina S.A., Telintar S.A.- Startel S.A.- CCT 201/92." Buenos Aires.

Ministry of Labor of Venezuela. 1989. "Annual Report of Activities." Caracas.

1990. "Annual Report of Activities." Caracas.

1992. "Annual Report of Activities." Caracas.

Molano, Walter. 1997. *The Logic of Privatization: The Case of Telecommunications in the Southern Cone of Latin America*. Westport, CT: Greenwood Press.

Molina, José, and Carmen Pérez. 1996. "Los procesos electorales y la evolución del sistema de partidos en Venezuela." In *El sistema político venezolano. Crisis y transformaciones*. Angel Alvarez, ed. Caracas: Universidad Central de Venezuela.

Molinar, Juan. 1991. *El tiempo de la legitimidad*. Mexico City: Cal y Arena.

Mora y Araujo, Manuel, and Ignacio Llorente, eds. 1980. *El voto peronista. Ensayos en sociologia electoral argentina*. Buenos Aires: Editorial Sudamericana.

Morris, John. 1998a. "Economic Integration and the Transformation of Labor Relations in the Mexican Automotive Industry." In *Transforming the Latin America Automobile Industry*. John P. Tuman and John T. Morris, eds. Armonk, NY: M.E. Sharpe.

1998b. "The Political Economy of Restructuring in Mexico's 'Brownfield' Plants: A Comparative Analysis." In *Transforming the Latin America Automobile Industry*. John P. Tuman and John T. Morris, eds. Armonk, NY: M.E. Sharpe.

Murillo, María Victoria. 1996a. "Los sindicatos frente a la reforma del estado en Argentina y México." *Sociedad* (Universidad de Buenos Aires), no. 8 (April): 147–66.

1996b. "Latin American Unions and the Reform of Social Sector Delivery Systems." OCE Working Paper no. 332, Inter-American Development Bank, Washington, DC, December.

1997a. "Union Politics, Market-Oriented Reforms and the Reshaping of Argentine Corporatism." In *The New Politics of Inequality in Latin America: Rethinking Participation and Representation*. Douglas Chalmers et al., eds. New York: Oxford University Press.

1997b. "A Strained Alliance: Continuity and Change in Mexican Labor Politics." In *Mexico: Assessing Neo-Liberal Reform*. Monica Serrano, ed. London: The Institute of Latin American Studies, University of London.

Murmis, Miguel, and Juan Carlos Portantiero. 1971. *Estudios sobre los origenes del peronismo*. Buenos Aires: Ediciones Siglo XXI.

Naim, Moises. 1993. *Paper Tigers and Minotaurs*. Washington, DC: Carnegie Endowment.

Navarro, Juan Carlos. 1993. "Propuestas y experiencias de reforma institucional en el sector educativo en Venezuela." Caracas: Proyecto de Desarrollo Insituticional del Sector Social.

1994. "Reversal of Fortune: The Ephemeral Success of Adjustment in Venezuela between 1989 and 1993." Instituto de Estudios Superiores de Administración (IESA), Caracas. Unpublished manuscript.

1997. "4 Notas sobre el sistema educativo venezolano." IESA, Caracas. Working paper.

Nelson, Joan, ed. 1989. *Fragile Coalitions: The Politics of Economic Adjustment*. New Brunswick, NJ: Transaction Publishers.

1990. *Economic Crisis and Policy Choice: The Politics of Adjustment in the Third World*. Princeton, NJ: Princeton University Press.

1992. "Poverty, Equity and the Politics of Adjustment." In *The Politics of Economic Adjustment*. Stephan Haggard and Robert Kaufman, eds. Princeton, NJ: Princeton University Press.

1994. *Intricate Links: Democratization and Market Reform in Latin America and Eastern Europe*. New Brunswick, NJ: Transaction Publishers.

Bibliography

Novaro, Marcos. 1994. *Pilotos de tormentas. Crisis de representación y personalización de la política en Argentina (1989–1993)*. Buenos Aires: Ediciones Letra Buena.

Novelo, Victoria. 1989. "Las fuentes de poder de la dirigencia sindical en Pemex." *El Cotidiano* (Mexico City) 28, March–April: 23–5.

———. 1991. *La difícil democracia de los petroleros*. Mexico City: Ediciones el Caballito.

O'Donnell, Guillermo. 1973. *Modernization and Bureaucratic-Authoritarianism: Studies in South American Politics*. Berkeley: Institute of International Studies, University of California.

———. 1976. "Estado y alianzas en la Argentina: 1955–76." *Desarrollo Económico* 16, no. 64.

———. 1982. *El Estado Burocrático Autoritario*. Buenos Aires: Editorial de Belgrano.

———. 1994. "Delegative Democracy?" *Journal of Democracy* 5, no. 1 (January): 55–69.

O'Donnell, Guillermo, and Phillipe C. Schmitter. 1986. *Transitions from Authoritarian Rule: Tentative Conclusions about Uncertain Democracies*. Baltimore, MD: Johns Hopkins University Press.

Offe, Claus, and Helmut Wiesenthal. 1985. "The Two Logics of Collective Action." In *Disorganized Capitalism*. John Keane, ed. Cambridge, MA: MIT University Press.

Oil and Gas Journal. 1995. "Privatization of State Company Catalyzes Argentine Oil Industry (YPF S.A.)." *The Oil and Gas Journal* 93, no. 7 (13 February): 45–54.

Olson, Mancur. 1971. *The Logic of Collective Action*. Cambridge, MA: Harvard University Press.

———. 1982. *The Rise and Decline of Nations*. New Haven, CT: Yale University Press.

Ornelas, Carlos. 1995. *El sistema educativo mexicano*. Mexico City: Fondo de Cultura Económica.

Ostiguy, Pierre. 1998. "Peronism and Anti-Peronism: Class-Cultural Cleavages and Political Identity in Argentina." Department of Political Science, University of California, Berkeley, CA. Unpublished doctoral dissertation.

Paglianitti, Norma. 1991. *Neo-conservadurismo y Educación*. Buenos Aires: Libros del Quirquincho.

Palermo, Vicente. 1995. "¡Síganme! La política de las reformas estructurales: el caso argentino 1989–1993." Instituto Universitario Ortega y Gasset, Universidad Complutense de Madrid. Unpublished doctoral dissertation.

Palermo, Vicente, and Marcos Novaro. 1996. *Política y poder en el gobierno de Menem*. Buenos Aires: Grupo Editorial Norma.

Palermo, Vicente, and Juan Carlos Torre. 1992. "A la sombra de la hiperinflación. La política de reformas estructurales en la Argentina." CEPAL, Buenos Aires. Unpublished manuscript.

Palomino, Héctor. 1995. "Quiebres y rupturas de la acción sindical: un panorama desde el presente sobre la evolución del movimiento sindical en Argentina." In *La nueva matriz política argentina*. Carlos Acuña, ed. Buenos Aires: Nueva Visión.

Pastor, Manuel, and Carol Wise. 1997. "State Policy, Distribution and Neoliberal Reform in Mexico." *Journal of Latin American Studies* 29: 419–556.

———. 1999. "Stabilization and Its Discontents: Argentina's Economic Restructuring in the 1990's." *World Development* 27, no. 3: 477–503.

Pellicer de Brody, Olga, and José Luis Reyna. 1978. *El afianzamiento de la estabilidad política*. In *Historia de la revolución mexicana*, vol. 22. Mexico City: El Colegio de México.

PEMEX (Petroleum of Mexico). 1987. "Contrato Colectivo de Trabajo cebrado entre el Sindicato Revolucionario de Trabajadores Petroleros de la República Mexicana y Petróleos Mexicanos." Mexico City: PEMEX.

——— 1989. "Contrato Colectivo de Trabajo cebrado entre el Sindicato Revolucionario de Trabajadores Petroleros de la República Mexicana y Petróleos Mexicanos." Mexico City: PEMEX.

——— 1991. "Contrato Colectivo de Trabajo cebrado entre el Sindicato de Trabajadores Petroleros de la República Mexicana y Petróleos Mexicanos." Mexico City: PEMEX.

——— 1993. "Contrato Colectivo de Trabajo cebrado entre el Sindicato de Trabajadores Petroleros de la República Mexicana y Petróleos Mexicanos por sí y en representación de Pemex-Exploración y Producción, Pemex-Refinación, Pemex-Gas y Petroquímica Básica, y Pemex-Petroquímica." Mexico City: PEMEX.

Pencavel, John. 1997. "Collective Barganing in Developing Economies." In *Labor Markets in Latin America: Combining Social Protection with Market Flexibility*. Sebastian Edwards and Nora Lustig, eds. Washington, DC: Brookings Institution.

Pérez Fernández del Castillo, Germán. 1992. "Del corporativismo de estado al corporativismo social." In *México, Auge y Crisis*. Carlos Bazdresch, Nisso Bucay, Soledad Loaeza, and Nora Lustig, eds. Mexico City: Editorial Fondo de Cultura.

Pérez Pérez, Gabriel. 1993. "El SME ante el reto de la modernización del sector eléctrico." *El Cotidiano* (Mexico City) 58, October–November: 4–6.

——— 1995. "El STPRM, bajo las cadenas de la subordinación y el control estatal." *El Cotidiano* (Mexico City) 67, January–February: 12–16.

Peschard, Jacqueline. 1991. "El partido hegemónico: 1946–1972." In *El partido en el poder*. Mexico City: IEPES.

Pessino, Carola. 1997. "Argentina: The Labor Market during the Economic Transition." In *Labor Markets in Latin America*. Sebastian Edwards and Nora Lustig, eds. Washington, DC: Brookings Institution.

Petrazzini, Ben. 1996. "Telephone Privatizationn in a Hurry: Argentina." In *Privatizing Monopolies*. Ravi Ramamurti, ed. Baltimore, MD: Johns Hopkins University Press.

Pirker, Elizabeth. 1991. "La participación de las empresas estatales en la economía argentina." In *Privatizaciones. Restructuración del Estado y la Sociedad*. Arnoldo Bocco and Naum Misnburg, eds. Buenos Aires: Ediciones Letra Buena.

Pizzorno, Allesandro. 1978. "Political Exchange and Collective Identity." In *The Resurgence of Class Conflict in Western Europe Since 1968*, vol. II. Colin Crouch and Alessandro Pizzorno, eds. New York: Holmes & Meier Publishers, Inc.

Pontusson, Jonas, and Peter Swenson. 1996. "Labor Markets, Production Strategies and Wage-Bargaining Institutions: The Swedish Employers' Offensive in Comparative Perspectives." *Comparative Political Studies* 29: 223–50.

Presidencia de la República de México. 1994. *Crónica del Gobierno de Carlos Salinas de Gortari. Cuarto Año, enero 1992–diciembre 1992.* Mexico City: Fondo de Cultura Económica.

Pripstein Posusney, Marsha. 1993. "Irrational Workers: The Moral Economy of Labor Protest in Egypt." *World Politics* 46, no. 1 (October): 83–120.

Przeworski, Adam. 1991. *Democracy and the Market.* Cambridge: Cambridge University Press.

1995. *Sustainable Democracy.* Cambridge: Cambridge University Press.

Przeworski, Adam, and Michael Wallerstein. 1982. "The Structure of Class Conflict in Democratic Societies." *American Political Science Review* 76: 215–38.

Quinteros, Cirila. 1990. *La sindicalización en las maquiladoras tijuanenses.* Mexico City: Consejo Nacional para la Cultura y las Artes.

Ramírez, Luis Enrique. 1993. "La reforma laboral." Buenos Aires: Instituto de Estudios sobre Estado y Participación.

Ramírez, Miguel. 1993. "The Political Economy of Privatization in Mexico, 1983–92." Occasional Paper no. 1, Latin American Studies Consortium of New England.

Rammamurti, Ravi. 1996. "Telephone Privatization in a Large Country: Mexico." In *Privatizing Monopolies: Lessons from the Telecommunications and Transport Sectors in Latin America.* Ravi Rammamurti, ed. Baltimore, MD: Johns Hopkins University Press.

Recalde, Héctor. 1994. *Reforma Laboral: flexibilidad sin empleo.* Buenos Aires: Organizaciones Mora Libros.

Reyes del Campillo, Jesús. 1990. "El movimiento obrero en la Cámara de Diputados (1979–1988)." *Revista Mexicana de Sociología*, year LII, no. 3 (July–September): 139–60.

Roberts, Kenneth. 1995. "Neoliberalism and the Transformation of Populism in Latin America." *World Politics* 48 (October): 82–116.

Robinson, Nancy. 1980. "The Politics of Low Income Housing in Mexico: A Case Study of Infonavit, the Workers' Housing Institute." Stanford University, Stanford, CA. Unpublished thesis.

Rock, David. 1977. *El radicalismo argentino, 1890–1930.* Buenos Aires: Amorrortu Editores.

Rodríguez, Miguel. 1991. "Public Sector Behavior in Venezuela." In *The Public Sector and the Latin American Crisis.* Felipe Larraín and Marcelo Selowsky, eds. San Francisco, CA: ICS Press.

Rodríguez Caballero, Francisco. 1996. "Understanding Resistance to Reform: Conflict and Agency in the Venezuelan Experience." Workshop on Economic Reform and Civil Society in Latin America, David Rockefeller Center for Latin American Studies, Harvard University, April 12.

Rodrik, Dani. 1994. "Comment." In *The Political Economy of Policy Reform.* John Williamsom, ed. Washington, DC: Institute for International Economics.

1996. "Understanding Economic Policy Reform." *Journal of Economic Literature* 34 (March): 9–41.

1997. *Has Globalization Gone Too Far?* Washington, DC: Institute for International Economics.

Rogosinki, Jacques. 1997. *La Privatización en México. Razones e impactos.* Mexico City: Ediciones Trillas.

Rogowski, Ronald. 1989. *Commerce and Coalitions: How Trade Affects Domestic Political Alignments.* Princeton, NJ: Princeton University Press.

Romero, Aníbal. 1997. "Rearranging the Deck Chairs on the Titanic: The Agony of Democracy in Venezuela." *Latin American Research Review* 32, no. 1: 7–36.

Rouquie, Alain. 1975. *Poder militar y sociedad política en la Argentina.* Buenos Aires: Emecé.

1982. "Hegemonía militar, estado y dominacion social." In *Argentina Hoy.* Alain Rouquie, ed. Mexico City: Siglo Veintiuno Editores.

Roxborough, Ian. 1984. *Union and Politics in Mexico: The Case of the Automobile Industry.* Cambridge: Cambridge University Press.

Salinas, Carlos. 1988. *El Reto.* Mexico City: Editorial Diana.

1992. "Cuarto Informe de Gobierno, Anexo Estadístico." Mexico City: Poder Ejecutivo Federal.

1994. "Sexto Informe de Gobierno, Anexo Estadístico." Mexico City: Poder Ejecutivo Federal.

Salinger, J.D. 1991 (1945). *The Catcher in the Rye.* Boston: Little, Brown.

Sanín, Alfredo Tarre Murzi. 1983. *Los adecos en el poder.* Caracas: Grupo Editor Interarte.

Savedoff, William. 1996. *La organización marca la diferencia. Educación y salud en América Latina.* Red de Centros de Investigación, Inter-American Development ment Bank, Washington, DC.

Savedoff, William, Ricardo Hausmann, and Claudia Piras. 1996. "Social Policy Reform in Latin America." Working Papers Series, no. 230, Woodrow Wilson International Center for Scholars, Washington, DC.

Schamis, Héctor E. 1999. "Distributional Coalitions and the Politics of Economic Reform in Latin America." *World Politics* 51, no. 2 (January): 236–68.

Schenone, Osvaldo H. 1991. "Public Sector Behavior in Argentina." In *The Public Sector and the Latin American Crisis.* Felipe Larraín and Marcelo Selowsky, eds. San Francisco, CA: International Center for Economic Growth.

Schmitter, Phillipe. 1974. "Still the Century of Corporatism." *The Review of Politics* 36, no. 1 (January): 9–49.

Schulthess, Walter Erwin, and Gustavo César Demarco. 1994. *Reforma presional en Argentina.* Buenos Aires: Abeledo Perrot.

Schwartzer, Jorge. 1983. *Martínez de Hoz: la lógica política de la política económica.* Buenos Aires: CISEA.

Scott, James C. 1976. *The Moral Economy of the Peasant: Rebellion and Subsistence in Southeast Asia.* New Haven, CT: Yale University Press.

Bibliography

Secretaria de Trabajo y Previsión Social (Secretariat of Work and Social Security).
1989. "Memoria de Labores." Annual report, Secretaria de Trabajo y Previsión Social, Mexico City.
1994. "Memoria de Labores." Annual report, Secretaria de Trabajo y Previsión Social, Mexico City.
1995. "Emplazamientos y huelgas estalladas en empresas de jurisdicción federal." Mexico City: Secretaria de Trabajo y Previsión Social, Subsecretaría "B."

Senén González, Santiago, and Fabián Bosoer. 1999. *El sindicalismo en los tiempos de Menem*. Buenos Aires: Editorial Corregidor.

Shalev, Michael. 1992. "The Resurgence of Labour Quiescence." In Marino Regini, ed. *The Future of Labour Movements*. New York: Sage.

Shugart, Matthew Soberg, and John M. Carey. 1992. *Presidents and Assemblies: Constitutional Design and Electoral Dynamics*. Cambridge: Cambridge University Press.

Sinclair, Upton. 1990 (1960). *The Jungle*. New York: Signet Classic.

SMATA (Union of Mechanic and Automobile Workers, Argentina). 1984. *Luchas Obreras Argentinas. José Rodríguez, secretario general del SMATA*. Buenos Aires: Editorial Experiencia.
1985. *Memoria y Balance 1984–85*. Annual report. Buenos Aires.
1989. *Estatuto Social*. Constitution. Buenos Aires.
1991. *Memoria y Balance, 1990–91*. Annual report. Buenos Aires.
1992. *Memoria y Balance, 1991–92*. Annual report. Buenos Aires.
1993. *Memoria y Balance, 1992–93*. Annual report. Buenos Aires.

SME (Mexican Union of Electrical Workers). 1992. *Estatutos*. Constitution, Mexico City.
1994. "El nuevo organismo, triunfo y nuevo reto del sindicato." Mexico City: SME.

Smith, William. 1989. *Authoritarianism and the Crisis of the Argentine Political Economy*. Stanford, CA: Stanford University Press.
1992. "Hyperinflation, Macroeconomic Instability, and Neoliberal Restructuring in Democratic Argentina." In *The New Argentine Democracy*. Edward Epstein, ed. New York: Praeger.

Smith, William and Carlos Acuña. 1994. "The Political Economy of Structural Adjustment: The Logic of Support and Opposition to Neoliberal Reform." In *Latin American Political Economy in the Age of Neoliberal Reform*. William Smith, Carlos Acuña, and Eduardo Gamarra, eds. New Brunswick, NJ and London: Transaction Publishers.

SNTE (National Union of Education Workers). 1992. *Estatutos*. Constitution. Mexico City: SNTE.
1995. "Informe de actividades que rinde el comité ejecutivo nacional del SNTE al III Congreso Nacional Extraordinario." Mexico City: SNTE, February 26–March 1.

Soules, George. 1991. "The Education Mess: Minister Roosen Directs Cleanup." *Veneconomy Monthly* (Caracas), May: 14–15.

Starr, Pamela. 1997. "Government Coalitions and the Viability of Currency Boards: Argentina under the Cavallo Plan." *Journal of Interamerican Studies and World Affairs*, forthcoming.

Streek, Wolfgang and Jelle Visser. 1998. "An Evolutionary Dynamic of Trade Unions Systems." Cologne: Max-Planck-Institute für Gessellschaftsforschung Discussion Paper 98/4.

Street, Susan. 1983. "Burocracia y educación: hacia un análisis político de la desconcentración administrativa en la Secretaría de Educación Pública (SEP)." *Estudios Sociológicos* 1, no. 2 (May–August): 239–92.

——— 1992. *Maestros en movimiento: Transformaciones en la burocracia estatal (1978–1982).* Mexico City: Ediciones de la Casa Chata.

STRM (Mexican Union of Telephone Workers). 1988. "Comisión de Modernización. Proyecto." XII National Ordinary Democratic Convention of the Telephone Workers, STRM, Mexico City.

——— 1994. "Propuesta General de Táctica y Estrategia. La democracia, el proyecto y el liderazgo del STRM ante el cambio y la modernización de México." XIX National Ordinary Convention, STRM, 30 September.

Sturzenegger, Federico. 1991. "Description of a Populist Experience: Argentina, 1973–76." In *The Macroeconomics of Populism in Latin America.* Rudiger Dornbush and Sebastian Edwards, eds. Chicago, IL: University of Chicago Press.

SUPE (Federation of United State Petroleum Unions). 1988. *Estatuto. Federación Sindicatos Unidos Petroleros del Estado.* Constitution, SUPE, Buenos Aires.

——— 1992. "Los emprendimientos conformados son un verdadero paliativo social para resguardar las fuentes de trabajo." In *Memoria y Balance, 1 Octubre 1991 al 30 Septiembre 1992.* SUPE, Buenos Aires.

——— 1993a. "Emprendimientos en formación (Estudio de factibilidad)." Internal document, SUPE, Buenos Aires.

——— 1993b. "Sociedades comerciales conformadas por personal desvinculado de YPF S.A." Internal document, SUPE, Buenos Aires.

——— 1994. *Memoria y Balance, 1 Octubre 1993 al 30 Septiembre 1994.* Annual report, SUPE, Buenos Aires.

Sweeney, John. 1989a. "The Labor Sector: Weak Link in CAP's 'Shock' Program." *Veneconomy Monthly* (Caracas): 11–12.

——— 1989b. "A Businessman in Education." *Veneconomy Monthly* (Caracas), October.

——— 1990a. "The New Automotive Policy: Consistent with the Economic Program." *Veneconomy Monthly* (Caracas), July: 23–4.

——— 1990b. "Wanted: A New Labor Movement." *Veneconomy Monthly* (Caracas), February: 6–8.

——— 1991. "CAP Offers Labor an Olive Branch." *Veneconomy Monthly* (Caracas), November: 3–5.

Sweeney, John, and Rita Funaro. 1990. "The Labor Law: Common Sense vs. Populism." *Veneconomy Monthly* (Caracas), May: 3–4.

Swenson, Peter. 1991a. "Bringing Capital Back In, Or Social Democracy Reconsidered." *World Politics* 43, no. 4 (July): 513–44.

——— 1991b. "Labor and the Limits of the Welfare State." *Comparative Politics* 23, no. 4 (July): 379–99.

Bibliography

Tamarin, David. 1985. *The Argentine Labor Movement, 1930–1945: A Study in the Origins of Peronism*. Albuquerque: University of New Mexico Press.

Tarre Briceno, Gustavo. 1994. *4 de febrero: el espejo roto*. Caracas: Editorial Panapo.

Teichman, Judith. 1995. *Privatization and Political Change in Mexico*. Pittsburgh, PA: University of Pittsburgh Press.

——— 1997. "Neoliberalism and the Transformation of Mexican Authoritarianism." *Mexican Studies* 13, no. 1 (Winter): 121–48.

TELMEX (Mexican Telephone Company). 1988. "Contrato colectivo de Trabajo." Mexico City: TELMEX.

——— 1990. "Contrato colectivo de Trabajo." Mexico City: TELMEX.

——— 1992. "Contrato colectivo de Trabajo." Mexico City: TELMEX.

——— 1994. "Contrato colectivo de Trabajo." Mexico City: TELMEX.

Thelen, Kathleen Ann. 1991a. "West European Labor in Transition: Sweden and Germany Compared." *World Politics* 46, no. 1 (October): 23–50.

——— 1991b. *Union of Parts: Labor Politics in Postwar Germany*. Ithaca, NY: Cornell University Press.

Torre, Juan Carlos. 1983. *Los sindicatos en el gobierno, 1973–1976*. Buenos Aires: Centro Editor de América Latina.

——— 1988. "La CGT y el 17 de octubre de 1945." In *La formación del sindicalismo peronista*. Juan Carlos Torre, ed. Buenos Aires: Legasa.

——— 1989. "Interpretando (una vez más) los orígenes del peronismo." *Desarrollo Económico* 28, no. 112 (January–March): 525–48.

——— 1990. *La Vieja Guardia Sindical y Perón*. Buenos Aires: Editorial Sudamericana e Instituto Torcuato Di Tella.

——— 1998. *El proceso político de las reformas económicas en América Latina*. Buenos Aires: Paidós.

——— n.d. "La trayectoria de las instituciones del sindicalismo argentino." Instituto Torcuato Di Tella, Buenos Aires. Unpublished manuscript.

Torres, Gerber. 1993. "La economía que podemos construir." In *Venezuela del siglo XX al sigl XXI: un proyecto para construirla*. Carlos Blanco, ed. Caracas: Editorial Nueva Sociedad.

UNIDO. 1998. "Industrial Statistics Database 3-Digit Level." Version 0.36.1. Vienna, Austria: United National Industrial Development Board.

U.S. Department of Labor. 1992a. "Argentina 1991–92." *Foreign Labor Trends*. Washington, DC: Dept. of Labor.

——— 1992b. "Mexico 1991–92." *Foreign Labor Trends*. Washington, DC: Dept. of Labor.

——— 1992c. "Venezuela 1991–92." *Foreign Labor Trends*. Washington, DC: Dept. of Labor.

Valenzuela, J. Samuel. 1992. "Labour Movements and Political Systems: Some Variations." In *The Future of Labour Movements*. Marino Regini, ed. Newbury Park, CA: SAGE Studies in International Sociology.

Vázquez Rubio, Oscar. 1989. "Los telefonistas cruzaron el pantano: concertaron con Telmex." *El Cotidiano* (Mexico City) 21, September–October: 31–2.

——— 1990a. "Conseguimos avanzar, pero esto no garantiza un triunfo." *El Cotidiano* (Mexico City) 35, May–June: 18–21.

1990b. "El telefonista sostiene su apuesta." *El Cotidiano* (Mexico City) 35, May–June: 25–6.

Vega Lopez, Eduardo. 1995. "La política económica de México durante el período 1982–1994." *El Cotidiano* (Mexico City) 67, March–April: 31–3.

Vegas, Emiliana, Lant Pritchett, and William Experton. 1999. "Attracting and Retaining Qualified Teachers in Argentina: Impact of the Level and Structure of Compensation." The World Bank, Washington, DC. Unpublished manuscript.

Villaroel, Gladis. 1996. "Las amenazas militares a la democracia y la opinión del venezolano." *Espacio Abierto* 5, no. 2: 224–48.

Von Bulow, Marisa. 1994. "Reestructuración productiva y estrategias sindicales. El caso de la Ford en Cuahutitlán 1987–1993." Facultad Latinoamericana de Ciencias Sociales-Sede México, Mexico City. Unpublished thesis.

1995. "Reestructuración productiva y estrategias sindicales. El caso de la Ford en Cuahutitlán 1987–1994." Paper presented at the Latin American Studies Association XIX International Congress, Washington, DC, September 28–30.

Wallerstein, Michael and Bruce Western. 1999. "Unions in Decline: What Has Changed and Why." Northwestern University and Princeton University. Unpublished manuscript.

Walter, Jorge, and Cecilia Senén González. 1998. "Empresas y sindicatos en la telefonía argentina privatizada." In *La privatización de las telecomunicaciones en América Latina*. Jorge Walter and Cecilia Senén González, eds. Buenos Aires: Eudeba.

Weldon, Jeffrey. 1997. "The Political Sources of Presidentialism in Mexico." In *Presidentialism and Democracy in Latin America*. Scott Mainwaring and Matthew Soberg Shugart, eds. Cambridge: Cambridge University Press.

Weyland, Kurt. 1996a. "Risk Taking in Latin American Economic Restructuring: Lessons from Prospect Theory." *International Studies Quarterly* 40, no. 2 (June): 185–207.

1996b. *Democracy Without Equity: Failures of Reform in Brazil*. Pittsburgh, PA: University of Pittsburgh Press.

1999. "Economic Policy in Chile's New Democracy." *Journal of Interamerican Studies and World Affairs* 41, no. 3 (Fall): 67–96.

2000. "Claryfing a Contested Concept: 'Populism' in the Study of Latin American Poltics." Paper presented at the workshop on "Old Populism, New Populism in Latin America," Yale University, April 7–8.

Williamson, John. 1990. "What Washington Means by Policy Reform." In *Latin American Adjustment: How Much Has Happened?* John Williamsom, ed. Washington, DC: Institute for International Economics.

Williamson, John, and Stephen Haggard. 1994. "The Political Conditions for Economic Reform." In *The Political Economy of Policy Reform*. John Williamson, ed. Washington, DC: Institute for International Economics.

World Bank. 1994. *World Tables 1994*. Baltimore, MD: Johns Hopkins University Press.

1995. *Reformas Laborales y Económicas en América Latina y el Caribe*. Washington, DC: World Bank.

Bibliography

Xelhuantzi López, María. 1989. *Sindicato de Telefonista de la República Mexican. 12 años: 1976–1988*. Mexico City: Mexican Union of Telephone Workers.

——— 1992. "Reforma del Estado Mexicano y sindicalismo." Facultad de Ciencias Políticas y Sociales, Universidad Nacional Autónoma de México, Mexico City. Unpublished thesis.

YPF S.A. n.d. "YPF. Transformación. Recursos Humanos." Department of Human Resources, YPF, Buenos Aires. Unpublished manuscript.

Zamora, Gerardo. 1990. "La política laboral del estado mexicano, 1982–88." *Revista Mexicana de Sociología* (Mexico City), no. 3: 23–48.

Zapata, Francisco. 1986. *El conflicto sindical en América Latina*. Mexico City: El Colegio de Mexico.

——— 1993. *Autonomía y subordinación en el sindicalismo latinoamericano*. Mexico City: Fondo de Cultura Económica.

——— 1994. "Crisis en el sindicalismo en México?" *Revista Mexicana de Sociología* (Mexico City), no. 1: 79–88.

Zazueta, Cesar, and Ricardo de la Peña. 1981. *Estructura dual y piramidal del sindicalismo mexicano*. Mexico City: Secretaria del Trabajo y Prevision Social, Centro Nacional de Informacion y Estadisticas del Trabajo.

Zepeda, Mario. 1990. "El Pronasol, la política y la pobreza." *Memoria* (Cemos, Mexico City) 36: 6–7.

Zorrilla, Rubén. 1983. *El liderazgo sindical argentino. Desde sus orígenes hasta 1975*. Buenos Aires: Ediciones Siglo Veinte.

Interviews

Alderete, Carlos. 1993. Secretary-general of FATLyF. Interview by author. Buenos Aires.

Alfonsín, Raúl. 1999. Former president of Argentina. Interview by author. New Haven, CT, 17 April.

Araoz, Gerardo. 1995. CTERA representative in OSPLAD. Interview by author. Buenos Aires.

Betancourt, Alejandro. 1995. Secretary of social affairs of SUPE. Interview by author. Buenos Aires.

Bucarito, Mirna. 1996. Chief of the office of recruitment and personnel selection in CADAFE. Interview by author. Caracas.

Callegaris, Nestor. 1993. Secretary of energy policies of FATLyF. Interview by author. Buenos Aires.

———. 1995. Interview by author. Buenos Aires.

Caro Figueroa, Armando. 1994. Ministry of labor and social security of Argentina. Interview by author. Buenos Aires.

Cassia, Antonio. 1993. Secretary-general of SUPE and secretary-general of the CGT. Interview by author. Buenos Aires.

———. 1995. Interview by author. Buenos Aires.

Castañeda, Rafael. 1994. AD union leader and member of the executive committee of the CTV. Interview by author. Caracas.

Cruz Bencomo, Miguel Angel. 1995. Former leader of PEMEX professional employees. Interview by author. Mexico City.

D'Amelio, Francisco. 1994. Secretary-general of Sutra-Automotriz Carabobo and secretary of labor problems of the Ford section of the union. Interview by author. Valencia, Venezuela.

De Gennaro, Victor. 1995. Secretary-general of the CTA. Interview by author. Buenos Aires.

Del Campo, Jesús Martín. 1995. PRD official and SNTE union leader. Interview by author. Mexico City.

Delpino, Juan José. 1996. Former president of the CTV. Interview by author. Caracas.

Díaz, Paul Bernardo. 1995. Former union leader in the local executive committee of the Ford Motors Workers Union. Interview by author. Mexico City.

Díaz, Rodolfo. 1992 and 1995. Former ministry of labor and social security of Argentina. Interview by author. Buenos Aires.

Domínguez, José. 1995. Advisor to the secretary of education of the CTM. Interview by author. Mexico City.

Dromi, Roberto. 1998. Former minister of public works of Argentina. Interview by author. Buenos Aires, August 24.

Durán, Jorge. 1995. Former secretary of external relations of the SME. Interview by author. Mexico City.

Elguea, Javier. 1995. Director of Inttelmex, training institute of TELMEX. Interview by author. Mexico City.

Espinasa, Ramón. 1996. Chief economist of PDVSA. Interview by author. Caracas.

Flores, Edmundo. 1994. Former labor director of CANTV and former president of the Caracas union of FETRATEL. Interview by author. Caracas.

García Solís, Victor. 1995. Secretary of social communication of the STPRM. Interview by author. Mexico City.

Giar, Juan. 1995. Manager of human resources of Telecom-Argentina. Interview by author. Buenos Aires.

Giordanengo Raúl. 1995. Subdirector of labor relations and social action, director of human resources of Telefónica de Argentina. Interview by author. Buenos Aires.

Hernández, Cruz. 1996. President of FETRATEL. Interview by author. Caracas.

Hernández Juarez, Jose F. 1996. Secretary-general of the STRM. Interview by author. Mexico City.

Iturraspe, Francisco. 1994. Professor of labor law, Universidad Central de Venezuela. Interview by author. Caracas.

    1996. Professor of labor law, Universidad Central de Venezuela. Interview by author. Caracas.

Kamkoff, Jorge. 1996. Former president of the IVSS of Venezuela. Interview by author. Caracas.

Lansberg, Ivan. 1996. Former presidential commissioner for the restructuring of the IVSS. Interview by author. Caracas.

La Riva Blanco, Edilberto. 1996. President of FETRASALUD. Interview by author. Caracas.

Lejarza, Mateo. 1995. Advisor to the secretary-general of STRM. Interview by author. Mexico City.

López Mayrén, Joel. 1995. Secretary-general of the COR. Interview by author. Mexico City.

Maffei, Marta. 1995. Secretary-general of CTERA. Interview by author. Buenos Aires.

Maguira, Carlos. 1995. Attorney to the Mar del Plata union of FATLyF. Interview by author. Buenos Aires.

Malavé, Joaquín. 1996. Secretary of finances of the Caracas union of FETRAELEC. Interview by author. Caracas.

Interviews

Marbrán, Ignacio. 1995. Former advisor to the SNTE and labor scholar. Interview by author. Mexico City.

Marmolejo, Pilar. 1995. Training manager at Inttelmex/TELMEX. Interview by author. Mexico City.

Martínez D'ector, Mario. 1995. CROC union leader in the state of Mexico. Interview by author. Mexico City.

Martínez Mottola, Fernando. 1996. Former president of CANTV during the privatization process. Interview by author. Caracas.

Mendoza, Eduardo. 1994. Manager of industrial relations of Ford Motors of Venezuela. Interview by author. Valencia, Venezuela.

Millán, Juan. 1995. Secretary of education of the CTM. Interview by author. Mexico City.

Miranda, Héctor. 1995. Secretary of external affairs of the FTSTE. Interview by author. Mexico City.

Mirkin, Alejandro. 1995. Under-secretary of energy, ministry of the economy. Interview by author. Buenos Aires.

Montero, Ricardo. 1996. Labor director in the CANTV. Interview by author. Caracas.

Navarro, Carlos. 1994. President of the Front of Copeyanos Workers and member of the executive committee of the CTV. Interview by author. Caracas.

Navarro, Juan Carlos. 1996. Professor at IESA and expert on education reform and decentralization. Interview by author. Caracas.

Olarte, Cesar. 1996. Former secretary-general of the CTV. Interview by author. Puerto La Cruz, Venezuela.

Ortega, Carlos. 1996. President of FEDEPETROL. Interview by author. Caracas.

Ortíz, Rosario. 1995. Dissident union leader in the STRM. Interview by author. Mexico City, April 18.

Paleta, Cuautemoc. 1995. Secretary-general of the CROM. Interview by author. Mexico City.

Pardo, Manuel. 1995. Secretary of collective bargaining of SMATA. Interview by author. Buenos Aires.

Penso, Rodrigo. 1994. MAS union leader and member of the executive committee of the CTV. Interview by author. Caracas.

Pérez, Carlos. 1996. Former president of Venezuela. Interview by author. Oripoto, Venezuela.

Pérez, Jesús. 1994. Union leader and national representative of Causa R. Interview by author. Caracas.

Raitano, Oscar. 1995. Secretary of social action of SMATA. Interview by author. Buenos Aires.

Ramírez, Jesús. 1996. President of Fetra-Enseñanza. Interview by author. Caracas.

Ramiroff, Marina. 1996. Vice-president of organization and human resources of CANTV. Interview by author. Caracas.

Ramos, Alfredo. 1996. President of the Caracas union of FETRATEL and national representative for Causa R. Interview by author. Caracas.

Recalde, Héctor. 1993. Legal advisor to the CGT and since 1994 to the MTA. Interview by author. Buenos Aires, August 10.

1995. Interview by author. Buenos Aires, June 28.

Reyes del Campillo, Jesús. 1996. Expert on Mexican elections. Interview by author. Mexico City.

Rigane, José. 1995. Secretary-general of the Mar del Plata union of FATLyF. Interview by author. Buenos Aires.

Rivas, Alberto. 1996. Manager of human resources of PDVSA. Interview by author. Caracas.

Rodríguez, Enrique. 1993. Former secretary of labor and ministry of labor and social security. Interview by author.

1995. Interview by author.

Rodríguez, José. 1992. Secretary-general of SMATA. Interview by author. August 8.

Rodríguez, José Antonio. 1996. Advisor to the secretary-general of the SNTE. Interview by author. Mexico City.

Rodríguez, Ruben. 1996. Former minister of labor of Venezuela. Interview by author. Puerto La Cruz.

Romo, Horacio. 1995. Secretary of external relations of the SME. Interview by author. Mexico City.

Roosen, Gustavo. 1996. Former minister of education of Venezuela, former president of PDVSA, and president of CANTV. Interview by author. Caracas.

Ruiz, Ramiro. 1996. Manager of industrial relations of CANTV. Interview by author. Caracas.

Salazar, Diógenes. 1995. President of OSTEL and secretary of press and propaganda of FOETRA. Interview by author. Buenos Aires.

Sánchez, Jorge. 1995. Former secretary-general of SME. Interview by author. Mexico City.

Simonotti, Fernando. 1995. Administrative director of OSTEL. Interview by author. Buenos Aires.

Smith, Roberto. 1996. Former minister of transportation and telecommunications of Venezuela. Interview by author. Puerto La Cruz, Venezuela.

Sozio, Torcuato. 1993. Former under-secretary of collective bargaining of the ministry of education of Argentina. Interview by author. Buenos Aires.

1995. Interview by author.

Taccone, Juan José. 1993. Founder and former secretary-general of FATLyF. Interview by author. Buenos Aires.

1995. Interview by author.

Teglia, Roberto. 1995. Manager of labor relations of YPF S.A. Interview by author. Buenos Aires.

Todesca, Carlos. 1995. Economist specialized in the automobile sector. Interview by author. June 23.

Tomada, Carlos. 1993. Legal advisor to the CGT. Interview by author. Buenos Aires, August 8.

Vallejo, José Beltrán. 1996. Former president of the CTV. Interview by author. Caracas.

Vazquez, Hebraicas. 1995. Leader of the dissident faction in the STPRM. Interview by author. Mexico City.

Interviews

Vera, Juan José. 1996. Attorney of the human resources department of PDVSA. Interview by author. Caracas.

Villalba, Julián. 1996. Former president of CADAFE. Interview by author. Caracas.

Xelhuantzi López, María. 1995. Advisor to the secretary-general of the STRM. Interview by author. Mexico City.

Zerpa Mirabal, Miguel Angel. 1994. AD union leader and member of the executive committee of the CTV. Interview by author. Caracas.

Index